Martin of Manchuria

A Torch in the Storm

Margaret Martin Moore

WESTBOW
PRESS®
A DIVISION OF THOMAS NELSON
& ZONDERVAN

Scripture taken from the King James Version of the Bible.

WestBow Press books may be ordered through booksellers or by contacting:

WestBow Press
A Division of Thomas Nelson & Zondervan
1663 Liberty Drive
Bloomington, IN 47403
www.westbowpress.com
1 (866) 928-1240

ISBN: 978-1-4908-8890-3 (sc)
ISBN: 978-1-5127-0617-8 (e)

Library of Congress Control Number: 2016906525

Print information available on the last page.

WestBow Press rev. date: 09/16/2016

Contents

Dedication

Remembering with love and gratitude – my parents.

Stanley Haviland Martin
1890-1941
Born in St. John's, Newfoundland

Margaret Rogers Martin
1887-1961
Born in New Britain, Connecticut

"...they rest from their labors; and their works do follow them." Revelation 14:13

Introduction

This book is not a "Treatise on Missions." It is simply the story of a man and his wife who followed the call of God to serve Him as medical missionaries.

The inspiration for writing this book came one day as I watched a television program. It was featuring a girl who had written a book about various dates she had had with her boy friend. She had sketched pictures of each dress she had worn for the occasion. Now the pictures were being shown, one by one on television.

"Well! Lah dee dah!" I thought. "How about that!" If she could write a book on such a subject, what about the story of a young man with a handful of surgical instruments going in to the wilds of Manchuria and building a hospital? Bandits, tigers, epidemics, and the saving of lives came to mind as I decided to try to record his adventures.

The title *Torch in the Storm* should be *Torches in the Storm*, for my father could not have done what he did, without the help of my mother Margaret Rogers Martin. Her background and her share in the adventures are included in the book.

Part of the information comes from my early childhood in Manchuria, family letters, my parents' stories, newspaper accounts, and the correspondence between my family and the United Church of Canada Mission Board added to the material.

Many precious letters were lost when my sister Betty died in a house fire. The loss of my sister was a far greater loss, of course. Also, my sister Edna and I were missionaries in Seoul, Korea at the time of the communist invasion on June 25, 1950. We escaped with only what we could carry. I had three sons with me including my two and a half month old baby, Ron. Again, many irreplaceable letters and pictures were left behind and were lost. Other information comes from my father's former patients, or Korean church women who told of their experiences in Manchuria.

I was fortunate to hear stories in person from the Honorable Dr. Lee Kap Song (Yi Kap Song), one of the signers of the Korean Declaration of Independence, and also from Suh Myung Hak, who had taken part in the Independence Movement on March 1, 1919, when she was a young girl. She later served as principal of Ewha High School.

The stories from Dr. Yi I heard at a dinner table in his home. His family commented afterwards, "He was telling you things we never heard before!"

At another time he stayed so late in the evening at my home, that his family called to see if he was all right. That night he showed us his hands – scarred from being hung by his thumbs when in prison.

I wrote this book for my family, my friends and especially for Korean friends who have not heard this part of their history.

Mrs. Ruth Seamands, missionary to India, was one of the first to encourage me to attempt this writing. I will always remember her encouragement and guidance. She is well-known for her book, *Missionary Mama*.

I am extremely grateful to Rev. Robert Wood, my editor, who was a Methodist pastor for many years, and a former editor of the Zondervan Publishing Co. Through the long months the chapters of my book that I sent to him came back to me through the mail, giving me courage to keep going.

A Korean translation was made by Mr. Lee Sung Kyu, who had been Director and Representative of the *Kukdan Kakyo Drama Troupe* in Seoul, Korea. The translating took years of work for which I cannot thank him enough. The title of this book was suggested by him. His wife, So Ya, also helped, and his son-in-law, Koh Young Bum, kindly reviewed the Korean script.

My son Alan was my typist. He did the most work, typing and retyping many chapters. I couldn't have done it without him. Thanks, Alan! Also thanks to granddaughter, Suzanne Moore Taigen for typing several chapters. Sons Bill and Ron did valuable proof reading and gave suggestions. Ron made two trips to Canada with me; for Archives material, and for the Plaque Dedication at Pagoda Memorial Park at the University of Toronto. Eldest son David gave encouragement and youngest son Kevin designed the front cover, so it was a family project.

Friends read the first draft with appreciative comment. I am grateful to General Paul Rader and Commissioner Kay Rader of the Salvation Army, Dr. Kenneth Kinghorn of Asbury Theological Seminary, Heidi Linton of Christian Friends of Korea, and many others who gave encouragement. Mrs. Linton said, "The North Koreans must read this."

I am especially pleased as my sons, nephews, nieces and grandchildren are learning of their family history.

My sister-in-law, Virginia Stevens Martin, provided important material about her husband Jerry (Dr. Gerald Martin) for the chapter, *Jerry's Story*.

Finally, I gratefully acknowledge Ms. Nicole Vonk, General Council Archivist, for granting permission to publish transcriptions of letters and reports sent to and from my parents and the United Church of Canada Mission Board, preserved by the United Church of Canada Archives, Toronto.

Prologue

Since the setting of the early days of this biography is in Newfoundland, I have included some background of the country and how some members of the family came to live there. Newfoundland is a country with a five thousand-year history of Indian settlements on the West Coast. The vanished Beothuks were the early aborigines, and in nearby Labrador were Eskimos as well as Native Americans.

Innus, Inuits and Mi Kmaqs are among the present tribes. In the year 2000, Newfoundland celebrated the one thousandth year since Leif Ericson and his fellow Vikings arrived at L'Anse Meadows at the northern tip of Newfoundland.

After years as a British colony it was for nearly a century a member state of the British Commonwealth. The governor was sent from England, but the country was autonomous with its own prime minister and Houses of Parliament in the city of St. John's. It became a Canadian Province in 1949.

The deepest impression one gets when visiting the country is of the people themselves. They blend cultures from England, Ireland, Scotland, France, Portugal and Spain. They are cheerful and fun-loving, ready with a witty answer or a joke. Some have called them the friendliest people in the world. Of course, they speak in many accents according to their background. England has had the strongest influence on them.

Historic St. John's is the oldest town in North America. Forty ships already lay in its excellent harbor by the time the Mayflower arrived at Plymouth, Massachusetts in 1620. The town overlooks the harbor, flanked by hills and is entered by ship through the "Narrows."

In 1890, the year of Stan's birth, there were many schools and churches. The cod fishing industry employed great numbers of people and was the greatest source of income for years.

Stanley's father, Arthur William Martin, of English ancestry, was first a merchant and then an accountant at the General Post Office. Stan's mother, Minnie Coultas Martin, a twin, was the granddaughter of the Rev. William Coultas, a clergyman of the British Wesleyan Conference in Gravesend, England. Rev. Coultas' great desire was to go to the West Indies. "A powerful impression was made upon my mind. No English circuit for me, I must first preach to the blacks, the gospel of the blessed God." He sailed with his family to the West Indies in 1810, labored successfully for six years and returned to England to continue his ministry. Later his son, Minnie's father, became a doctor and went to Newfoundland, practicing medicine at Conception Bay and Carbonear. He was well known as the "beloved doctor." There were also two ministers among Stan's forebears on his father's side of the family. They were the Rev. George Bellewes and the Rev. Cecil Bellewes, a father and son.

I

"Embryo Missionary"

The young man stepped out from the ship's wireless shack to survey the scene. A fresh salt breeze and the smell of cod-fish cakes hit him in the face as he crossed to the railing. An unusually large iceberg floated nearby on the brilliant blue water as the hospital ship, the *Strathcona,* approached the Narrows. He was tired. Even though he was the wireless operator, he had taken turns to be on watch in the night with a desperately sick man. The doctor came up behind him as he stood. "Remember Signal Hill?" he asked as he pointed to the high hill above the channel. "I hear you were there when it happened!" Stan nodded, and memories flooded him as his hometown slowly came into view.

Stanley Haviland Martin was born July 23, 1890, in St. John's, Newfoundland. Since a person is profoundly influenced by one's early days and surroundings, Newfoundland and Labrador helped to form this man. When one thinks of this area, images of cold winters, suffering, and tragedies of fishermen and sealers come to mind. Nevertheless it is a land of rugged beauty, surrounded by water teeming with life. Northern lights, the *aurora borealis*, light the skies with spectacular beauty on many nights. Majestic icebergs float by in summer; ten-thousand-year-old mountains of fresh water ice from the Arctic and Greenland.

The spring of 1892 saw two significant happenings. The town of St. John's almost completely burned to the ground. At that very time Dr. Wilfred Thomason Grenfell was on the ship *Albert* arriving from England. The doctor was coming for the first time to determine the needs of the fishermen of Newfoundland and Labrador. Those on the ship could see the frantic activities of the people near their homes, and the flames moving beyond to the forests. Dr. Grenfell and his fellow workers docked, and immediately began to distribute some of the relief clothing they had brought, and to care for burned and injured victims. Quite an introduction to the people he had come to serve!

The great doctor was to have a profound influence on the country, and later on the life of Stanley Martin. Stan was then a two-year-old, probably in his mother's arms watching the burning town. Family records do not indicate whether their house burned, although three-fourths of the city was destroyed.

After doing what he could to help, Dr. Grenfell proceeded to the Labrador coast. He spent the summer of 1892 there caring for the sick and laying the foundation for his ministry.

When he returned to St. John's on his way back to England, word had already reached there of his fine work. The government of Newfoundland became interested and a wealthy merchant donated a warehouse that was to be Grenfell's first cottage hospital at Battle Harbor on the Labrador Coast. The doctor was greatly encouraged. He then returned to England to gain support and to make plans for future service to the deep sea fishermen of Newfoundland and Labrador. As the years went by, St. John's was rebuilt and lives gradually became normal again.

Stan's family was headed by his devout Victorian father and gentle mother. He had three sisters, Mabel, Gertrude and Eva and a brother named William. They had the usual childhood illnesses. Stan had in his youth a streptococcal infection causing rheumatic fever with resultant heart damage that showed up in his adult years as an enlarged heart. Stan said that when he and his brother had the mumps, his mother tied socks filled with warm baked potatoes around their necks. When their mother wasn't looking they ate the potatoes. Playing cards were forbidden. They were so strictly taught at home, that when William as a boy, saw a pack of playing cards fluttering on the ground, he bolted to the other side of the road.

Great excitement reigned in St. John's every March, when the sealers gathered by the thousands to leave for their annual seal hunt. Stan and his brother often went down to the wharves to watch while the men loaded their ships with food and equipment. Barrels of flour, molasses, corn meal and other provisions were hoisted aboard. Gallons of water were stored. Later at the "ice-field" men had to go overboard to bring in fresh water ice to be melted and boiled to replenish their supply. Tons of coal had to be on board for the steam engines. These were sailing ships augmented by steam. Bows and sides were reinforced with "greenheart," a wood that would not shatter when pounded by the ice.

At last, departure time arrived. Stan and William stood on the crowded docks, everyone cheering as the small fleet moved out with flags flying and whistles blowing. Weeks later the boys again joined the crowds to welcome them back home. This time the decks were piled high with the seal pelts. As the men returned to their homes, St. John's buzzed with stories of blizzards, shipwrecks, and of brave men lost at sea. Little did Stan realize that some day he would be closely associated with the rough and dangerous life of men such as these.

The children found time for mischief too. He told friends, "We were young Turks!" One time he and his chums stuffed the chimney of the house where a wedding party was going on. Bride and groom and all the guests were smoked out!

Once he hid under the great horsehair couch in the formal parlor of their house and heard his sister Gertrude's "gentleman friend," propose to her.

His father, the well-respected Sunday school superintendent was recommending a wonderful cough syrup he had bought at the apothecary. He told all his friends about it. However, Stan with a growing interest in chemistry tried an experiment. He lighted a spoonful of the syrup with a match. To his father's chagrin it burned with a blue flame! It was alcohol based --- probably brandy! His father stopped recommending it.

Much of his family's life was centered around their church, the Wesleyan Methodist church founded in 1873, now known as the George Street United Church. His father was Sunday school superintendent for thirty-eight years, and his mother served many years as president of the Woman's Missionary Society. His sister Gertrude later married the Rev. Ira F. Curtis who served as minister at the church from 1930 to 1936. (Stan had heard the marriage proposal.)

The church building was erected of Newfoundland stone obtained from the Southside Hills. Captain Edward's sealing crew, prior to their departure for "the ice" on the sealing vessel *Neptune*, had pulled the stones on heavy wagons from Southside quarries to the site of the church. It was built near the waterfront to be of service to "all those that go down to the sea in ships." The church also sponsored a Southside Mission on the waterfront as part of their ministry.

So Stan grew, nurtured by the teachings of a church that emphasized service to others.

His father wrote in a letter concerning him:

> He was then the chum of Taylor Clouston and Jim Thompson, boys who attended 'The Quiet Hour' conducted by Dr. Andrew Robertson on Friday afternoons at four o'clock. He told many fine stories of missionaries like Moffat and Livingston, and the explorer Stanley who found Livingston in the heart of Africa, of Duff and Morrison all heroes in pioneer Christian work. Stan came home when about fourteen filled with enthusiasm and gravely said one evening; 'The first medical missionary was Jesus the Son of God, the great example.' It moved our hearts. At prayers that night, he was again dedicated to God's service, and we prayed that the way may be opened for the boy's education, because the motto of his life was 'My supreme duty is to serve others'. He was always thoughtful and helpful to old people, bringing pails of water from tanks, when the approaches were covered with ice, or carrying loads of wood up hill for old men too feeble to do it.

On a cold windy day, December 12, 1901, high on top of Signal Hill overlooking St. John's harbor, an experiment took place that affected not only Stan's future, but the future of the whole world.

For some time before that date, newspapers were reporting that an Italian inventor was coming to try to receive a wireless signal from across the Atlantic. Newfoundland had been chosen because of its far eastern location on the Atlantic. The signal was to come from a place called Poldhu on rocks jutting from the southwest tip of England.

Many people were skeptical, but curiosity overcame the people of St. John's on the day they watched the handsome inventor Guglielmo Marconi disembark at the dock with his assistants. When all was ready by December 12, crowds trudged up steep Signal Hill to see what would happen. Among them were excited eleven-year-old Stan and his nine-year-old brother, William.

There they saw a big kite holding up a four hundred foot wire, attached to instruments in the old barracks building. Marconi and his two assistants waited for impulses to come from the twenty-kilowatt spark outfit at Poldhu. They concentrated their attention on a tiny hammer to see if it would give three clicks on a little glass tube. The historical moment came just after noon, December 12, 1901. Marconi heard the letter "S," three taps on the glass! The letter "S" for *SUCCESS*! It was the dawn of a new world-wide communications system! What a thrilling moment!

Marconi was sure of the experiment when he heard the signals again the next day. He then made a short announcement that a wireless signal had come across the Atlantic. The world was astonished, but some scoffed. Then Thomas Edison said, "If Marconi says it's true, it's true." Marconi was grateful for this encouragement.

Over the years, lavish praise and expressions of gratitude came to Mr. Marconi. Stan, who was to meet him later in another country, summed up his admiration for Marconi with, "It was a never-to-be-forgotten hour to see again the face, and talk with the man who had made possible for humanity the famous SOS call!"

That December night in 1901 there was excited talk at the supper table, as Stan and his brother related what had happened. The sparks that flew over the Atlantic that memorable day had reached young Stan.

We don't know all that ensued as Stanley Martin finished high school in the years to follow. However, his father wrote, "Stan was self-taught in telegraphy. He served his apprenticeship as Marconi operator at Cape Ray. At seventeen he was appointed operator at Anticosti Island in the mouth of the St. Lawrence River. Later he served at Saint John, New Brunswick, Canada."

At eighteen he received a remarkable request. Out of all the young men in his hometown he was asked to come to St. Anthony near the northern tip of Newfoundland. They wanted him to install wireless equipment and to be the wireless operator for the famous Dr. Wilfred Grenfell's hospital ship, the *Strathcona*. He was about to walk through the door of a new world, into a new and exciting chapter of his life.

Dr. Stanley H. Martin, MD, CM

II

T'Doctor

That June in 1908 the days seemed to drag as young Stan finished his school year at the Methodist college in St. John's. The wireless equipment had been purchased and he had said good-bye to his friends. Finally, it was time to leave for St. Anthony, and he boarded the coastal steamer, the *Fogota*.

With his few belongings in his cabin, and the wireless equipment stashed safely below, he returned to the railing and waved as the ship slowly moved from the dock. His family and friends grew smaller and smaller until he could barely see them. He knew they were proud of him and thrilled for this opportunity, but he remembered tears. He felt in his jacket for the package that his mother had given him. At last he turned to observe his fellow passengers. They were all older men, rough and hardy, tanned with years of work in the open. Probably fishermen, he thought, as he made his way to the bow of the ship. The deck was piled high with boxes and barrels. He found a large chest directly behind the bow and settled himself. As the cool breeze blew on his face he tried to imagine what it would be like to be at the wheel of the ship. Soon they passed through the "Narrows" to the open sea, and the ship swung around to the north. Automatically his eyes scanned the waters for the spume of whales. None were visible at the moment.

He tried to comprehend what was happening to him. It all seemed like a dream. He had heard of the Grenfell Mission ever since he could remember.

That very spring in 1908 news had flashed around the world that the famous Dr. Grenfell had nearly lost his life. He was returning from visiting a patient, traveling by dogsled across a frozen stretch of sea when the ice began to melt. He was adrift with his dogs on an ice-pan for about twenty-four hours before he was rescued. He had to kill three of his dogs to use their skins to keep himself from freezing to death. The publicity from this fearful adventure made people more aware of this remarkable man and his work.

Stan wondered what it would be like to work with him. He remembered last summer as a seventeen-year-old wireless operator, the SOS calls, the messages he had sent and received. There had been storms with ships in distress, and medical emergencies, life and death matters. What messages would the new equipment receive? What dangers were ahead?

Soon they were passing Quidi Vidi on the port side where the waves were splashing high onto the cliffs. The sea was heaving now with a steady roll. He loved it, relaxing completely with every movement.

Stan reached in his pocket and drew out the little package his mother had given him. It was carefully wrapped in tissue paper and tied with a blue ribbon. "Of course," he chuckled to himself as he opened it, "a little New Testament that's easy to carry." Opening to the flyleaf he read his mother's handwriting. "They that go down to the sea in ships, that do business in great waters; These see the works of the LORD and his wonders in the deep. ...he bringeth them unto their desired haven." (Psalm 107:23-24,30)

At the bottom of the page she wrote, "My prayers for protection will be with you. Your loving Mother."

He put the little book back into his breast pocket over his heart. "All will be well." he said to himself as he leaned his head against a barrel and fell asleep exhausted from the past hours.

The clanging of the ship's bell woke him. He turned to see men behind him jostling toward the passage to the galley and the large dining salon. Soon he was seated with them as they all were served a hearty lunch. He was the youngest there and listened quietly to the conversation. They were a cheerful bunch, joking and laughing the whole time. These meal times, he discovered, were to be valuable preparation for the days ahead. Stan had had contact with fishermen before but never like this. When they heard of his mission they were amazed that one so young was entrusted to install the wireless equipment. "You will be working with T'Doctor?" one asked. Some had seen Dr. Grenfell; others had relatives living today because of his medical help. They were unanimous in their praise of the work at the northernmost hospital station.

The trip to St. Anthony was a distance of three hundred miles but mail was to be delivered at ports along the way, so it was to take twelve days.

The sharing at meal times became more somber as they told their stories. One man told of a fisherman's wife who on a stormy night heard a knock on the door three different times. Each time she opened it, no one was there. The fourth knock was heard and when she opened the door, fishermen friends carried in the body of her husband who had drowned.

Jake, the oldest of the passengers, knocked the ashes from his pipe, cleared his throat and said in a gruff voice, "The strangest story I've heard, was of the man at the wheel of a ship steering according to his captain's orders off the coast of Labrador. Suddenly a man with a scarred face came up beside him and said, 'Turn her fifteen degrees to port.' The mate at the wheel was puzzled, but obeyed thinking the Captain had sent him. In about a half an hour their ship came upon a vessel wrecked and stranded on a rock. There among the stricken passengers was the man with the scarred face! All were rescued and brought to safety."

The faith of the men shone through as they told of amazing deliverances in fierce storms. They knew God had answered their prayers.

The days passed with intervals at port calls. New passengers came on board. Some were on stretchers, others on crutches, all bound for the hospital.

At last on a sunny morning they sighted the islands near St. Anthony, and then St. Anthony itself came into view. It was a low-lying village with hills beyond. A few large buildings gleamed in the sun with a scattering of small houses. Two churches flanked the harbor that was filled with schooners.

"Which is the *Strathcona*?" Stan wondered as he leaned forward to see more clearly. Then he spotted her, a trim black steamship with a red cross on her smokestack. A blue flag with the letters MDSF was flying in the breeze from one of her masts. He knew it stood for Mission to Deep Sea Fishermen. His heart pounded in anticipation.

As the ship dropped anchor, little boats called punts swarmed to her and freight and passengers were precariously loaded for the trip to the small wharf.

Stan requested that the wireless equipment should stay on board until time for transfer to the *Strathcona*.

Carrying his duffel bag he jumped from the punt that had brought him to shore and hurried toward the hospital. As he went, he read the Bible verse written in large letters across the upper story of the building. "FAITH, HOPE, AND LOVE ABIDE; BUT THE GREATEST OF THESE IS LOVE."

As he entered the front door, he saw a man in white emerging from an operating room, pulling his surgeon's mask from his face.

"Dr. Grenfell?" Stan asked breathlessly. "Yes." The doctor stopped and looked at him. "Are you Stanley Martin the Marconi Man?"

"Yes, Sir." The doctor grasped Stan's hand in welcome. Whatever apprehension or awe Stan had before coming, vanished as he looked into the twinkling friendly eyes of this famous man. He heard an English accent as the doctor continued.

"We've been expecting you! Did you have a good trip?"

"Yes Sir."

"Jolly good. Where's the equipment?"

"Still on board the *Fogota*, sir."

"We'll see about that later, now come and have lunch with us."

They walked down the hall to the large dining room, where many were seated. Some were nurses in their long white uniforms and nurses caps. Some were doctors, others wore the dark sweaters and baggy pants of the village people.

Dr. Grenfell stopped at his place at the table. "Ladies and Gentlemen," he said jovially, "We're in touch with the world again! This is Stan Martin from St. John's. He brought our wireless equipment and will be our operator on the *Strathcona*."

There were cheers and applause as they sat down. Stan was surprised and pleased at their reaction, but he knew from experience how desperately important communications meant to them, and the people who would be served by the *Strathcona*. Later many of them came around to shake his hand with sincere words of welcome.

He realized at last how hungry he was, as they settled to eat a lunch of fish chowder served with hunks of bread and butter. Dr. Grenfell talked to him as they sipped mugs of steaming tea.

"We're still loading our supplies, but soon after you install your equipment we will be off to Labrador. I hope next week."

The doctor then talked with those sitting near, inquiring news of the critically ill patients upstairs. Having spent the morning in surgery he had been out of touch. As Stan listened he began to understand the respect and love they had for him.

Arrangements were made that several of the villagers were to accompany Stan to the waiting steamer that afternoon. Soon the precious crate of equipment was hoisted aboard the *Strathcona*. Stan climbed the ladder and followed the crate, as it was carefully placed in the chart room. He looked around eagerly examining every detail of the space.

He knew that the ship was named for Lord Strathcona the chief donor. Originally, this man was a poor young fellow from Scotland named Donald Smith. He became president of the Hudson Bay Company, the Canadian Pacific Railroad and the Bank of Montreal. In appreciation for his fine work he had been elevated to the peerage by the English government. Because he had spent thirteen years of his early life on the Labrador, Lord Strathcona was keenly interested in Grenfell's work.

As soon as he could, Stan took a tour of the ship. The men who had come with him followed him eagerly, explaining everything. She's "ninety-seven feet over all and eighteen feet abeam with a displacement of 130 tons. Her up-to-date machinery [can] produce 150 horsepower and a speed of nine knots." [1] Stan could see how proud they were of her.

They toured the wheelhouse and chart room on the upper deck, then went below.

Here he saw the "usual crew accommodation and a saloon that could be transformed into a mission hall. There were spaces for a dispensary and a hospital equipped with specially contrived swinging cots and x-ray apparatus." [2] This was all built according to Dr. Grenfell's specifications in Yarmouth, England. She was brought across in 1899.

When Stan returned to shore, the friendly staff at the hospital did all they could for the young teenager, so clever with his knowledge of the "new fangled" equipment. He was given a room near the men's wing and soon knew all the patient's names and their ailments, as well as the names of the doctors, nurses and volunteers.

Each day he rowed out to the ship and worked with the wireless equipment until all was ready. He was excited when the first incoming messages were tapped out. They were pleas for help, medical emergencies from the coast south of them. When Dr. Grenfell was notified he shook his head sadly, "Wire them, 'Sorry, but we're leaving for Labrador and can't come now, but get the patient to St. Anthony if at all possible.'" The sobering thought came to the doctor as it did so often. *We can't help them all, we're limited.* He then set his heart and mind to be ready for the thousands of fishermen and their families who would need him on the coast of Labrador. Stan too was ready and eager to do his part in the new adventure "down North."

---

[1]   Rompkey, Ronald. *Grenfell of Labrador.* University of Toronto Press Inc, 1992. p. 101.

[2]   Ibid

Mrs. Margaret Rogers Martin, RN

III

Down North

It was a blue and gold morning that June day in 1908 when Dr. Grenfell shouted down to the engineer to start the engine of the *Strathcona*. Stan stood at the ship's railing watching the now-familiar St. Anthony harbor scene. The ship blew a farewell whistle and started to move. Those at the hospital who could, crowded onto the verandas to watch and wave. Some of the nurses were holding little children. This was the yearly ceremony as the *Strathcona* headed out for another busy summer "down north."

The ship's course had been set for the northern tip of Newfoundland and later a swing to the west. Life settled into a busy schedule. One was checking bearings, the mate was at the wheel, Dr. Grenfell was in the chart room, and Stan by his wireless apparatus.

Mealtimes were a time of congenial fellowship and learning. Most of the crew were old timers, but since Stan and one of the engineers were new on the ship, Dr. Grenfell shared many of his adventures.

He told of the history of the St. Anthony hospital, of how the people of St. Anthony requested the hospital be built in 1899. The way it all came together was amazing! Eager, concerned men of the village of St. Anthony, about forty of them, had volunteered to work, so they went to the woods to build a logging station. There were about a dozen teams of dogs to pull the logs on sledges. They built a kitchen and the lodgings in six feet of snow. The favorite foods were doughboys [dumplings] served with a slice of pork. Sometimes they had bird soup. After two weeks they returned with the dog sledges hauling enough material to build the thirty-six by thirty-six foot hospital. Six months later it was complete.

The conversation often turned to the conditions they could expect on the Labrador coast. They had heard that the part of Labrador that belongs to Newfoundland begins near the mouth of the St. Lawrence River. It's a broad peninsula that juts out from the Atlantic Coast and goes up as far as Cape Chidley near the Hudson Bay. Because of the terrain most of the people lived on the coast. These people were mostly of a mixed race – white and Indian or white and Inuit. The Indians of Labrador were of the Montagnais tribe which is part of the great Algonquin group. Most of them lived farther inland. Some of them came to the coast to sell their furs. There were

Moravian missionaries (German United Brethren) who worked at mission stations caring for the Inuits. Inuits are much like the Eskimos of Greenland. At this time of year the summer families came from the south. There would be about 30,000 of them, white fishermen who just spent the summer months. Their women and children were an important part of the work as they flaked the codfish –- splitting, cleaning, salting and setting them in neat rows to dry.

The *Strathcona* turned northwest and the air was noticeably colder as they plowed through the waters of the Arctic current. The first fishing schooners were beginning to appear on the horizon. Even though it was summer, a sharp watch was always kept to avoid icebergs or low ice pans floating on the blue-green waters.

They were heading first for Battle Harbor, Grenfell's first cottage hospital on the coast. When he was free, Stan stepped to the railing to watch for the shoreline, or to enjoy the spouting of whales, or the dolphins leaping in the sun. Once in a while a majestic iceberg appeared and he called to the others to come and admire "This one!" Icebergs were in many shapes and some were of lovely colors but they were dangerous.

More days passed and the doctor shared more stories from his years of summer visits. The doctor told of the "Liveyeres" the courageous fishermen, sealers and trappers who stayed near the coast the year around. Soon they would be seeing their "tilts," the little shacks near the shore where the families of the summer fishermen lived while the men were out at sea. He told of the poor diet of the people, because of the short growing season. Even turnip tops were a luxury. Bread, tea, molasses, fish and summer berries, were the staples for food. Stan listened as Grenfell warmly praised the people there.

As the Strathcona steamed ahead, the numbers of schooners on the horizon suddenly increased, and the coast of Labrador loomed in sight. When the hospital ship came within hailing distance of the schooners, the fishermen waved enthusiastically. They recognized the vessel with its blue MDSF (Mission to Deep Sea Fisherman) flag. The ship proceeded past coves and inlets, Dr. Grenfell consulting his charts or scanning the shoreline. There were no lighthouses so they sought safe harbors at night.

At last one day a shout rang out from the deck, "Battle Harbor ahead!" They were approaching their first destination of the summer. This was all very new to Stan and he took in every detail. The hospital which was now visible, had been strategically placed to be available to all ships that passed. It was also the terminal port for three mail steamers.

The ship's whistle blew as they entered the harbor. Then a drama took place that was to be repeated over and over as Stan spent that summer and summers to come on the Labrador.

This was the *Strathcona's* first visit of the year and it was a shot in the arm, an exhilarating time for the hospital staff and the villagers. They crowded to the wharf to welcome them. As they came ashore, Dr. John Grieve the hospital director and his staff greeted the newcomers and they all moved up to the hospital. The nurses and the housekeeper were standing at the door.

Stan followed, noticing the ragged clothing, the bare feet, and the brown, berry-stained faces of the children who trooped along with him. One little fellow wore pants that were obviously made from a blanket. It was always so exciting for the little ones when the hospital ship came. As the visitors walked through the wards they learned of the events of the winter. Dr. Grieve told of dogsled trips and of their winter days after the sea froze. It had been an unusually hard winter.

Stan, with the St. Anthony hospital floor plan fresh in his mind followed close by on the doctors' heels. He never dreamed that hospital plans would one day be on his desk in a far country. The Battle Harbor hospital was a twenty-bed hospital and at full capacity. Stan noticed how Dr. Grenfell greeted each patient. They moved from room to room, the men's wards, the women's wards and the operating room. They also saw a large hall used for many purposes. Dr. Grenfell had often held services there. Stan listened as the illnesses and treatment procedures of the current patients were discussed. Tuberculosis was a tremendous problem as well as scurvy and beri beri caused by malnutrition. Part of the reason that tuberculosis spread so rapidly was because of small, crowded living quarters.

Dr. Grenfell consulted further about the more critically ill patients, then ordered that new medical supplies, books and relief clothing be brought from the ship. Stan was in charge of the books and the relief clothing. The books were carefully packed as small libraries with a variety to suit many age groups. He soon had some eager teenagers helping in a procession carrying boxes to the lecture hall. The *Strathcona* didn't stay long, for more urgent needs were farther north. After a night spent on the ship as their hotel, the anchor was hoisted and they moved out. Those left behind in the little hospital faced the future with new courage.

This next trip would include several stops. The first was at a small cove with several little shacks lining the coast. As soon as they dropped anchor small rowboats drew near and people started climbing on board.

"Please, doc, there are some sick ones we couldn't bring. Could you come to shore for a while?"

Dr. Grenfell held clinic for those who had come aboard, and then he was rowed in to see the most seriously ill. There he saw heartbreaking cases, often too late for help. The tilts and sod houses that smelled of fish and seal oil were pathetic to see. Bunks were against the walls and the floors were of packed earth. There were dilapidated stoves and people sat on the bunks instead of chairs.

As the doctor moved from shack to shack and examined the sick, sometimes medicine was all that was needed. At other times an old sail was used as a stretcher and a patient would be carried by his friends and rowed out to the ship for surgery. The problem always was, who could provide post-operative care if the patient stayed in his shack? Then it was that the swinging cots on the *Strathcona* slowly filled up for a trip to the nearest Grenfell hospital. This time it was to Indian Harbor. It was "all hands needed now" as they cared for the many seriously ill patients on board.

Stan had a natural knack for assisting the doctor. Being a Newfoundlander he seemed to understand the patients in a special way as they spoke in their strong dialect. Whether it was feeding them, pulling teeth, dressing wounds, or giving medications, Stan was becoming an expert teenage nurse.

The wireless was often crackling with messages calling for help. Dr. Grenfell made note of the locations and planned his schedule to help if possible.

One late afternoon they arrived at Indian Harbor crowded with schooners. The harbor name is derived from an interesting rock formation that looks like an Indian lying on his back. Dr. and Mrs. Paddon and three nurses came down to meet them at the wharf. The familiar cordial greetings took place. It was always with the deepest respect and gratitude that the mission workers received the doctor who made their vitally needed work possible. This time, patients were to be unloaded and transported up to the hospital. One teenage patient named John, who was in great pain, was anxious for Stan to walk beside his stretcher as he was taken to the strange place. Stan stayed with him as the boy was admitted, bathed and laid in a clean hospital bed. Stan patted him on the shoulder and said "Aren't you lucky!" as a pretty nurse approached to administer a pain shot. Stan waved goodbye from the door, and went to check on the others brought from the ship, then quickly observed the layout of the hospital.

He had heard how the building had been constructed in St. John's and sent by pieces on the mail steamer. At first it housed only nine patients and was badly crowded, but now it was a fine two-story building, 32 by 32 feet.

The *Strathcona* crew enjoyed the meals after many days at sea. The plan was to stay four days this time for Dr. Grenfell to do surgery on the many waiting patients.

The time passed quickly, and with fine weather smiling on them they again hoisted anchor and were off, leaving behind them many grateful people. Now there would be weeks of medical stops on a course that would take them all the way up to the Inuit and Montaignais Indian area. The greatest adventure that marked Stan's first Labrador summer in 1908 was just ahead.

They received the usual messages concerning medical emergencies on Stan's wireless, but on July 28 a message came from Anticosti, an island south of them. "Storm brewing, possibly a hurricane. All ships at sea take warning." Stan was tickled that the message came from the place where he had been wireless operator the year before. He quickly responded with, "Heard you. Thanks. Stan Martin on the *Strathcona*."

Dr. Grenfell was used to storms, but he kept careful watch of the falling barometer. They anchored that evening about twenty miles from Indian Harbor in an open unsafe harbor. However as winds increased, they got up steam and headed back for Indian Harbor, the best possible place for them. Dr. Grenfell later wrote: "It was blowing so strongly by this time that the hospital yawl *Daryl* had already been driven ashore from her anchors, but still we were able to keep ours in the water, and getting a line to her, to heave her astern of our vessel with our powerful winch. The fury of the breeze grew worse as the day went on. All the fishing boats in the harbor filled and sank with the driving water. With the increase of the violence of the weather we got up steam and steamed to our anchors to ease if possible the strain on our two chains and shore lines – a web which we had been able to weave before it was too late. By Sunday the gale had blown itself entirely away and Monday morning broke flat, calm, with lovely sunshine…" [3]

It's one thing to survive a hurricane when on shore, but to live through a night like that on board a small steamship was unforgettable. No wonder they called her "the brave old hospital ship." One could add, "It was a brave crew that lived to tell about it."

The eventful summer passed and after miles of service along the whole Labrador Coast the *Strathcona* returned to St. Anthony.

---

3   Grenfell, Wilfred T. *A Labrador Doctor*. Houghton Mifflin Company. The Riverside Press Cambridge, 1919. p. 316-317.

Stan boarded a coastal steamer and returned home to St. John's and another year at Methodist College. When he walked again into his home at 171 Le Marchant Road he knew his life had changed completely. He would never forget the brave, cheerful, suffering people he had seen that summer. As for him, he was now ready to face any hardship in the future.

He reveled in the family's welcome. His brother, Bill, had grown taller. His sisters Mabel, Gertrude and Eva hovered over him. "Did you see any pretty girls?" they asked. He only grinned at them as he stood before the open fireplace glancing around at the familiar furnishings. That night his comfortable bed didn't rock all night. He was home. He especially enjoyed his mother's good cooking with the variety of fruits and vegetables he hadn't tasted all summer. But "Please, Mother, no fish for me for a while." His mother smiled and understood.

Soon he was back into the rush of college life – hockey, hours of study and a new interest in his science subjects. The church people and his chums were eager to hear of his adventures. A new seriousness in Stan was obvious as he told of Dr. Grenfell's work, describing the tremendous changes in the lives of desperately needy people. He told of open-air hymn sings and services by the sea or on board the *Strathcona*. He had heard Dr. Grenfell's many messages and had come to understand his philosophy of life. "I believe in the gospel of Jesus Christ as it is translated into the everyday lives of those around me. In other words, roll up your sleeves and make the world a better place, right where you are, in the name of Jesus." This creed became Stan's own as he prepared himself for the future.

After his college year of 1909, Stan was welcomed back to St. Anthony for his former summer job. He found the hospital busier than ever, with the fine surgeon, Dr. John M. Little, in charge. The *Strathcona* lay waiting and Stan checked the wireless equipment. There was exciting news of Dr. Grenfell's future plans.

The doctor had made his usual trip to England that fall to report to the Mission to Deep Sea Fishermen Council, and for a lecture tour to raise funds. In the spring, when he was returning on the *Mauretania*, he met a young lady named Anna Elizabeth MacClanahan. It was a four and a half day trip across the Atlantic, but before they reached New York he had proposed to her. "Why, you don't even know my name!" she exclaimed. He answered to the effect that he was more concerned about what her name was going to be. A trip to her home at Lake Forest near Chicago won her consent, and the approval of her family, and their wedding date was set for November 18 that year. During the doctor's visit to her home the couple planned and designed a house that was to be built on a beautiful hill overlooking St. Anthony. But the Labrador summer work had to come first. Thousands of people were waiting for Dr. Grenfell. When all was ready the *Strathcona* blew its farewell, and he and his crew were off again.

Dr. Grenfell had outlined the tour schedule: The cottage hospital visits, then Hamilton Inlet, the Hudson Bay post, Rigolet where the Montagnais Indians brought their furs for sale, Indian Harbor where they had withstood the hurricane, and then they would go up as far as Hopedale and Turnavik Eskimo country. If time and weather permitted, the plan was to go even farther north past Nain to Okak, near Cape Mugford. A new member sailed with them this time, Francis B. Sayres from Brown University. He was one of the WOPS (work without pay) typical of the fine college recruits Dr. Grenfell was able to attract. He was to be the doctor's secretary. As was expected, he pitched in with the rest of the crew and did all kinds of work. Later he married Jessie Wilson, President Woodrow Wilson's daughter, at a ceremony in the White House with Dr. Grenfell as best man.

As the *Strathcona* made her stops, it was gratifying to Stan and the others to meet former patients who were well again and hard at work on their schooners. The staffs of the hospitals welcomed them as long-lost friends. The coastline was familiar and life took on a happy routine as they traveled, although there were many days of storm and fog.

There were deep discussions on board ship far into the night, and Stan absorbed a tremendous amount of knowledge while he shared in the companionship of the men. His summer trips were an education in astronomy, marine life, seamanship, and meteorology, as well as medicine. If they ever took a day off, they went ashore and climbed up into the hills to enjoy the scenery. Years later from Manchuria, Stan wrote to Grenfell about that summer. "I think of the afternoon in Saglek Bay (Northern Labrador) when Sayre, you, and I climbed the peak near the bay. I cannot forget the glorious sunsets and Labrador twilights, and the colors of the little glacier near the top. Another year, I remember the night we ran ashore in the old *Strathcona* with Bill at the wheel. We were eating goose and cranberry sauce at the time and you went over the side with your wife's photo and the cash box. Ha! Ha!"

Dr. Grenfell told of the near disasters and the number of dents on the bottom of his ship. There were fifty-two!

The summer was passing quickly with hundreds of patients examined and treated. On a memorable day in August, they were cruising near Indian Harbor when some distinguished looking men hailed the ship and came on board to use the ship's wireless equipment. The leader of the group was Harry Whitney. He said they had met Dr. Robert Cook on the west side of the Gulf coming from his Polar Expedition. Dr. Grenfell welcomed them saying he had met Dr. Cook several times and stayed at his home in Brooklyn. Whitney and his party were firm in their belief that Cook had discovered the North Pole. They also brought news that the explorer Commodore Peary was returning that year, also claiming to have reached the Pole. In fact Whitney had traveled with the returning Peary part of the way, but had transferred to another ship.

A few days later as the *Strathcona* was cruising in the Gulf of St. Lawrence, Stan went to Dr. Grenfell and said, "There can be no harm telling you, Doctor, that Peary is at Battle Harbor. He is wiring to Washington that he has found the Pole and also is asking his Committee if he may present the Mission with his superfluous supplies, or whether he is to sell them to you." Seeing that it is not easy to know whence wireless messages come if the sender does not own up to his whereabouts, Dr. Grenfell at once ordered Stan to wireless to Peary at Battle Harbor the simple words "Give it to them, of course, and sign it 'Washington.' Dr. Grenfell knew the commander would see the joke.'" [4]

When they arrived at Battle Harbor, Commodore Peary's ship the *Roosevelt* was at the wharf. The place was swarming with newspapermen.

4   Grenfell, Wilfred T. *A Labrador Doctor,* p.341. Houghton Mifflin Company, The Riverside Press Cambridge 1914

"Peary not only claimed that he had found the Pole, but also that Cook had not, and he was realizing what a hard thing it is to prove a negative." [5] In spite of the furor the *Strathcona* crew enjoyed the members of the expedition. The photograph that Stan took of Peary later appeared in Dr. Grenfell's book *A Labrador Doctor.*

Stan wrote later to his family, "I handed Peary *a telegram from Cook* saying he had discovered the North Pole one year earlier. Peary was very angry." Thus it was that the little *Strathcona* got a glimpse of a whirling controversy that still has not been fully settled.

After Stan's exhilarating second summer with Grenfell, life back in St. John's and his college classes, seemed very quiet. Nevertheless, he made excellent grades in all his subjects. It began to be clear in his mind that he should study to become a doctor. Dr. Grenfell encouraged him in this for he had watched him work with the Labrador patients. The doctor wrote of an incident involving a seriously ill pneumonia patient on the *Strathcona*. "While we have had our watches to keep on deck, a regular watch has been kept day and night by his bedside and though we are under full sail and steam, scudding southward along the Polar current, the crisis came last night. The watches are being kept by a Medical University volunteer assistant from Johns Hopkins and our Marconi operator who is an embryo medical missionary." [6]

When Stan broached the subject of medical school to his parents his father asked, "Where will you get the money?" His mother quietly said, "God will provide."

The mother's faith and trust were honored by God, for after two more Labrador summers with Grenfell, Stan enrolled at Queen's Medical School in Kingston, Ontario to fulfill his dream and God's calling. He was able to do this with his summer earnings and generous help from Dr. Grenfell.

Stan had traveled a lot, and had met many strangers in his life, but he still had a feeling of trepidation that day as he stood facing the beautiful buildings of Queen's University at Kingston, Ontario. This was Canada, Canada with English-speaking people but very different from his home country. The sunlight filtered through the gold and scarlet maple leaves as he approached the massive entrance. Some college students were loping by in sports uniforms, and pretty girls were eyeing the newcomer. He steeled himself to concentrate and disappeared into the building. At the Registrar's office he presented his papers. The Registrar adjusted his spectacles and perused them slowly "You are from St. John's, Newfoundland?"

"Yes, sir."

"Ummm. You worked with Dr. Wilfred Grenfell?"

"Yes, I spent several summers with him on his hospital ship."

"Dr. Grenfell is well-known here because he visited our campus. More than that he is well thought of, all over Canada. You must have had an interesting time with him." "Yes, I did." Stan was grateful for the kind words. Stan handed over his precious earnings, enough for the first semester. He then moved to the bulletin board to study the lists of addresses of homes that took in boarders. He chose NR 100 Clergy West noting that it was not too far from the school. He had his duffel bag, but he knew he would have to take a carriage to the river dock for his trunks.

[5]   Ibid
[6]   *Deep Sea Fisherman.* July, 1910. p. 17.

Fortunately the home he had chosen had a vacancy, and by evening he was settled bag and baggage into his comfortable room.

School started soon and he relished his first class. It was anatomy. He found he knew much of the material already from a dog-eared copy of an anatomy book that Dr. Grenfell had given him. His fellow medical students eyed the young Newfoundlander with curiosity.

As the days passed he joined in some of the sports programs. Later he played his mandolin and sang at social gatherings. When a chance to act in Shakespeare presented itself he joined the Drama Club and was readily accepted. In his classes the professors and students were impressed with his medical knowledge and skills, learned by hands-on experience working with Dr. Grenfell.

He enjoyed having a role in *Hamlet*, but was mortified that the "props" person had forgotten to put the button on his rapier in his fight scene. So the curtain came down, as he hurried to give first aid to his buddy! It was nothing serious however. He laughed to tell about it.

Always a churchgoer he attended the Methodist Sydenham St. Church. At the University he joined the Student Volunteer Group, continuing his membership from high school days in St. John's. Soon he was the enthusiastic president of the Student Volunteer Band, with a growing interest in foreign missions.

The first school year passed quickly and each summer he returned to the St. Anthony hospital. In 1912 he worked again with Dr. John Little, the brilliant surgeon from Boston. In the summer of 1913, he was given increasing responsibilities as an X-ray technician.

As he unpacked and settled in for the summer's work he found many new faces. There were new nurses, as well as eager men college students called WOPs meaning "work without pay." Dr. Grenfell was able to attract them from some of the finest schools and hospitals in the United States and Canada. St. Anthony was buzzing with activity!

"THE HOSPITAL SHIP. STRATHCONA"

The Strathcona Dr. Wilfred Grenfell's hospital ship at Labrador

IV

God's Mosaic

✦

The wind blew hard that cold November morning in New England. However the great white homestead was snug and warm. It had braved many winter storms since Revolutionary Days.

Lincoln Albion Rogers, a scholarly gentleman, was seated in front of the roaring fireplace finishing the morning paper. He was pleased when he read that his friend Henry Wadsworth Longfellow was coming for another visit to their alma mater, Bowdoin College, at Brunswick not far from there. That's good, he thought, I will plan to see him. He took out his pocket watch to check the time. It was almost time for the mail.

It was lonely there at Cathance, Maine, but as Christmas was coming, Roger's only daughter, Margaret, would be there soon. He brightened at the thought. His eyes went to the portrait of his beautiful wife who had died in childbirth many years ago. He always kept flowers in front of it. Little pink chrysanthemums smiled there, the last of the fall flowers. He remembered how he had had to give up his little daughter, who was six at the time of her mother's death, to be sent to her Uncle Francis Barne's home at Houlton, Maine. He was her mother's brother. As Lincoln was then principal of the New Britain Seminary, New Britain, Connecticut, and later in charge of the science department in the New Britain high school, there was no one to care for her at home. Lincoln was extremely grateful that her Uncle and his family had raised her so well, encouraging her in her studies and piano lessons. The cousins were older, but loved her as a little sister. It had been a home with books and music, and a busy church life at the First Baptist Church that her Uncle Francis had founded in 1863. He was its first deacon and served as superintendent of the Sunday school for many years. He had attended Harvard University but returned home early because of ill health. Each Sunday at church, the young child Margaret noticed the large globe of the world to the right of the pulpit area. It was in the days when Adoniram and Anne Judson had gone to Burma as missionaries, and the church had followed their ministry with prayer and concern. Through her high school days, Margaret constantly heard of missionary work around the world.

She had had visits with her father as she took nurses training at St. Luke's in New York City. Later she transferred to the New England Baptist Hospital Training School in Boston and had graduated in 1911. Now her father was looking forward to more frequent visits.

Going to the hall he put on his warmest coat and cap to brave the storm and went out to the mailbox. The path he had shoveled was holding, but snow was streaming on to it from the piles on either side. Letters? Yes, and bills, of course, but one letter was from Margaret. He was content and hurried back to his warm fireplace.

Some days dawn innocently with no announcement that a watershed in life may occur on that day. Such was this day for him as he read:

Wednesday November 20, '12
Dear Papa,

I have some news for you. I have been offered a position for a year in one of Dr. Grenfell's hospitals in North Newfoundland and have practically decided to go. It is the sort of work I have wanted to do all along, so the opportunity did not find me unprepared. It is a position with a small salary, no expenses, and Dr. Grenfell himself with his wife and children are to be at the station to have charge of the hospital in person this winter.

I have been out to see Aunt Addie [her mother's sister] today and talked it over with her. She approves and I think realizes that it is the chance of a lifetime for me.

The surgical experiences alone, for a year is a great inducement. Nurses who have returned, say it is as good as a postgraduate course. There are two other nurses, and Dr. Grenfell sent for another one who has fallen ill with appendicitis and failed them. That is how I got the call. You may be interested to know I first heard of it in Boston at the Dudley St. Church. I have been more or less discontented with private work, it costs a lot to live and the temptation to spend a lot for clothes and good times makes it seem like pouring water into a sieve. And while the work is pleasant enough you don't get anywhere. Now, up there, one's work is really needed and it will be a grand chance to see a little of the work of a great missionary in his own mission station.

It is only for a year, which is not so bad as the long and lonely times that I spent in New York. Nor is it as far away as India, where one would have to stay for several years.

I have talked it over at my Nurse's Registry and the one in charge thought it an excellent experience for a young nurse to have.

About the climate, it is cold, of course, but we had it 40 degrees below in Houlton and I know how to dress for it.

The hospital is at St. Anthony's on almost the extreme northern point of Newfoundland, a well-equipped operating room, steam heat, and electric lights. Am enclosing a circular which I should like returned.

The boat goes from St. John's to St. Anthony every two weeks and I would like the one leaving December 11th, which would oblige me to leave Boston December 6th, going by train to Sidney, Cape Breton, across the channel to Newfoundland and by rail to St. John's.

I am thinking of coming to Cathance Friday or Saturday to see you and talk it over. It is not a thing that I would rush into and regret, but I have been planning and shaping my course for just such a chance, and now that it has come, I am ready. I am glad it has come in this way for it will not take me away from America and it will not keep me away too long. I had been thinking of trying to get some such work in the west or south, in home missions.

This is a thing which I must decide for myself but it would make me very happy to go with your entire approval and consent, to do my little part in the Master's work. Think over it, sleep over it, and don't answer in haste.

Lovingly,
Daughter

Lincoln sat quietly for a while as the news sank in. The letter slid onto the floor. He was stunned. In a few moments he stood with his back to the fire and gazed around the room. The thought of the long winter months ahead seemed to descend on his heart like a black cloud. The room darkened. He thought of his brothers' families – yes, he had them nearby. The pictures of Brother George and Brother Charles in their sea captain's uniforms smiled reassuringly from the library bookcase. But they are gone for months at a time overseas – their wives, with nephews and nieces will surely have me for Christmas. But this news, he paused, this news will have to be thought through.

His daughter Margaret's visit came and went like a whirlwind. She was so excited and so beautiful in her long Boston skirts, and her dark hair in a bouffant hairdo. Her eyes shone as she explained further details. As she had written in her letter, she was prepared for this. "I'll write often! When the boats can sail it'll be every two weeks, and when the sea freezes they say there's dog-sled mail from Deer Lake."

They pored over a large map together. Gradually, in watching her happiness, he began to accept the inevitable, and gave his consent.

During the precious few days together he prepared their favorite steaks and New England baked beans and Boston brown bread. He was an excellent chef. She played the piano for him. "Loves Old Sweet Song," the classics he loved, and many hymns. On pretense of stoking the fire, he often used his big handkerchief, before going back to sit down and listen. Sometimes they just sat holding hands while watching the flames dance in the fireplace.

Upstairs in her room at night she looked through the treasures he had given her that had belonged to her mother. She chose an embroidered handkerchief and a gold brooch with daisies on it, to take on her new adventure.

Then the day arrived for Cousin Alex to come with his horse and buggy to take them to the Brunswick railroad station. After Lincoln returned he slowly went back in to the empty house, stirred the fire, put on another log and sat in his favorite chair.

A postcard from Sydney, New Brunswick, and one from St. John's Newfoundland, were the first communications. Nearly six weeks later her first letter came from St. Anthony. It had been forwarded from his sister-in-law. Eagerly Lincoln settled himself to read it on January 4, 1913.

> SS *Prospero*
> Seal Cove
> White Bay
> December 23, 1912
>
> Dear Aunt Addie,
>
> Such a trip as this has been!
>
> We expect to reach St. Anthony by Xmas day. Last I wrote you was mailed from Exploito and this will go back by the *Prospero*. Now if the weather is good, the ship will make one more trip as far as St. Anthony; otherwise, there will be a period of five weeks or so, when you will not hear, while the first dog teams are making their way to Deer Lake.
>
> I saw my first iceberg this morning, a stray that was left in a cove at Baie Verte. It was a beauty, pale green and snowy white. The seawater is wonderfully clear along this coast. You can see the bottom in places where it is deep enough to float the good ship *Prospero*. At Fortune Harbor last Saturday was our first experience with ice breaking. She sailed into a deep winding harbor in the shape of a letter "S" and went through thin ice to the wharf. The open sea was quite hidden by the hills when we were in that port. At the entrance was a tiny lighthouse perched high on a cliff with a roped path leading to it from the light keeper's house.
>
> As we passed it, the captain blew the ship's whistle and they (on shore) dipped the English flag in salute to His Majesty's Royal Mail.

It has been growing steadily colder and our portholes are now white with frost. I have been out every day for a long time and have found my heavy sweater and black coat quite sufficient. Am wearing the worsted shoes inside my boots now.

Saturday evening we reached Pilley's Island and Mr. Blackburn and I went ashore and called on the doctor and nurse at the hospital. It is quite as barn-like as the picture in the magazine, but there are comfortable beds and good stoves inside, an operating room of a sort, dispensary, library and two isolating wards for TB.

December 24, 1912

We made good progress last night and this morning after breakfast we were within an hour's run of Englee; a beautiful clear day, sun low in the southeast, blue sea and white hills along the shore, one sail in the distance, and on our starboard, low large islands which can be seen from St. Anthony. So we are on the home stretch.

Englee is in a broad bay, surrounded by hills, and our first glimpse was of a wee white church spire. After winding around an inner point, we came to the harbor that was thick with "slob" ice, and pushed our way up to the wharf. The ropes were thrown to a schooner that was lying there frozen in, and the freight was landed across the deck. We did not stay long, and are well on our way to Conche, which will be our last stop before St. Anthony. We ought to get in early this evening.

At nearly all harbors now, we have to break ice to reach port. In Tilt cove with a brilliant moon, we pushed our way beneath an almost overhanging cliff, black and grim, with frozen cascades down its sides. We were there a long time on account of freight, and the misty moonlight on the more distant hills was weird enough. From one of those hills came a snow-slide that buried several people and houses last year.

Nippers Harbor was another picturesque place with very comfortable houses. On shore there, I met a boy with a large can of cow's milk. Some fresh butter also was brought aboard. Again the clear deep green water at the wharf. The rise and fall of the tide here is only about four or five feet, I am told.

I was talking with Mr. Ford, a Hudson Bay man, and he says that in the southernmost bay of Hudson Bay, a place about 200 miles wide, there is a very great rise and fall for which they are not able to account – 45 feet. The Bay of Fundy tide rises 60 feet.

We have on board Mr. George Reid, the man who rescued Dr. Grenfell, when he was "Afloat on an Icepan." Mr. Reid said he expected to find a dead man. He did not know it was "T' Doctor" when he spied him with the glass, but had seen him cross the bay on the ice earlier in the day. But it was all the same to him, a life to be saved, and he took his sons and some other young men and went to the rescue.

We visited several little harbors yesterday where a dozen small boats came out to meet the steamer. The ship's boat is lowered away at these points with the "Royal Mail."

We have been traveling night and day, thanks to good weather, and a brilliant moon.

Last December 24th, I was helping you get the turkey ready. I wish I could help you today. As it is, I have been out on deck enjoying the fine air and scenery most of the morning. We have breakfast at eight, and when the first bell rang at seven-thirty, there was a big moon shining through the porthole, and the *Prospero* was steaming smoothly through a sea of soft "slob" along the French shore. "Slob" makes for very smooth sailing.

Sunday we had a fine sing. There is a piano and there were about twenty or thirty people, mostly local fishermen. And how they did sing, and they asked me again in the afternoon to play for them, and in the evening when I was away up on the top deck, they sent for me to play some more! "Throw Out the Life-Line" was a favorite, and they sang verse after verse of "Nearer, My God, to Thee" and "Abide with Me." "The Harbor Bell" was another. It was quite touching to hear those big fellows sing. We had a Methodist minister from Newfoundland aboard, the St. Anthony rector who is a Scotchman, a French priest and some Salvation Army people, besides Mr. Blackburn and I of the Grenfell mission. The Captain sings well and came down and helped us out for awhile.

No more surf now, and the rocks are ice-covered white.
Nearing St. Anthony – about three hours more, should arrive 9:00 p.m.

Lovingly,
Margaret

With the first communication from Margaret at St. Anthony, her father was remarkably encouraged. She had arrived safely and he could wait for the next events. A growing pride in his daughter helped cheer the long winter days.

That night on the ship, after Margaret finished her letter she eagerly went on deck. As the *Prospero* approached the harbor, lights from little houses along the shore shone with a warm yellow glow. They were from oil lamps or candlelight. The hospital and surrounding mission houses were brighter, with precious electricity. She was struck by the deep darkness all around the little settlement. It was fortunate that the *Prospero* could still make it to the wharf. When they docked, staff members were there to greet her and to help her with her bags on the short walk to the hospital. There the door was opened, and she was swept in to a bright, colorful room to cries of "Welcome! Glad you're here!" Dr. and Mrs. Wilfred Grenfell were at the door. There were introductions all around. Since it was off-season for new personnel she was the only new nurse at that time and greatly needed.

They were in the midst of a Christmas Eve program, and the little children from the orphanage nearby were about to sing. Margaret was seated near them and she had a chance to look around the hospital living room. It was decorated with tinsel, and red and green paper chains. A Christmas tree stood in the corner. She studied the eager little faces of the children as they sang. Later she was to hear of the tragic background of some of them.

There were presents for the children, and tea and tinned cookies from England for refreshments. Evidently the cookies were a very special treat. Margaret had an introduction to the cheerful, irrepressible Dr. Grenfell, who kept them all laughing as they chatted together.

They sang more carols, the party broke up, and Margaret was shown to her room. It was not long before she fell into a sound asleep. It was the end of a journey, but the beginning of the greatest adventure of her life.

The next morning she dressed in her nurse's uniform and cap, taking time to peer through the frosted window at the view of the harbor, and the glittering landscape nearby.

Breakfast was down the hall, and again the staff members welcomed her as she sat with them. Miss Cannon the senior nurse said, "After morning prayers, I'll show you the ropes."

Many questions were directed to the newcomer. Since the staff members were isolated, they were eager for news of the outside world. They were especially following the situation of Captain Scott and his exploration party in the Antarctic. She noticed the different nationalities as they spoke. One of the nurses, Miss Bryce, a charming lady, was Scottish. She was to become one of Margaret's best friends. Dr. Seymour Armstrong, a surgeon, was English. The others spoke with their Newfoundland way of speaking that fascinated Margaret as she traveled aboard ship.

One of the men said, "You'll be facing the coldest winter of your life here. A Hudson Bay man who visited us, told us, 'Northern Newfoundland is far colder than the Hudson Bay area.'" He also said "The Finlanders, the men Grenfell brought over to herd his reindeer, complain that they never faced cold like this before." Margaret only laughed and said, "I'll be all right. It was cold in Maine, too. I'm used to it."

After scripture and a prayer, they scattered to their duties to start the busy day. Miss Cannon led the way for Margaret. They went first to the wards. There, friendly curious eyes watched the new nurse as she moved among the beds, and greeted the patients. The wards were bright in the winter sunshine, with scripture verses on the wall. In the operating room they were preparing for surgery that was scheduled for 8:30 that morning. They expected Dr. Grenfell at any moment, down from the "Castle," his home on the hill.

It didn't take long to tour the facilities and learn where all the equipment was kept. Margaret was to start with night duty, so she could unpack and rest until then.

Her first night on the wards went smoothly. She was thoroughly accustomed to hospital routine. She wrote her papa, "After dinner when on night duty I go around, take temperatures, give out medicine, extra blankets, and get people settled for the night. Last evening Dr. Armstrong was giving tuberculin tests to a number of the patients and it was after nine before I got the lights out. Dr. Armstrong likes tea, English fashion, before retiring."

"After all the staff members have gone to bed I sit in the nurse's room and read, or write, or sew, and listen for any calls from the wards. The house is so quiet now. But in the summer when it's full, the nurse has to fly around like an owl."

She noticed how everyone was greatly affected by the comings, and goings, of the ships. The *Dutchess* was the first one to come in, limping with a broken propeller, bringing twenty-four letters for Margaret. The hospital staff was astonished! Her father, and nearly every Barnes and Rogers relative had written her.

The *Prospero* returned to them January 14th after a stormy trip, and had to stay far out beyond the ice. Even then she became frozen in during the night. Two of the patients returned home on her. One was a little lame girl who was pulled by hand on a komatik [sled] by Dr. Grenfell to the water's edge to catch the boat. The mission dog team was away on a trip.

Then came the big freeze, and a hush came over the harbor. They were frozen in for the winter. The new situation called for a greater appreciation for human companionship, and for the social events to keep up one's spirits. Sunday services were held in the wards with many of the villagers attending. Dr. Grenfell often led them. He read "The Other Wiseman" on Margaret's first Sunday. Other Sundays, the Methodist Rev. Allenby or the rector of the Anglican church presided and preached. The patients appreciated the messages, the music and the visitors. They helped the long winter days go by.

Margaret and the other nurses often gave dinners or tea parties or were invited to the Guesthouse, orphanage or Dr. Grenfell's for meals. Sometimes there was a "Sing" at one of the homes. Margaret wrote later, "Everyone (back home) seems to think that this place is cheerless, far from it! We are as cozy and comfortable as we can be, and too busy to have time to fret for the luxuries and amusements of city life, making the most of what we have, our music and our outdoor sports. The out-of-doors here is just perfect, such sunrises, such hills and snow and ocean ever changing, never the same."

Her small world expanded when she walked across the harbor to a little store, passing deep holes dug in the ice for fresh water holes. She bought some Baffinland moccasins, and admired an Eskimo princess' fur costume, and Inuit ivory curios, kayaks and reindeer and seals.

V

The Long Winter

S oon after she arrived, Margaret was invited by Mrs. Grenfell up to the "Castle" for tea. It was slippery going up the hill. Mrs. Grenfell led her to the spacious living room and they had tea before the open fireplace. A great white polar bear rug was spread out before them. Miss Dunn, the English governess for little Wilfred, Jr., had tea with them, while two-year-old Wilfred, toddled around them and begged for cookies. Mrs. Grenfell was interested in Margaret's background, and that her father had taught at Dearborn Seminary in Chicago not far from Lake Forest, Mrs. Grenfell's hometown. She showed Margaret around the home; especially the great glassed-in front area, with the magnificent view of the mission complex and the harbor. Guns, snowshoes and mounted heads of deer and caribou graced the walls. A place of honor was given to a plaque honoring Moody, Watch and Spy, Dr. Grenfell's dogs that he had to kill when he was stranded on the ice-pan. Their skins saved his life, keeping him from freezing to death.

The two women stood before it, sober with the memory of the near tragedy. Margaret said, "Mr. Reid who first spied the Doctor out on the ice-pan, and went to rescue him, was on the ship last month as we were coming to St. Anthony. He told me about it. What a story!"

To Margaret, the Grenfell home was to be a welcome oasis in future days.

On January 24 she wrote to her father:

> Yesterday we had two cases in the operating room, and were rushed all day. Did not get through our ward dressings 'til 4:30 p.m. Dr Grenfell stayed for dinner with us at the hospital and did dressings afterwards. He is most entertaining at table. You can imagine. Such sparkles of fun. Everything is original. In the P.M. he sent Burton (our medical student) to Gricquet, ten miles in 10-degrees-below weather, by dog team on a sick call, and to see patients along the way. He is expected to be back today. But it has been "dirty" weather, a smother of drifting snow and high wind, the temperature 18 degrees. So he hasn't shown up yet. We have no cases of lung tuberculosis, but a number of TB bone and joint cases.

In summer they have an outdoor shack for TB patients on the side of Fox Farm hill, where the Tea House is. I visited the Tea House twice last week. The view was quite different from the first day, as the Arctic slob has come well down into White Bay. The horizon was white instead of blue.

In the evening Miss Appleton asked me to go up again by the light of the full moon. A perfect night. Thermometer -4 degrees below zero. Just lovely with proper garments, skin boots, sweaters and dickey, I was almost too warm climbing the hill.

Our little Methodist church is just square, with pointed spire and good lines. It stands where it can be seen out to sea. To the right were the rugged cliffs of Fishing Point, and the big moon shimmering over the harbor ice. This is a place an artist would revel in!

Have been here a month tonight! In some ways the time has flown. I can't always realize I am here.

Tomorrow I am invited to the orphanage for dinner, and I shall take my thimble along to help with the mending. Miss Storr and Miss Spalding, two fine English women are in charge.

When I first came, I used to look out of my window at the orphan children in their elf-like costumes, funny little pixies playing about in the snow. It was like fairyland.

In the hospital now, we have four children, three boys and a girl. Little Evelyn came on the boat with me. Poor Tommy, one of the little boys, has been in bed for several weeks with a bad abscess on his leg, which had been operated on, but is slow in healing. He has to wear a heavy brace from his shoulder to his feet to keep his poor little leg straight. He has been in the hospital now nearly a year. His father came down to see him this week from Cape Norman. He is here as a patient for rheumatism just now. He's a big husky fisherman. Tommy can catch a good lot of fish too, when he is well.

We have another fisherman who has lost one foot, and is suffering intense pain at times. He has deep bone abscesses in the other hip. He has been ill for a long time and it doesn't seem as if he can stand it much longer. He's bright and cheery though, when he has spells of being free from pain. He taught me a bottle knot the other day, quite an intricate affair but "not a circumstance" to a top-mast head knot or some such thing as he called it. He cannot read and uses quaint phrases such as you read in Dr. Grenfell's stories. "Can I have a hot brick? He [the brick] is cold now.

A cold snap spoiled the plumbing in the Guest House. The hospital and the "Castle" are the only places that have water now. The orphanage pipes froze up some time ago, and the older boys have to haul water from the brook.

The next day Margaret picked up her sewing kit and made her way over to the orphanage for dinner. The children were excited knowing they would have something special to eat because "company" was coming! They clustered around as the gracious Misses Storr and Spalding greeted her. She was introduced to each child.

She was shown around and was especially interested in the nursery, where three little ones were in cribs, and two toddlers were being fed in their highchairs. Martha, a rosy-cheeked teenager from the village, was feeding them. Miss Storr pointed to a little blonde girl and said, "Susie there, arrived just recently, her widowed mother died and neighbors found her just in time to save her from starving. These others were gathered from the Labrador coast last summer, and came on the *Strathcona*."

During the meal the children kept up an excited chatter. The special treat was the dessert, rice pudding with raisins! They had heard that "this Miss Rogers nurse" could play the piano and they could hardly wait to hear her. Believe it or not, there was a piano in the corner of the living room.

After dinner Margaret played for them. She started with Sunday school hymns they knew, so they could sing with her, then ended with a flourish by playing "The Mosquito March." None of them sat down to listen, but crowded around her to watch her flying fingers. They cheered as she finished.

Then it was time for afternoon chores for the children, and Margaret went to the sewing room with Miss Spalding. As they patched and mended, the gray-haired English woman spoke in low tones. She told of shipwrecks and drownings, of malnutrition, of drunken fathers and 'flu epidemics. Always she was grateful that these children were found in time. Here their future was bright. They were well-fed and educated, and some of them were to go on to careers in the outside world, or to be employed as good workers in the Mission.

The weeks flew by in the hospital, but at last Margaret was to have her first trip away from the Mission.

She wrote home about it:

February 12, 1913

St. Anthony, NFLD
[Received March 28 in Houlton, Maine 6 - weeks.]

Dear Aunt Addie:

I hope you received my telegram today. I sent it the 10th, to make sure. Did not write the last mail, thought the telegram would do.

I had been on a trip, and we have had two operations, and one a big amputation this week. So you see we have been busy!

The trip was to Gricquet, ten miles by komatik to bring back a sick baby, and to carry medicines to various patients along the way. I would not have missed it for anything, and hope to have more experiences like it. Mr. Burton and Miss Cannon divided the night duty in the hospital.

To begin with, we had a dangerously ill pneumonia case, one of the reindeer herders in the hospital, and Miss Bryce and I were taking alternate nights.

I had just gone off duty, after noon dinner, when Mr. Burton came up and said Dr. Grenfell wanted to know if I would like to go and get that baby. I was delighted with the chance for the trip, and got ready as quickly as I could. It takes time to dress in these Arctic costumes. All the stockings one owns, skin boots, three sweaters, canvas shirt and dickey and woolen hood.

Then after getting my orders and various pills, I went down to the ice, where a fine dog team was waiting. This same team had just brought Dr. Grenfell over from Gricquet in an hour and a half. They took me back in two hours. You pile on the komatik, wrapped in a steamer rug if you are wise, and hang on tight and away you go. The way a good Newfoundland driver manages his team of dogs and keeps the komatik from upsetting, rouses my greatest admiration.

A komatik is long and low, almost like a toboggan, and one would not have far to fall. But I have not been spilled yet.

Well, away we went across the harbor up, up on the wind-swept hills, and down again to the harbor light on the other side. There was such a steep pitch, I jumped off, and slid down, as there were too many "ballicaters" or piles of rough ice at the bottom to suit my fancy for riding. Then, away across smooth ice with the white frozen ocean on the right and Fishing Point behind.

Then up again towards the deer camp. We saw several beauties of the herd in the distance. And on the return journey next day, we followed about 20 or 30 of them. And how the dogs did run!

Once we crossed a lake and took a thrilling coast down to sea level again and went several miles along St. Luman's Bay, solid ice and so blue, white and pretty along the shore. At St. Luman we stopped at a house to get warm and saw the young sister of one of the dog-drivers. It is amazing the number of pretty girls there are in this country. But the women age very quickly. A hard life they lead.

Unfortunately, I carried to Gricquet some medicines that should have been left at St. Luman. I called to see a girl with a sore throat, and gave her some medicine. Looked in at the little pneumonia boy Dr. Grenfell had just left. Then I called at

Kenneth Adams, whose baby was to come back with me. Such a forlorn place, dirty, you never saw such a place. I took a basin of soap and water and showed the father how to bathe the baby. He did have a cake of soap!

Five children were downstairs; two older girls about 14 and 15, sweet and pretty and quite deaf, and little Jimmy, who had been a patient for a long time at the hospital. "Ken" Adams (the father), who was a happy-go-lucky, good-natured and kind-hearted man said he would take me back with the medicines to St. Luman with his dogs and thought we could easily reach Gricquet again by ten, about a four-mile trip. It was then getting dark, but the light on the snow made fair going, and the man knew the way so well, I was not afraid. So back we went in the cool sweet air.

Coasting over some fine hills again, we found a dear little old lady, another pneumonia (case) in a wee bit of home that was "spick and span" clean, quite a contrast. Just she and the "skipper' lived alone together. She told me how Dr. Little came there drenched through with rain one night, and how she worked 'til three o'clock to dry his things for him. Then she said she was afraid the "skipper" had not put on a white tablecloth for my tea! All this while she was breathing 50 to the minute. I have since heard the dear old soul has recovered.

A message was delivered for some man to come with dogs to haul wood for the Dr. (Grenfell). Another box of pills for a "beriberi" case, and we got back to Gricquet quicker than I thought. But still more patients were asking to be seen, though I had no medicine for them. A regular epidemic of colds and pneumonia. Later Dr. Grenfell, Mr. Burton, and Miss Bryce made six trips to Gricquet within the week. There were so many who were ill.

I stayed at Mr. Esau Hillyer's that night, the best place in Gricquet, comfortable and clean. His young wife gave me delicious crackers and cheese and a "bake-apple" drink. "Bake-apple" is a small white berry which they gather and preserve, and the drink tastes not unlike baked apple. In the morning I made a call on foot on two pneumonia cases. When I returned found the "coach box" or woman box (these boxes are put on the komatik for more comfortable and warmer travel) waiting for me to go after the baby. Another call was to see two or three more patients and by the time I had the baby bundled up, it was eleven o'clock.

It was a beautiful clear day, a little below zero. We made good time stopping in a "Brahut" to "mug up" [probably drank hot tea] and to feed the baby. We arrived at St. Anthony about 3:30. We were glad to see the Light House and Fishing Point looming up. It was not a hard journey except that I was anxious about the baby. I had two hot stove lids to keep him warm. He lived for several days, but was too far gone when we got him, for us to be able to save him. He died last Sunday, just after service. It was so sad.

Mr. Dahl, the Anglican rector, took the hospital service and stayed to tea with us. Mrs. Boone and I went to church in the evening and heard the Dr. [Grenfell] preach a fine Lenten sermon. He was so tired. He had been up all night before at Gricquet. But he preached splendidly as always.

Tuesday, Dr. Armitage and Miss Cannon returned after a month's absence. They had been up to Cape Norman, down the West Coast to Flower Cove and Brigg Bay where the epidemic proved to be chicken pox.

Dr Armstrong went on a call to "Port-au-Choix" after he recovered from his pneumonia. They are both tired but none the worse for the trip. A glorious country to be out-of-doors, if you can keep from freezing. Fingers, toes and noses "frost-burn" very easily. Please send this letter on to N.Y. and Houlton.

Lots of Love,
Margaret

St. Anthony, NFLD
March 27, 1913
3:00am

Dear Aunt Addie,

The mail came in last night, bringing your letter, the first in three weeks from you. We all came eagerly down to the sun parlor where Dr. Armstrong and Mr. Burton were sorting it. "Now, don't grab!" Burton said, and well he might, for we nearly fall over each other when the mail comes. Your pictures in the sleigh arrived and I was <u>delighted</u>!

You wrote about seal meat. I have not eaten any, but the odor in most houses, and about the skin boots, is very strong and rather disgusting at first, but one gets used to it. Miss Bryce had some seal meat when she was at Gricquet and she said it tasted fishy. Reindeer meat is very lean and rather tasteless. Also, the wild ducks, which we have had, sometimes have a fishy taste. We have bunny to eat a good deal and it is delicious. This certainly was not what I started to write about!

Mrs. Grenfell says that people ask her such foolish questions. One well educated lady asked if her eyes hurt after coming out of the Arctic night! And we are latitude 70 degrees, miles south of London!

Prospero is due to leave St. John's May 7th and should be here the 15th. We'll have about six more weeks of isolation.

You wanted to know more about our surroundings. My favorite spot is Fox Farm Hill. There are some live foxes up there now in the pen. I have not seen them. When they are first caught they are easily frightened, so that they die if too many people go near them. Three of them have died.

They say there was a steam ship sealer outside the harbor Tuesday. I did not see it. This is the time of year when they go. Captain Kane of the *Prospero* takes the *Stephano* to the ice fields. The *Stephano* is a beauty. I've been aboard her. When she goes to the ice all the nice staterooms and first class passenger part is closed and boarded up. They say the filth and gore on a sealer is unspeakable!

The patients were very much pleased with the Easter cards Mary sent. I gave them out on Easter morning. Postcards and picture papers (comics?) are appreciated by the patients. There are even some grown-ups who can't read.

We received several *N.Y. Times* with accounts of Captain Scott. What a pity! A fascinating story and one which, we can well understand in this climate. [After discovering the South Pole Captain Scott and all of his party perished on the way back.]

Rev. Allenby had a preaching service at his church Good Friday evening, which I attended. I helped a little with the music Easter Sunday morning, practiced an anthem with the choir, and some Easter hymns, the lovely "Christ is Risen! Alleluia!" that's sung so much, was a favorite and we opened the service with that. Miss Appleton's school children sang two hymns and repeated a chapter of Scriptures. There was a good attendance.

In haste for the mail,
Margaret

April 6, 1913 to Papa,

There will only be one more dog-mail they say as the going is getting soft south of here.

We have just had Sunday service in the ward with good attendance from outside the hospital. Dr. Grenfell led the service. He read the 23rd Psalm and spoke of the heroic self-sacrifice of Captain Scott and members of his party.

I have not been able to tell the temperature this winter, for Dr. Armstrong's thermometer was broken, but 30 degrees below was reported somewhere, awhile ago. It is quite delightful here now, with crust on the snow. But when it thaws! There have been days when the slush is ankle deep!

A steam sealer came in last week, the first boat since the *Prospero* last January first. She stopped out at the edge of the ice. At least a hundred men came on shore, and most of them came to the hospital including the Captain and the ship's doctor.

One former patient was among them, and several were from along the coast who knew patients still here. The ship was called the *Narrascopic* and had caught 35,100 seals! Our good Captain Kane had caught 37,000 about $60,000 worth.

I saw a few seal skins with the blubber inside, down at Moore's wharf the other day, each weighing about 150 pounds, just skin and blubber without the carcass, big black and white "harp" seals.

My year will not be up until the end of December, and if you are willing I am thinking of staying another six months.

We had a great time at a Sports Festival the day after Easter, and some fine pictures were taken by Miss Appleton.

The dog-team race started from the head of the harbor and went away down and around a schooner (frozen) in the ice, and back to the Mission wharf. The number of dogs was limited to five, and one team of three dogs came in second. The prize was a barrel of flour. Fine prizes were given, axes, sweaters, and gloves. They call gloves "cuffs" in this country.

The candy scramble by the children was very pretty. Miss Cannon seated on a komatik with a good dog team, rode out on the ice throwing handfuls of candy with the children rushing for it. The harbor ice is not always slippery you know, but has lots of snow on it.

There was an eight-mile marathon run for the young men, and a very funny sack fight which I did not see, all men tied in sacks – Dr. Grenfell and everybody. The Sports lasted two days. I will send you a program.

Night of May 26-27, 1913

To Papa,

Telegram received tonight. "*Prospero* left Seal Cove at noon" so she should be here early in the A.M. The last trip she turned back without reaching St. Anthony to our great disappointment. We have been more cut off this month, with neither steamer nor dog-mails, than we were all winter. But we have not suffered for food and goods, and plenty of it.

The harbor people are getting short of supplies and two or three cases of scurvy have been seen.

There is little snow now, and the scrub on the hills is a soft red brown, with gray rock and green tuckamore. An iceberg is grounded on Cape St. Anthony and the harbor ice is fast breaking up. It is clear water as far as the place where we landed on Christmas Eve. The schooner, which was frozen in, has been towed to a wharf, and there are chunks of white ice floating in the bluest water. The doctors have answered several calls by boat.

Miss Bryce and Miss Cannon are to open the Battle Harbor hospital and I am to stay here for the present.

Miss Brown the former head nurse from Johns Hopkins is coming with a Dr. Little, a surgeon. We shall be rushed from now until the summer nurses come, as there are only three of us. I am taking a full month of night duty now, as Miss Bryce will have a lot of it at Battle. Dr. Grenfell promised I need not have any more night duty this summer, if I would take a month now on Miss B's account. She is one of the most charming girls I have met in a long time, a little Scotch lady.

Yesterday they sent home five cured patients and we only have twelve in the house now. Tonight we are quite likely to have thirty after the boat comes! Three more are going away on her, including Evelyn Boone and her mother. Evelyn's hip is in good condition now, though she will have to be in a cast for some time yet.

That's all for now.
Love,
Margaret

Jottings from Margaret's diary tell of the coming of spring. April 25, 1913 -- Heard the sound of a brook running "the rush of many waters." Snow going fast. April 26th – heard a bird sing.

May 28th I saw the first blade of green grass this A.M. My winter coat was too warm for the first time. We have had lovely song birds for a month.

> To Aunt Isa Putnam Barnes (Uncle Francis' wife)
> May 28th

There is some satisfaction in writing when you know the letter will not be more than ten days on the way now. It will be taken by the *Prospero*. The ship came in last night, and we were so glad we could have almost wept for joy! She had been expected all day and reported en route by telegraph. At last, at half past eight in broad daylight we saw her smoke over the hills, and very quickly she came smashing her way through the rotten ice directly to the Mission Wharf.

I was on night duty. Little Tommy wanted to see the boat come in, so I wrapped him up in a blanket, and carried him to the front ward, where he could look out the window to his heart's content.

She was a pretty sight with the lights shining from the portholes and her side and masthead lights trembling, more beautiful to us, because she brought letters from home. On this boat I had thirty-two in all.

The summer rush will soon begin, with a boat every week or two. There will be lots of patients, new nurses, and summer people.

Cousin Anna made me laugh when she supposed the season here was a month later than in Maine. It's about three months later! There is still ice in the harbor and it's almost June.

July 12, 1913

Dear Papa,

Orangeman's Day is a big holiday here, with lots of ammunition wasted. It sounds like the Fourth of July. The *Duchess* came in at ten last night in the rain, and brought your letters. She took away my dear Miss Appleton the teacher who is going home for a short holiday.

I have given up all idea of coming home for the present. Aunt Addie doesn't need me now, and it would mean going back to private nursing, which would be dull and uninteresting after this. My life is here now, and I hope I may be useful and grow more capable under Miss Brown's kind supervision.

I'm glad you had such a good time at the Bowdoin Commencement. I thought of you often. I am sorry to be so much away from you dear, but I see no help for it. I'm glad you have the college and the library, which is always peaceful and full of friendly books. President Hyde belongs to the New England Grenfell Association.

I don't begin to know all the students here but we have some fine medical ones in the hospital. One is from Johns Hopkins, one from Queens University, Kingston, Canada who is also Dr. Grenfell's Marconi operator on the *Strathcona*, and one student from California. Mr. Martin, the Marconi man is a Newfoundlander, and is a very talented fellow. He runs the X-ray apparatus, and is most kind and helpful to the nurses. Mr. Dayton the Hopkins man is a fine chap too. He is only 24 and has finished his third year in medical school. Mr. Martin is 23 and has finished his second year of medical school.

All I have time for tonight to catch the *Duchess*.

Love from
Daughter

VI

"A Wonderful Kind Feller"

Stan lay luxuriating in the warmth of his bunk for a few more minutes before dressing and rushing over for staff breakfast. He was thinking of Margaret Rogers, the nurse who was new to him, when he returned to St. Anthony that summer. When had he first noticed her? Was it the music he heard that first day? Someone was playing the piano in the hospital sun-parlor with a group of the orphans standing around, singing at the top of their voices. That person can really play, he thought then.

Was it the time her eyes caught his, as they worked across the operating table from each other? Smiling brown eyes above her surgical mask? Was it her laugh? She laughed a lot, especially responding to Dr. Grenfell's constant bubbling humor. Where is she from? He knew she was an American from her speech. Perhaps she'll come with me to the Tea House after work today, I'll see. He bounded out of bed and was off to face the day.

Stan looked for her in the Supply Room after morning surgery. She was rolling bandages. He stood in the doorway in his white coat. "Excuse me, Miss Rogers?" She looked up – "Yes."

"I'm Stan Martin – I guess you know – I've seen you at work." He paused. "I wonder, would you be free to go to the Tea House with me this afternoon?" "Why, yes," she said slowly. She stood up and the rolled bandages fell to the floor. Both of them scrambled to retrieve them, and his cheek brushed her hair as they stood up. Flustered, he continued. "Could you meet me at the front door, at 5:00 then?" "That'll be fine." "Good." Then he was gone.

That was easy, he thought, as he went whistling down the hospital corridor, but his heart was pounding.

Five o'clock found them at the front door dressed in other than their hospital whites. They felt a joyous release from their routine as they walked rapidly up the hill. She was wearing a cream colored blouse and a long dark skirt. Her chestnut brown hair was shining in the sunlight. He was wearing his favorite blue sweater and baggy brown pants, the kind that the Harbor men wore. Blue, she thought as she eyed the sweater, the color of his eyes, the bluest I have ever seen – China blue.

The usual questions flew back and forth as they walked. He learned of her New England background, about Houlton, Maine, and Boston at nursing school. She talked of her family especially of her father. "It's hard on him, my being out of the country, but letters help a lot."

Stan told of his St. John's background, and of recent days at Queen's University.

They sat talking, as they sipped tea looking out over the beautiful harbor. There were ice pans in the water even though it was June, but the expanse of blue water was growing every day. Margaret had been at the Tea House many times before, but now everything seemed new and exciting. To Stan, talking to her, and seeing the view through her eyes was like a tonic. She liked the same things he did.

As they walked down the hill, back to their busy life, it seemed as if they had been friends forever. Their work brought them together daily. Stan was transferring patients to and from the wards for X-rays. They were in surgery together assisting Dr. Little. Sometimes Margaret was the anesthetist; sometimes Stan was the surgeon. He recorded his operations in his diary with careful sketches of the procedures.

When they had time off they walked for miles, exploring places that were new to Margaret. Stan was familiar with boats, so he was able to take her for rides in a sail boat that belonged to a Harbor friend. Some evenings they sailed near sunset. On an unforgettable evening, the crimson and gold sky, and the reflected colors on the sea were all one world. They sat in the little boat holding hands, drenched in the color. At St. Anthony, far from the city lights, the stars were brilliant at night. Stan was able to point out to Margaret the constellations, planets, and first magnitude stars. His love and knowledge of astronomy followed him all his life.

On Sundays, the young couple attended the little white spired Methodist Church, and were on hand at the services held in the wards for the patients. Stan sang tenor and was often at Margaret's side, as she played for "Sings" at various places. They had been brought up on the same hymns and Christian teachings.

To agree in so many ways in spiritual matters made it easy for Stan to ask her one day, "Would you ever be interested in foreign missionary work?" She dropped her head wondering if this were a proposal. "If God could use me," she answered softly. He pulled a little book of Whittier poems from his pocket. "Here, read this. It is one of my favorite poems." He opened the page to "The Missionary." She read as they sat in the grass, leaning against a rock while the sea breeze blew on them. They were at Fishing Point, one of their favorite places.

Margaret's letters to her father told the story. She was careful not to upset him when she knew he was counting the days until her return. She had written of the many times spent with Stan, but now she was getting more specific.

"I know you will like my friend Stan Martin! Everybody likes him. So do I! The patients say he is a 'wonderful kind feller', and the people in the Harbor would do most anything for 'Dr. Martin'." He is not of the type who would be satisfied with ordinary private medical practice. You could hardly be that after years of association with Dr. Grenfell!"

Stan proposed to Margaret on a night when the northern lights danced in a blaze of glory. She wrote the exciting news to her Father.

"We believe it is all as God meant it to be. I am very happy; it seems that our life will be of real service to the Master. I know dear, that this must come as a blow to you, but I believe that you love me so much you will rejoice in my happiness.

We have not decided this in haste; we have been together all summer. It was only last Sunday that we finally promised ourselves to God and to each other. This has been the happiest week of my life. We know absolutely that it is the Lord's doing, and feel safe and strong in this assurance. There are many problems to be worked out but Stan has a good head on his shoulders. He's an expert electrician, and he is coming to Boston to Massachusetts General, in December, to do some special X-ray work. I hope you can go to Boston and meet him then. He is not at all snobbish. His home is a very simple one. Dr. Little's father has invited him to be his guest. Dr. Little is so good to us here at the hospital. He is just fine. He is good to everybody, the poor patients that come and all the workers in the Mission. Also his sister has given $10,000 to enlarge the orphanage here. They're a wonderful family."

As the young couple watched the calendar, the days were flying until it was nearly time for Stan to return to medical school. They dreaded the coming separation. All summer the coastal steamers brought more patients to St. Anthony. By August fifteenth, Stan was packing his trunks. The *Prospero* came in bringing forty-five patients. They were all finally processed by ten o'clock that night. His diary described the last operations he performed, before boarding the ship the next day for St. John's.

This time Margaret was on the hospital verandah waving good-bye, as once again Stan saw the St. Anthony harbor slide from sight. Through her tears Margaret watched as long as she could, then turned to go back to her patients. There was a bright spot in her life however, as she was soon to take a trip to St. John's to visit Stan's family. She was determined to busy herself in the hospital work so the time would fly until then.

Stan's first stop was at his home at St. John's as he repacked and waited for his ship to Sydney, New Brunswick. His family listened intently as he told of his summer, and especially about this wonderful girl, Margaret Rogers, who was now his fiancée.

"She's beautiful! A brunette, with a lovely ivory complexion. You should hear her play the piano!! Most of all she is a loving, capable nurse and she loves me! We knew from the very first date that our relationship would be special."

He showed pictures of her in her Inuit costume, and in her nurse's uniform taken with members of the Staff. His parents were gratified that she was fully committed to missionary work, for they had watched Stan, as God was preparing him for this. They were eagerly looking forward to her visit.

At last September 11, Stan's departure date for Canada arrived and he made his farewells. His diary gave snatches of his trip.

Up all night waiting for the boat, the *Sanfyorro*. Went to bed, got up at 1:00 a.m. and walked out in the dark to the pier. Ghostly night. Waited around in the dark. She got in at 2:00am and loaded for four hours. Went aboard, men were playing poker, and drinking whisky. Found my bunk, but couldn't sleep. We passed Cape Race at 5:30pm. Noticed smoke of steamer, *Mouvenna*. It's a race now. Sunday September 13th. A heavenly glorious day. Good meals. Captain fine. My, but its calm! Wrote Margaret. *Mouvenna* is twenty miles ahead at noon. Expect to miss her at Sydney. Got some fish yesterday off Cape Race. They paid for them with whisky and tobacco Arrived Sydney 10:30pm. The *Mouvenna* already at our pier. Monday 14th. Captain Abrahamsen was very kind. Had breakfast. Just missed the *Stiklestat* bound for Montreal with coal – 500 feet long. Waiting for the Immigration Officer. Still waiting for Immigration. Customs officer kind, takes some notes from me, and I go aboard the *Mouvenna*. Had glorious day. Dead calm. Left Sydney at 11:00am. We're due at Montreal Thursday AM. The Marconi operator on board is a perfect gentleman. He played some great music with a bow and a stringed fiddle made of a cigar box and a hockey stick. The music was simply exquisite. "I Hear You Calling Me." etc. All in the bowing. Stop at Montreal, held up in the fog in the river. Went to Western Hospital and saw my friend Bill Fraser – observed two operations – fastidious asepsis – two operating tables using the N.O. ether. Walked around town. Sick of dresses etc. [He had no use for ladies dressed in their fancy fashions.] Arrived at Kingston the next day, found my former boarding room unavailable so I obtained a room at Smith's, with my friend Mosely.

During the last few days before classes began, he wrote to Margaret telling of time spent with his friends swimming, sailing and canoeing. The weather was getting colder, and the campus was gorgeous with the fall colors. He knew it was time to write to his future father-in-law. He began in his neat handwriting on Queen's University stationery:

Medical School
October 15, '13

My Dear Mr. Rogers,

As requested by Margaret, and I assure you because I wanted to, I find myself at last attempting to write a few lines.

Since leaving the Coast I have been quite busy arranging my hospital work and settling down to study. We are preparing for a large intercollegiate conference here, which is being held in the interests of Foreign Missions and we expect a large number of delegates from the other universities. We number ourselves about 2000 in all schools, and with the large body of Student Volunteers from Toronto and McGill Universities we will have our hands full.

The large majority of our graduates take up Home Missions work and I believe rightly so. But Queens has been unique in her fostering of the true Missionary spirit "Christ for all." Although our Student Volunteers band here only numbers twenty — we have been for the last ten years sending out an average of four. Last year two women went to China, one woman to Turkey, and one doctor to Formosa.

Many stay home because it's much easier, since our West is so wealthy etc. There are still a few of us who love to tackle the harder problems and go to the far countries. Please read Whittier's poem "Missionary." It expresses the challenge well. Margaret has often read it and it is my favorite poem.

As you know I was a wireless engineer in the Marconi Co. of Canada, and still am, though in my third year in medicine. But I always craved for a larger scope and better training to help those who could not help themselves.

It was the sermon that Frank Sayre, who married President Wilson's daughter, and I heard from Dr. Grenfell that finally fixed our ideals. I have been six summers with Dr. Grenfell now and am even more ready to accept God's plan for my life. It wanted but the kindred spirit found in your loving daughter to help me realize to the fullest my true sonship to our heavenly Father, and to reach Him through the medium of fervent prayer. As you know Margaret and I took communion together and vowed that we would live for "God and humanity." When I last heard from her she was at my home in St. John's NFLD enjoying a rest which she much needed.

My sister, Eva, who is a trained nurse is going to keep her company and take care of her. My father whose name is known and honored throughout the country will always be ready to look after her in any way. I am enclosing paper cuttings from the "Labrador Mission," to give you an idea of the great increase in the work in our hospital. I may say that before leaving I had 150 cases in two months in X-ray work alone.

From the nature of things and seeing that you are probably interested in who I am, I must apologize if this letter seems at all bombastic.

You may send the "Paper Cuttings" to Aunt Addie as Margaret asked. A chum has just come with his car so I must close with

Sincere good wishes,
Stan H. Martin

In the meantime Margaret had made her journey to St. John's to visit Stan's family. She wrote about it to her Father:

St. John's, NFLD
Oct. 16, 1913

Dear Papa,

It is nice to know that this letter will go through to you in four days. Dr. Little telegraphed me that I may have another week's vacation leaving here on the next *Prospero* trip October 22.

Mrs. Martin is so pleased with seeing me getting rested and putting on weight! Says I'm a different girl since I came a week ago. She is so good and kind to me papa dear, just as if I were her own daughter. Truly I am in good hands and have many things for which to be thankful. This bit of home life is delightful after the long months of hospital.

We have had some splendid walks, and a drive in the country round about. St. John's isn't very big and you can soon walk out of it, and into lovely country. It's just like home in New England with farmhouses and pasturelands - the "country of the pointed firs." Then there is a little park called Bowring Park up in the Waterford river valley with ponds and brooks and waterfalls, more beautiful even than Merry Meeting though on a smaller scale. We drove all about there one day, Mrs. Martin and Eva and I.

Twice, Eva and I have walked out to what is called the Battery, around the foot of Signal Hill, on the cliffs right out to sea. Here the narrow channel was guarded from the French attacking forces, by a chain stretched all the way across. The old fortification now serves the peaceful purpose of shelter for a turnip garden! The lighthouse and Fort Amherst are on the opposite or "Southside" of the Narrows.

Out there the scenery is like wild and rugged North Newfoundland, quite a contrast to the peaceful farming lands within.

How little one can write in a letter! You can hardly realize now the difference in my life, the joy, and the sorrow of parting, the faith that must bear us through the long winter months, and the hope we have to be united again when they are past.

I bought my ticket for St. Anthony this morning to sail October 22nd. I will telegraph my arrival to Stan and ask him to notify you immediately.

That is all for tonight.

Lovingly,
Daughter

Weeks later her father responded with his blessings and expressed joy in her happiness, but his heart was heavy. Margaret returned from St. John's to the hospital at St. Anthony and soon winter descended again on the little community. She wrote often to her father to catch the last mails before the big freeze.

What and where Stan's and my work shall be, we must leave to our Heavenly Father's guidance. But you are not going to lose me right away, Papa dear. Thank you for your good letter, it was a very precious one indeed, for I am glad to know that you feel as you do about it. Your letter tells of the "friendly fire" on the wooded shore of the Cathance. I think you have a singularly sweet nature to find your contentment as you do, with your books and the friendly stream. I wish I could have made life a little easier for you of late years. But you have your sacred memories, and I too now am learning what it really <u>means</u> to <u>live</u> and be happy.

Dr. Grenfell converses with the King of England, the Archbishop of Canterbury and the President of the United States with equal ease and pleasure, just as he talks with these poor people here, I fancy. I should like to have seen the White House wedding, Stanley says he knows Frank Sayre but wouldn't change places with him! Strange!

Stan wrote that he had been on an emergency ambulance run in Kingston, sitting in the front seat with the driver. They were speeding to save the life of a child, when the driver had to stop suddenly. The two of them flew right through the windshield, but came off with minor cuts and bruises.

Margaret wrote of the winter activities at Saint Anthony.

December 27th, '13

Dear Papa,

Dr. Grenfell has built a beautiful snow arch by his front door, and encased it with ice. On one side he has carved a little fisherman about two feet high, very clever, holding a British flag. On the other side a beautiful pussycat with a handsome fluffy tail and an American flag. He calls Mrs. Grenfell "Puss' and always represents her in his sketches as a cat, so we suppose these two represent the family.

Around our hospital you can often hear the sound of barking or howling dogs. Most of them are those trained to pull the dog sleds. Others are pets of the villagers or staff. The most famous dogs are the ones that survived the Ice-Pan adventure with Dr. Grenfell. There are five left--Jerry, Doc, Sue, Brim and Jack. The one named Jack a black spaniel is one of the Doctor's favorites. He likes to sleep beside the Doctor when he works at his desk.

Poor Jack got caught in a trap one day and we thought him lost. But someone brought him back, a very sad little dog with two toes frozen off. He was brought to the hospital yesterday with such a bandage as I tried once to put on Tommy [one of the patients mentioned earlier]. There was a stocking over that, if you please! He sat up very quietly while the doctor held him for me to <u>sew</u> on the bandage with needle and thread.

I've been up to the Doctor's to tea this afternoon. We had it in his workroom or den. Mrs. Grenfell was making curtains for the Tea House and Doctor was doing a water color illustration for a new story of his.

Time to close for the mail.
Lots and lots of love,
Daughter

With his fall studies well under way Stan knew it was time to make his application for service with the Methodist Mission Board in Toronto. He wrote December 5, 1913 to Dr. J. Endicott in Toronto.

Dear Sir:

As a medical student and also as one who has spent five years in medical mission work, I would like to know exactly what are the chances of being sent to the foreign field in the spring of 1915. I would prefer that my own denomination send me out (Meth.)

Yours in His service,
S. H. Martin

He was answered much later, January 9th, '14 by J. H. Arnup.

Dear Mr. Martin:-

Owing to my almost continuous absence from the office I was unable to attend earlier to your letter of December 15th, addressed to Dr. Endicott. In the division of work the securing of candidates falls to me, and it is a great privilege to be allowed to confer with young men about their life work.

In answer to your specific question as to the prospects of being sent out to the field in the spring of 1915, you could not be sent to the field before October or November of that year.

It is altogether probable that we shall need one or two additional doctors for the party of 1915, and I should be very glad if you would fill out the enclosed form and also write me as fully as possible whatever facts concerning yourself and your life that you think will help us in forming a judgment as to your qualifications for our foreign work.

Awaiting your reply, and in the meantime expressing the hope that you may be led to put your life where it's most effective service can be rendered, I am,

Sincerely yours,
J. H. Arnup

Stan answered this the next day:

My dear Mr. Arnup:-

As this has all to do with my life's work I am rather anxious about the relation between myself and your board. 1ˢᵗ, Who am I? And what are my qualifications?

My grandfathers for generations have been ministers and missionaries in the Methodist Church.

I have been five seasons with Dr. Grenfell in Medical Mission Work, having traveled the whole Labrador Coast 2000 miles several times and put in 30 months of hospital and itinerating medical work. Have studied medical missions in all its branches. Have just finished a training of five years in X-Ray work. Saw 100 cases a day in the Massachusetts Gen. Hospital of Boston, also saw the best of surgeons doing wonderful work. Have been associated with one of the ablest surgeons in America for the last three summers. Am engaged to be married to a thoroughly Christ-like woman whose aim has always been to do foreign mission work simply because she sees the wider vision and knows the need. She is a thoroughly trained nurse from one of the best hospitals in the world, and is now in medical mission work and waiting for me, and like myself anxious to start our life's work where most needed. My mother – Pres. of W.M.S. of Meth. Church, Father Supt. of Sunday School 38 years, etc.

Now sir, with all this holding me to the Methodist Church, yet I would go to the field under any board which could send me in the fall of 1915. For reasons that I will not mention now, I must start practice in the fall of 1915. I have all sorts of offers for research, for work with Dr. Grenfell and hospital appointments, and yet

I don't want to tackle any of these. My fiancée is a wonder at most languages, and I don't want either of us to get too set in our ways. You know what I mean. But what I want is to know as <u>definitely</u> as possible whether our church can send us in the fall of 1915. If not, I must go under the Presbyterian Board. I am a member of Sydenham St. Church here, a Student Volunteer for 8 years, president of the Band last year. But you see that if I know where I am liable to go, how much better I can plan. I am doing work here in the hospital and college.

Now, being born in Newfoundland – St. John's – and living in Labrador it would be silly and not according to God's will to go to a tropical country. My life among fishermen and my love for the sea is another thing. Then my knowledge of X-Ray with which they now diagnose all diseases almost that you could mention, will be of great value to humanity. But that would entail living near or in a large hospital. Then my fiancée's ability for training native nurses, etc. Taking this into consideration you may be able to tell approximately where I would be best able to do the best work. Of course I know that God will guide you in your decision. I may never get to the field, but God will answer all those questions in the future. At present I feel that I was only carrying out His plans for me by writing to you.

If you can satisfy me as to the future we shall be glad to sign any papers you send. Please write me as soon as possible.

Very sincerely yours,

In His service,

S. H. Martin

As Stan waited for Mr. Arnup's reply he also applied for service with the Canadian Presbyterian Foreign Missions Board. Mr. Arnup's letter arrived nearly three weeks later.

Toronto January 29, 1914
Mr. S. H. Martin
Queen's University,
Kingston, Ontario

Dear Mr. Martin:-

Your letter arrived during my recent absence from the office, which was unfortunately prolonged by serious illness in my family. The letter was not acknowledged by anyone in the office because it was marked "private" and therefore left to me.

It is perfectly natural for you to be anxious for definite information concerning your prospects of appointment to West China. I have gone in to the matter of our needs and prospective candidates, and allowing for anything like a reasonable maintenance or increase of revenue I can see nothing which does not strengthen my thought that we shall be anxious for your services by the fall of 1915. In saying that I am of course assuming that your medical examination, etc. will all prove to be satisfactory in the usual course.

You will see too that no secretary could make you an absolute promise nearly two years in advance that yourself or any other man will be sent to the field at a given time. No one can foresee what developments may take place either at home or abroad. But you will be very much pleased and I think satisfied with my personal assurance that all the information to hand gives me a confident expectation of securing your appointment by our Board against the time when you would be ready to sail.

In the ordinary course of events, your appointment would not be formally made by the Executive of our Board until January or April of 1915. It would be to our mutual advantage, however, for you to submit to medical examination and send me a preliminary medical report on the enclosed form.

Sincerely yours,
(Signed) J. H. Arnup

Margaret was keenly interested in the reports of the Board correspondence, but was absorbed in the hospital routine and activities. She wrote to her father " I have given up all thoughts of coming home at this time – I plan to stay until June 25, 1914." She wrote of a hand amputation with Dr. Grenfell as the surgeon and she was anesthetist. She told of victrola concerts when she played the records for the patients, and of playing the piano for frequent "Sings." She also learned to ski. "It was the most fun I've had in a long time!"

At last the spring of 1914 was coming but there was to be another severe onslaught of winter weather. The hospital staff knew the sealers were off to the ice fields. One day the sky was ominous with dark clouds and a terrible blizzard swept over the area. Even in the daytime hours the sky became darker and darker. Margaret had never seen anything like it. In the next few days, tragic news came in. Hundreds of the men were caught on the ice and nearly all died. Those who were rescued alive had suffered severe frostbite and some lost limbs. Many were taken to St. John's Seamen's Institute. The whole country was in mourning. Once again Margaret and Stan, who heard the news in Canada, were profoundly moved by the suffering and bravery of those men of the North.

In June, Stan came back to St. Anthony for the summer work, and Margaret stayed a little longer for a few precious weeks with him before going back to her father in Maine.

Stan's summer passed quickly with more opportunities for surgery and x-ray work than ever before. War clouds were on the horizon and he rigged up a wireless outfit to get the war news from

Belle Isle. In the fall he was back at Queen's for his last year of medical school. Mail service was quick and efficient again as the young couple made plans writing between Boston and Kingston, instead of waiting for the slow coastal steamers.

In January 1915 he had received some wonderful news and he wrote to his family:

January 17th, 1915

My dear ones at home,

I think I told you that I was gladly accepted by the Presbyterian Foreign Missions Board and that I am going out this fall God willing. I consider myself very lucky in going to Korea – especially from a health point of view. We are quite close to southern Russia, near the sea and in the mountainous part – so that it will be much like Newfoundland. The Japanese are rapidly civilizing the whole country, which is well covered with railroads and postal, and telegraph systems.

The Korean people are mostly farmers. They are becoming Christians by the 1000's. They build their own churches – support their own ministers and schools. This I have gathered from letters from missionaries in Korea. I've not decided what I shall do in the six months after I graduate. It will need to be hospital work, however, Dr. Guvenneti of Belle Isle wants me to take his practice for one month at $100.

I should like to get into an American hospital where I could get six months of heavy hospital work and experience – about ten operations a day. There are posters up here wanting electricians etc. for the war front. I am going down soon to see if Will can join the Canadian engineers, I think he would get good treatment and better pay. Margaret is spending a months holiday with her friend Dr. Baker at Philadelphia. She is then going for a month with cousins in Albany and then wants to help me by doing private duty in the U.S. Yesterday I had a glorious skate on the lake. Every week I get the *American Medical Journal* Margaret's Christmas present to me. I am in every night in the week, working. I am going out to tea tonight to Mrs. McLellands. Everybody seems to be very happy that I am going to Korea. I don't suppose you are, but remember I'll come home every six years. Eva will be home in three years and will get a position here in Newfoundland. I believe this war will commence to be finally over by the end of June.

John R. Mott is here this week for special meetings on missions.

Sincere love to Mother dear, and Father,
Love,
Stan

At the age of twenty-four on April 15, 1915, he was graduated from Queen's Medical School with high honors. He received his M.D. and also a degree in surgery. When his course was completed he was $250 in debt and prayed about the matter. A few days later while on Wolfe Island, he received a letter with a check for exactly $250. He testified later to his supporting church, "That is only one of the many instances I have had of direct answer to prayer."

Eagerly Stan and Margaret made plans for a fall wedding, but the war situation became more serious, and Stan volunteered for service with the British Royal Army Medical Corps. These new circumstances broke like a sudden storm over their lives. He was in uniform and under orders to proceed to Cairo, Egypt. However, the Presbyterian Mission Board prevailed on the military authorities to release him, because they were short of doctors for their work in the Far East. It was Rev. Andrew Robertson D.D., who was formerly of St. John's, who was the one to have him released. He had taken a great interest in the young Newfoundlander. Indeed he was the one who held "The Quiet Hour" that Stan attended in his youth.

With his release from the military, Stan was able to get further training and experience at Western Hospital in Montreal, from May until October. Their wedding date was set for November 3rd.

Then word came from the Mission Board, that their work was to be mostly with Korean people, but their assignment was to a mission station in Manchuria, in North China. The town was Yong Jung, the Korean name. The Chinese name was Lungchingtsun, meaning "Dragon Well." The board also wrote that the Orillia, Ontario Presbyterian Church was taking on their support, and would appreciate a visit from them on their way to the mission field.

In the meantime Margaret was preparing for the wedding and gathering supplies for their new life overseas.

She stood in Aunt Addie's bedroom in Boston, with a list in her hand. [Aunt Addie was her mother's sister.] Her aunt sat by her in her favorite rocking chair. Margaret had written several items, sheets, towels, table linens, bedding, silverware, and pots and pans. Any bride would have this list, she thought.

"What do I take away out there to China and we won't be back here for years? Aunt Addie look at this list. It looks as if I've just begun. I'll have to get some more trunks and suitcases."

"Well, let's see."

Aunt Addie adjusted her spectacles and pored over the piece of paper.

"There's a lot of tea, in China." She chuckled, "But what about coffee, ummm – raisins, baking powder, yeast, why you need a whole grocery store!"

"Well, we've heard they have good fish, and chicken, and some beef, lots of rice, of course. Also, they have a few fruits and vegetables, especially in the summer. Oh yes! I'll need canning supplies. That goes on the list. It's our special Western foods that they don't have. After St. Anthony where the food was so simple, Stan and I will manage all right."

"What about some baby clothes? You'll be gone several years."

"Oh Aunt Addie!" Margaret laughed and stooped to hug her aunt. "I hope I'll need them! Since packages take forever to cross the Pacific I had better be prepared and take a few baby things. That's a good idea."

Money ran out before the list was completed, but soon two sturdy trunks, and four wooden boxes were ready for shipping to Victoria, B.C. to await the sailing date.

Margaret then left for Brunswick, Maine, to stay with her father for the last days before the wedding. There they had a carpenter prepare a heavy wooden box for her "Ivers and Ponds" piano. It was sent to Boston to go with the other heavy baggage. At last it was time to go to the wedding in Houlton, Maine.

Stan finished his work at Western Hospital in October, then made a trip home to St. John's to say goodbye to his family. He too spent time packing trunks to be sent to the Canadian west coast. In them were his medical books, warm clothing, and what precious medicines and instruments he had been able to gather. His pride and joy, his four-inch telescope, was in its rosewood box also ready to go.

As he packed, he wondered what the future would hold for him and his Margaret. It was the great unknown, but he felt the strong hand of God upon him. His George Street Methodist Church, and the St. Andrews Presbyterian Church were good to him, adding basic supplies. The newspaper reported his coming departure, and Dr. Grenfell sent a farewell letter from St. Anthony.

The time was all too short. His friends dropped by, and special times of prayer were held with his parents every night. Finally the day of departure came. Stan was at the cold and windy pier surrounded by a large crowd. As Stan looked down at his mother's eyes filled with tears, the awareness of the great distance that would come between them, and the thought of years of separation facing them, crushed him for a moment. He hugged her close. After shaking many hands, and receiving hearty pats on his back, his ears were ringing with shouts of his well-wishers. "Good luck!" "God bless!" He broke away and boarded the ship.

As he turned to wave from the railing, the thought that every moment brought him closer to Margaret, the wedding, and the great adventure beyond, buoyed him up as once again his beloved town of St. John's passed from sight. In Boston, which was now familiar to him, he took the train to Houlton and to a joyous reunion with Margaret and her father who met him at the station. They drove to the edge of town to a large New England house surrounded by ancient pine trees. It was the Barnes' homestead on Bangor Road. This house had been Margaret's home from the time she was six-years-old. He was given a hearty welcome by the Barnes and Rogers relatives "cousins by the dozens," and Uncle Francis and Aunt Isa Barnes who had raised Margaret. He also met her cousin Anna Barnes who was the Houlton librarian. Margaret showed Stan through the house.

The smell of baking pies and cakes filled the kitchen. Ladies from their Baptist church were preparing for the wedding dinner the next day. Stan noticed that the walls of the living room and study were lined with books. Uncle Francis' Harvard plaque was over his desk. Some of the church men arrived at the backdoor with armloads of fragrant balsam branches they had brought from the woods. They then proceeded to make an archway between the dining room and the living room, for the place where the bride and groom would stand for the ceremony.

Stan was introduced to the little blonde cousin Margaret Barnes who was to be their flower girl. She followed Margaret and Stan up the stairs to the room that had been Margaret's those many years. The mirror reflected the flushed and happy bride, while Stan stood beside her. The little flower girl busied herself with some precious old dolls, and the couple melted into a quick embrace, scarcely believing their joy.

Evening came and most of the crowd left. The closest family members stayed for a familiar dinner – baked beans! Afterwards they asked Margaret to play the piano, and they all gathered around and sang. Stan sang "In the Time of Roses" in his beautiful tenor voice, then they settled down to hear of some of Margaret's and Stan's adventures in Newfoundland and Labrador.

Uncle Francis brought out the family albums and Stan learned more about Margaret's relatives. He learned that her great uncle, the Rev. Nathaniel Butler, had been personal secretary to Hannibal Hamlin, vice president of the United States under President Lincoln during Lincoln's first term. Her cousin, his son, also named Nathaniel, had recently been president of Colby College at Waterville, Maine.

Her uncle Phineas Barnes was then at work with Andrew Carnegie in the steel industry in Pittsburgh. They plied the young couple with questions about China and the situation they would find there. The pleasant evening finally came to a close. With warm hugs all around, the family members scattered to various homes.

The morning of November 3, 1915 dawned crisp and clear. Once again, the ladies of the house busied themselves, setting the long dining room table and decorating it with greenery, candles and white carnations. Although frost had killed the flowers in Maine, the florist had provided the carnations and a gorgeous wedding bouquet of prize chrysanthemums from a flower show in Boston.

In the afternoon the Baptist ladies returned. This time, they brought casseroles, muffins, and roast chickens. Many of these women had watched Margaret grow up in their church. With their deep faith, and interest in foreign missions, they were so proud that she was going to be a missionary, they wanted to help in every way they could. Margaret thanked them and invited them to be seated in the living room. Soon other guests began to arrive.

Margaret was in her bedroom as five o'clock drew near. Aunt Addie was there to flutter over her. She helped her dress in her ivory silk wedding gown, and adjusted her veil fastened with wax orange blossoms. Little cousin Margaret watched wide-eyed, as she stood near with her basket of flowers.

Aunt Addie then stepped back smiling, to have a good look at the bride.

"You're so lovely! You have dark hair and your mother was blonde, but you do look like her! How I wish my dear sister could see you now."

"She's watching from heaven, I know it." Margaret said, as she twisted herself to see the back of her dress in the mirror.

"No time for tears." Addie said as she quickly dabbed her eyes with a lace handkerchief. "Little Margaret," would you go down and tell Uncle Lincoln we're ready, and ask him to come upstairs so we can start the procession? You can leave your flowers here for a minute."

When the door opened, Lincoln Rogers stood there for a moment. As he saw his daughter, he gasped, then controlling himself he moved forward and kissed her on the cheek. He proffered his arm to her and whispered,

"You're so beautiful, dear!" This is going to take all the strength I have. God help me! he thought, as they moved to the stairs. When the grandfather clock struck five, it was time to go. Little Margaret started down first. The wedding march was played on the piano which the bride had played ever since she was a little girl. Her feet were on the stairs she had trod for so many years. Now she was walking toward her new life, her love, her husband. Stan stood in the archway and smiled as she approached.

The kind Baptist minister, the Rev. H. G. Kennedy, married them as the friends and family watched. From there they moved to the dining room, to the lovely table that was lighted by many candles. A large wedding cake was in the center.

There were so many people, half of the group socialized in the living room, while half were served dinner. Then they switched places. No one seemed in a hurry. The church organist, who had played the wedding march, went to the piano and played love songs.

At last Aunt Isa called for attention and asked, "Margaret and Stan would you please cut the wedding cake now?" The young couple complied as all the guests gathered around, to the sound of cheering and clapping. A sense of deep joy fell upon all as they shared in the occasion. Also unspoken sadness gripped everyone because the couple was to leave for a far off country. It was especially poignant for Margaret's father as he studied the radiant face of his only child. Another chapter for Stan and Margaret opened before them. But this time, future adventures would be faced together with God's help.

Dr. & Mrs. Martin and little cousin Margaret. Wedding, November 1915.

VII

New Horizons

They were on the train to Orillia, Ontario, Canada on their way to their supporting church. It was the beginning of their trip to Manchuria. They had left Margaret's father standing alone on the railroad platform. Margaret had waved from the window until he was out of sight, and then she collapsed sobbing beside Stan. She had used up his only available handkerchief and now she lay asleep exhausted from the last days of preparation for the trip.

Stan took out the lists of their baggage, but his thoughts went back to his mother and father at the ship's dock in St. John's. He remembered his mother's tears. There is only one sacrifice, he thought, one sacrifice to missionary life, it's the wrenching apart of families, the long separations.

He studied the lists. Ten pieces were waiting in Vancouver, including the food supplies, the piano, and the precious telescope. Four suitcases were checked on their train, and they had their carry-ons. He shook his head. Oh Lord, he thought. We'll need every bit of this. Will it all get there safely? He patted the bag by his side containing his small packet of surgical instruments.

They were met in Orillia by the presiding minister and his wife, Reverend and Mrs. F. W. Anderson, and taken to the Manse. There followed a busy week. On Sunday morning, Stan was designated Medical Missionary to Korea. [In those days when there was a missionary couple, only the man was designated.] The beauty of the church, the music and the excitement of the congregation overwhelmed the young couple. They were definitely being held up in prayer. It was fitting that the ceremonies were conducted by Reverend R. P. MacKay, D.D., of Toronto, the general secretary of the Foreign Mission Board of the Presbyterian Church. Rev. MacKay was the one with whom Stan had corresponded. He presented them with a copy of the Scriptures. At the request of the Bible Society, he also presented them with a Korean Bible. Greetings were brought by other Presbyterian officials, some from the nearby towns Barrie and Oro Station. Then Stan and Margaret were received as members of the Orillia church.

During the week, Stan was ordained an elder of the Presbyterian Church, and was made a member of the Session. There were receptions and opportunities for Stan and Margaret to speak to the eager people. The church pledged $1200 per year from its Mission Funds. They were showered with gifts, including two steamer blankets for the trip. Then it was time to leave. Another suitcase full of gifts was added to the checked baggage. Their church paper told the story:

> "During their brief visit to Orillia they have completely won the hearts of the congregation, and they leave for their distant field of labor with the good wishes of everyone, and knowing that they will be supported by a sympathetic and praying people."

Weeks later, Margaret's first letter reached her father, Lincoln Rogers:

> We crossed Canada and the beautiful Canadian Rocky Mountains on the Canadian Pacific Railroad – so high, a mile above sea level, and the moon shone on the snow covered peaks. Next evening we were down to the Pacific shore and were soon ready to board our ship bound for the Orient sailing December 4, 1915. It was the *Sado Maru* of the Nippon Yusen Kaisha Line.

At departure, they stood on deck watching the fading shoreline as the ship left Vancouver. Stan's arm was around Margaret's shoulders as the cold winds of December blew on them. Their hearts were thrilled at this crucial moment. Turning, they sought the warmth of their cabin to read the "steamer mail" from friends and family. Pacific crossings are often rough in the winter, but they were good sailors. Stan was never more at home than on a rocking boat. As the days past they spent many hours reading history books on China and Korea. These books were fairly rare at that time.

Stan asked, "Did you know that the Manchu Empire came to an end just seven or eight years ago?"

"No, is that right?"

"Yes, when the Empress Dowager Tzu Hsi died in 1908. Umm, I wonder what kind of government they'll have in Yong Jung."

Margaret just shook her head.

Time passed swiftly on the nineteen-day trip, as they enjoyed their fellow passengers. As the ship approached Japan, the harbor of Yokohama presented a gorgeous sight. Fujiyama, the snow covered volcanic mountain peak, was clearly visible miles out to sea. Some travelers have said that though they visited Japan several times, they have never seen Fuji because of the clouds and mist. The passengers crowded to the rail to watch. What a stunning welcome to the Orient!

It was Christmas Eve when they landed in Japan, and as the ship was to stay some time in Yokohama, they went ashore to see the sights. They soon found themselves walking with throngs of kimono-clad people on a busy street. The sound that the Japanese wooden *gaita* made on the cobblestones was pleasant to hear. There were curious glances at the foreign couple as they moved slowly through the crowd. The little Japanese shops piled with colorful merchandise fascinated them, and unexplainable smells from the food shops assaulted them as they walked. They could see dumplings steaming on charcoal braziers, and recognized the smell of roasting chestnuts. They decided to try a rickshaw ride. Margaret wrote in a letter about this:

The ride in a little rickshaw, high on two wheels, was a new and strange experience. It was our first contact with a part of the world where men are "the beasts of burden" and human life is cheap. "Rickshaw coolies do not live to be old, for their hearts give out," Stan said as he helped me up into the strange contraption.

After a rickshaw ride about the picturesque streets, we decided to walk. We got lost. It was a scary experience when everyone was speaking a strange staccato language, not one word of which we could understand.

They stopped walking and Stan looked down at Margaret. "Well, here we are, we're lost and we can't even ask directions. We don't know even <u>one</u> <u>word</u> of Japanese. We'll have to remember some landmarks."

"Let's see," Margaret said. "There was a China shop on one corner and I remember the fruit market – oh – wait a minute, I know one word of Japanese!"

"What's that?"

"*Maru* – it means boat. We came on the *Sado Maru*!"

It was worth a try, and Margaret approached an elderly Japanese lady coming toward them. "*Maru*? Boat? Do you speak English?"

The lady was startled to be addressed by the foreign lady. Then, waving her hand in front of her face, the Oriental way of saying "I don't understand," she smiled, bowed and stepped aside, continuing on her way. "Well, that didn't work," Stan said. "Let me try."

This time a young fellow, probably a student, approached. Stan went up to him. "Excuse me. We're lost. Do you speak English?" We came to Japan on the *Sado Maru*." *Maru* – boat. Where are the docks where the boats come in?"

The fellow stopped, listened and scratched his head. "*Maru – maru*? *Ah so*!" [I understand.]" He laughed and then pointed in the direction from which the couple had come. Then he made a sweeping movement to the left, and then straight up, that probably meant go straight again. "*Maru*? *Hi*! [yes]. Boat – yes!"

He smiled showing a gold tooth. Stan grasped his hand in thanks and as they parted, the young fellow went clacking down the street in his *gaita*, very pleased with himself.

"Well, let's see if he's right," Stan said as they retraced their steps. The man was right, for soon they saw the smokestacks of vessels lying at anchor. They gratefully went up the gangplank of their ship, the *Sado Maru* where English was spoken. A strange activity was going on at the ship. Margaret's letter continues:

Another first contact with their way of life which I shall never forget was seeing women putting coal on our ship, a dreadfully hard task. They sat in rows on a sort of ladder gangway and passed baskets of coal up from one to another over the side of the ship.

From Yokohama we continued to Kobe on the same ship. We then made a side trip to the old city of Kyoto, where for centuries, coronations of the Emperors of

Japan have taken place. We saw the palace and the throne where the Emperor and Empress sat, and the great court where princes and nobles gathered to pay their homage.

There is a great temple in Kyoto called the *Kyomitsudera* or the "Temple of Cleansing Water." When we visited it, the people were throwing money into a box with a grating on top, then they were clapping their hands and standing with bowed heads praying toward the temple. I will never forget the first time I saw men and women bowing at a great heathen temple and realized they were worshiping idols of wood and stone.

We saw a young Japanese girl go to a little shrine to pray. It contained a fountain of running water and up above it were idols and bells. First, she rang the bells to call the god's attention. Then she came down and stood under the stream of water, wearing a special kimono. She clapped her hands again and agonized in prayer, quite unmindful of us as we sat quietly at a little distance. It was one of the most pitiful things that I have ever seen.

During the first week of January, 1916 they proceeded to Shimonoseki to catch the ferry boat to go across the Tsushima Straits to Pusan, Korea. After their night in a Japanese inn, they hurried to the dock at the appointed time. When they reached the harbor, the strip of water between the ship and dock was widening. They had missed the boat by about three minutes!

There they stood, with all their baggage around them. Stan recounted the event later. "It was the Japanese New Year and a soldier with a long clanking sword laughed uproariously at the predicament of these foreigners. He was gloriously drunk."

Sadly, they hired the men with the carts again to haul the trunks and boxes, including the piano crate, back to their lodgings. The next day, word came that the ferry they had missed had gone down in a storm, all hands lost!

"Go ye into all the world – and, lo, I am with you always," came vividly to their minds, as they rested on the straw *tatamis* of their room. What if they had caught that boat! This was the first, the beginning of many crucial events to take place in their lives. They felt the strong presence of God and His protection.

The storm passed and they made a safe crossing to Pusan, Korea. Japan had annexed the country just five years before, so they were processed by Japanese customs officials at the busy port. They changed some money into the Korean currency.

On their way to the train station, they were bewildered by another new world. Fortunately, they didn't have to walk too far as they followed the baggage carts. White clad Koreans surrounded them as they walked. They knew that the white clothing was a symbol of mourning, a silent protest by the Koreans because Japan had taken over their country. There were women with babies tied onto their backs, or carrying all kinds of loads on their heads. Old grandpas, with their strange stovepipe hats and their long bamboo tobacco pipes, strode along with great dignity. Always there were bright-eyed little children running about, or stopping to stare at the strange foreigners.

At the station, they telegraphed their arrival time to Dr. O. R. Avison in Seoul, a fellow Canadian missionary. They checked their heavy baggage, and at last were settled into the crowded train for their long trip.

"I feel like I'm under a microscope," Stan said as he hunkered down trying to read. They were under the steady gaze of many eyes, friendly eyes, but extremely curious.

They had an overview of the country, as the train traveled north. There were miles of rice paddies lying fallow in winter, and beautiful snow-covered mountains. The journey took them halfway up the peninsula. Hours later they arrived in Seoul. They were amazed to see that the station was a magnificent structure, as beautiful as any in Europe. Later they learned it had been designed by a German architect.

The busy Dr. Avison met them, and helped them as they checked their heavy baggage at the station to wait for the next leg of the trip. From there he took them to the hospital compound to his home. There followed a kaleidoscope of events in the huge ancient city.

Stan and Margaret were shown the famous Severance Hospital, which had been founded by Dr. Avison. They stayed long enough for Stan to do some expert X-ray work. Margaret visited the nursing school and observed some of the nurses at work. It was their first contact with Korean people on a personal basis. They were warmed by their friendliness and appreciation for anything done for them.

They also visited palaces and saw the ancient South Gate. Seoul used to be a walled city, one hundred years before Columbus discovered America.

In the evenings, they were invited to dinners in the small Western community and heard hilarious stories of the early days. Most of them were about missionaries trying to talk Korean, or Koreans practicing their English.

One told of the missionary preaching on Jesus' triumphal entry into Jerusalem. He said in Korean, "Jesus came riding in on a butterfly." He then wondered why the congregation was convulsed with laughter – hiding their faces in their sleeves to be polite. The word for donkey is *tahng naqui*, the word for butterfly is *nahbi*.

Another told of the Korean trying out his English, bringing news of his friend's death. "He's expi – he's expi – he's dedicated!"

Many similar stories kept them laughing for a long time. Then Stan in a more serious vein said, "As you know, we're heading for Manchuria. We're surprised there are so many Koreans there. Could you tell us why this is so?"

One of the older missionaries answered. "Well, there are several reasons. Perhaps the most important one is that many of the most patriotic Koreans were <u>not</u> going to live under the Japanese and fled north. Others had their land expropriated by the conquerors, or were forced to sell their best farmland at a loss. There was a famine at one time, and that led some to leave. About 500,000 of them live up there now, and many of them are Christians. Sometimes whole villages migrated together. The land is excellent for farming and the Chinese, for the most part, have welcomed them."

Then it was time to continue their journey. They left by train for Wonsan on the east coast. It was the first of the northern Canadian Mission stations they would visit on their way to Yong

Jung. They were heartily welcomed there by the Reverend Doctor Alec Robb and his wife, Bessie. Dr. Robb rejoiced that at last there would be a medical man for the many thousands who would need him farther north. The mission compound overlooked Wonsan harbor. Margaret wrote later that the view from there was one of the most beautiful sights she had ever seen, especially in the morning when the sea was like glass – the "Land of the Morning Calm," as the Koreans called their country.

A whirlwind of visits to the Mission work followed. They met the famous sisters Elizabeth and Louise McCully, and saw their Mission School for Girls and the Bible Institute where they trained women church workers. Stan was interested in the little hospital run by the Methodists. Everywhere, they were greeted by smiles, bows and cups of barley tea. They noticed that many North Korean women wore a white cloth wrapped around their heads called a *soogun*.

Stan's practiced eye diagnosed illnesses as they passed crowds of people. He saw goiter cases, eye diseases, people coughing, and many limping with crude crutches. But his work was to be later.

The McCully sisters were caring for a blind girl in their home. She had been cast out of her family as useless. While Stan and Margaret were there, another blind girl was brought to them. News had traveled fast. The question was what could they do with her? They needed a special home for the blind. Everywhere, there was a need of some kind. Margaret wrote to her father, hoping their church would take an interest in the girl.

Again they were on their way. This time it was by coastal steamer from Wonsan harbor. After farewells to their friends, with the help of carts and "jiggys" (the A-frames that Korean men used to carry loads), all of their freight was loaded. Even the precious piano was hoisted aboard ship. Providentially the sea was calm, because humans and baggage were rowed out and transferred over a strip of heaving water.

Margaret and Stan thought of the many times they had traveled the coasts of Newfoundland and Labrador. How different the cargo was now. They watched as squealing pigs, bundles of dried fish, great earthenware crocks and bags of rice were hauled aboard.

Then came a three-day voyage up the coast to Chongjin, visiting pretty little harbors with long stopovers.

It was getting colder and colder as the little steamer plowed north. At Chongjin, they breathlessly watched as all their worldly goods landed safely at the dock. They followed the carts to a nearby inn.

The next morning they boarded a narrow-gauge railroad train that went only part of the way to Hoiryung, the mission station near the border of Manchuria. After a short trip, baggage and passengers transferred to another line, also a narrow gauge, but wider. This line ran on the Korean side, parallel to the Tumen river dividing the two countries.

Hours later, traveling west, they arrived at the Hoiryung station. A telegram from Wonsan had informed D. A. Macdonald of their arrival time. It was so cold they stamped their feet to get warm as they watched their baggage getting unloaded in the midst of clouds of steam from the engine. Shouting Koreans grabbed at the boxes and suitcases.

"Wait! Wait!" Stan shouted in English. Again, that feeling of utter helplessness gripped them. What next? Where would they ever find the missionary compound? Just then, they saw a tall foreigner, head and shoulders above the crowd, approaching with a big smile on his face. It would be hard to say who was happier - "D. A." as he was called, welcoming the new young couple, or the Martins, feeling secure again and hearing English words.

"Welcome! Welcome! How was your trip?"

"Fine. Fine! A little long, but we're all right. As you know, I'm Stan, and this is my wife, Margaret."

Margaret's face was so cold she could hardly smile her greeting.

"We've been looking forward to your coming. Wait a minute, I'll bring the cart men. Let's see, we'll need at least three carts. What's in the big crate?"

"My piano. I'm glad it's gotten this far," Margaret said, shivering.

"Oh splendid! The Koreans love music. We'll check a lot of this here, for your next trip of course! We'll take only the small things."

Towards dark, they approached the missionary compound and were met at the Macdonald home by Hazel and their two little boys, Bruce and Ross. What a relief it was to get out of the cold wind! Margaret could hardly walk she was so stiff from the horse-cart ride. Hazel showed them to the guest room. As they passed the kitchen, they could smell something delicious, maybe chicken. Hazel said, "Supper will be ready soon." They could see a Korean woman with a white *soogun* on her head, working by the stove.

"I want you to meet our cook Kitooki Omanee." The woman came to them and smiled as she was introduced. She said several words in Korean. Stan and Margaret could only smile and bow. They did a lot smiling and bowing in the coming weeks.

As they sat down for supper, they looked around at the simple room. It all seemed especially delightful as they heard the wind blowing eerily outside. Soon, steaming bowls of rice, chicken and vegetables were brought in. The grace included fervent thanks for the newcomers' safe arrival. The little boys plunged right in to the good meal, and Stan and Margaret said they had never tasted anything better.

The conversation led to D.A. and Hazel's mission work. D.A. was a minister and he told of his travels over a wide area where he was responsible for helping and encouraging the little Korean churches. Hazel was home-schooling the children and also worked with the Hoiryung church women. She dreaded the time when they would have to send the children to Japan or Pyeng Yang, Korea, for further schooling.

D.A. continued as they passed the food around. "Hoiryung is a border city as you know, and is quite large. It's a center of trade with Manchuria. The Japanese have a garrison here. They've been buying up the land, but we were able to buy two properties, one for the dispensary, and one for our three residences. You'll see them tomorrow. We've only been here six years. You're going to a newer work than ours, the Yong Jung property was bought only four years ago. The Yong Jung station has extraterritorial rights – an agreement between the Chinese and British governments. They fly the British flag at the main gate. Reverend Archer Barker and his wife are there now. We're all pioneers in these mission stations."

"You'll enjoy the Barker's a lot. He's a minister from Knox University, Rebecca is a teacher and a graduate of Toronto University."

Stan laughed. "Our arch enemy in sports! I'm from Queens."

D.A. said, "We'll telegraph them tomorrow. He'll have to meet you at Sambong, at the end of the rail line, to get you safely into Yong Jung. There is another missionary there, the Rev. Dr. William Foote. He's a minister and does work like mine in the country churches. His wife had to stay in Canada because of ill health. He's one of our pioneers."

The time spent in the snug little home was enlightening to the newcomers and added to their understanding of what was ahead: missing their home country, the sense of isolation, yet the tremendous challenge of their work. A Dr. Mansfield had manned the dispensary for a short while, but had been transferred to Wonsan. So now they were without medical help. In case of serious illness, they would have to make the rough journey down to Wonsan. The Martins, having just come from there, could share their concern. Stan brightened, however, and said cheerfully, "But now, Yong Jung is closer. I'll take care of you. I'll come to you if necessary."

Hazel smiled as she hugged her two little ones. They all played games with the children before bedtime, then Stan and Margaret retired for the night. They were exhausted.

In the night they heard strange animal sounds. The mission compound was at the edge of town. "That one sounds like the wolves we had in Labrador!" Stan said, sitting bolt upright in bed. Margaret shivered and listened, but they soon fell asleep again.

At breakfast they inquired about the sounds they had heard in the night. "Oh yes," Hazel said. "You may have heard wolves, we have them here. And there are tigers out there, but farther out in the hills. You've heard of the Korean tigers I suppose. You're heading for Siberian tiger country. That's why we don't travel after dark."

Margaret gulped She remembered being scared of bears when she was a little girl in Maine. She asked Stan, "Where is your gun, dear?"

"It's in the telescope box, but we'll be all right, if, as Hazel said, we travel only in the daytime."

D.A. gave Stan a knowing glance. He knew a lot of tiger stories, but he decided it wasn't the time for that just now.

After breakfast, Hazel started a new batch of bread with the cook. She wanted to have plenty to send with the Martins on their trip the next day. D.A. went to the post office to telegraph Yong Jung, while the Martins repacked. Afterwards, D.A. and the children took the guests for a tour of the mission work. The doctor's residence stood empty and so did the dispensary. Stan peered in the windows and saw sparse equipment. The third missionary home was Edna McClellan's. D.A. explained, "Sorry, she's away now. She's in a distant village at a Bible Woman's Conference. She travels by bullock cart, a very brave lady. You'll meet her later."

They visited the beautiful Girls' Mission School at the adjoining property. As they opened the back door, they saw the backs of about forty girls, all dressed alike in white *choguris* (jackets) and black skirts. Each one had her black hair in a braid down her back, tied at the end with a red ribbon. They looked like pretty dolls.

It was chapel time and they were standing and singing a hymn in timid sweet voices. It was the first time the Martins had heard Koreans sing. A pump organ graced the corner, but no one was available to play it because Miss McLellan was away.

The Korean principal caught sight of the guests and came eagerly to them. Again many strange Korean words assaulted the young couple's ears. He bowed deeply, then brought the visitors to the front to be introduced.

The students then bowed and stared frankly in curiosity. They had seen very few foreigners. D.A. spoke to the students saying, "This is the new doctor and his wife, a nurse, on the way to Yong Jung."

Margaret said, "Perhaps I could play something on the organ for them." A quick interpretation of her words to the principal and he said, "Good, please do."

Margaret chose the hymn the girls had been singing. This time the girls began to join in singing, with joyous abandon. After a few more bows and smiles the guests left, but as they closed the door, they could hear the excited chatter of the girls, their new friends. It was Margaret's first time to share her music on the mission field. Music – a bridge to people's hearts.

They returned to the warm home, fragrant with newly baked bread. Ross and Bruce scurried to the kitchen to have a cinnamon roll. Hazel said, "I sent Lee Sa Bahng to the post office to see if Archie had answered the telegram and he has already. Here."

She read the message to Stan. "Welcome Martins. Meet me at Chonan Inn Sambong. Archie Barker."

Hazel continued, "Also, while you were gone, I had Lee Sa Bahng buy these two metal hot-water bottles, and two heavy Korean quilts for your cart journey from Sambong. You'll freeze without them. Just keep them as a welcome gift." The Martins received the gifts gratefully.

The next morning came too quickly, and they were off to the railroad station. After a safe baggage transfer and farewells, they again found themselves in a crowded train coach. It didn't seem strange to the Chinese and Korean passengers that these foreigners had the two bulky quilt bundles besides their hand-baggage. Everyone seemed to have large bundles. There were even baskets of chickens at their feet. Egg shells and apple peelings covered the floor and sometimes someone cleared his throat and spat on the floor. "Tuberculosis," Stan thought, as he turned his head away.

As usual, the foreigners were objects of curiosity and the passengers, both Korean and Chinese, never tired of staring at them as the hours went by. Quietly, the Martins observed the Chinese dressed in padded dark blue clothes – a new people and the sound of a new language.

The smoky coal stove in the center of the coach didn't give much heat, but that and the warmth of the human beings made it bearable. The air was heavy with the smell of garlic. Stan and Margaret were glad they were dressed in their Newfoundland winter clothes and boots.

At last they arrived at Sambong. Stan knew he'd have to use the only two Korean words he knew, as the eager cart drivers surrounded him. *Chonan Yokwan.* (Chonan Inn).

"Ne, Ne." (Yes, Yes). They understood. Before long, and as if unseen hands assisted, all the boxes and barrels, and the large piano crate were safely unloaded in the courtyard of the Chonan

Inn. D.A. had suggested the amount to be given to the cart drivers. So Stan placed the sums of money in their hands. It must have been right, because they drove off smiling and waving.

It was twilight when Stan was standing near the gate of the courtyard, checking over the baggage. Margaret was inside, resting on the warm Korean radiant-heated floor of their room. Stan looked up and there to his surprise was a tall lanky Westerner riding toward him on a donkey. It was so small that though he was seated on a high Korean saddle, his feet touched the ground as he rode.

"Dr. Martin?" the rider called out.

"Yes, are you Archer Barker?"

"Yes!"

Stan helped him dismount and embraced the stranger in instant friendship. "Thank God you're here," Stan said. The pleasure was mutual. Once again, in the vast, desolate surroundings, Stan felt secure and cared for – the touch of God's hand on his shoulder. "Come and meet Margaret."

Margaret sat up as introductions were made, and the men sat beside her on the warm floor. "I came by donkey from the Chinese side. We'll get our cart rides from there tomorrow," Archie said, and then asked Margaret, "Are you feeling all right?" She nodded.

"Rebecca can hardly wait to see you. How are the Macdonald's?"

"They are all well."

"Did you meet Edna McClellan?"

"No she was away at meetings."

"Did you order supper?"

Margaret laughed. "We couldn't really – we don't know how to, we don't speak Korean. We just mimicked eating and drinking."

"Of course. I'll check on it."

Soon, small low tables were brought in with the most delicious Korean meal the Martins had ever had. It included grilled beef (*pul koki*) that had been marinated in soy sauce, garlic and sesame seed oil; rice, spinach, and, of course, the incendiary pickle called *kimchi*, red with pepper. They had tasted that at Wonsan.

Archer spoke enthusiastically as they ate, telling about the work at Yong Jung. He was especially happy that there would be medical work there now. "It's pitiful, the sight of desperately sick people that we see so often and can't do a thing to help. Now you'll be there."

Rebecca and I moved there in June four years ago. We rented a Chinese house while I had to supervise the building of the missionary houses. There are four of them, and they're really fine, if I do say so. There's a good grade of clay there for brick making and excellent stone in the hills. The Chinese are fine builders."

"We have 26 acres that the Mission bought for five hundred dollars in 1912. Right now, we are in one of the houses, the Reverend Rev. Foote is in another. There's a vacant one that will be the single ladies' house and the doctor's house, No.4, is waiting for you.

"China, as you know is quite different from Korea. Ever since the Empress Dowager died, things are very fluid. Here on the Korean side we have some protection from the Bolsheviks.

There, primary dangers are Chinese warlords with their bandits, the Bolsheviks, both Korean and Chinese, trained in Moscow, and the activities of the Korean Independence fighters. So far, we haven't had any trouble; you know we work mostly with the Koreans. They are some of the most wonderful people in the world."

Stan and Margaret nodded in agreement. "We realize that already. We are most impressed," Margaret said.

That night Archer unrolled his sleeping blankets in the corner of the Martins' room and was soon snoring heartily.

"Pioneers," Margaret whispered to Stan as she settled down beside him. "Pioneers. We're already sharing our room with a stranger. Well, he _is_ like a brother, although we just met him."

"That's right," Stan replied. "It's good to get even one room in this area."

They slept while the wind blew straight from the Gobi Desert and moaned eerily around the snug little inn.

The next morning after a Korean breakfast of hot rice and seaweed soup, Archer requested hot water for the metal bottles, and headed out on the donkey to bring the carts for the baggage. He explained that the carts would take them only across the river to the Customs office. The better carts that he had arranged for would be waiting there with Korean drivers.

Margaret had thawed some of Hazel's bread on the warm floor during the night. Now she made peanut butter sandwiches with peanuts that had been ground in the Macdonald's kitchen in a little meat grinder. They were oily, but would be most welcome on the trip. She filled thermoses with tea made from the precious English tea she had brought from home.

Archer was back, the baggage loaded, and they began their walk to the river. It was bitter cold, and Margaret wrapped her scarf around her face so only her eyes were exposed. As they crossed the frozen Tumen on foot, Stan held Margaret's arm firmly so she wouldn't slip on the ice. The baggage carts rumbled beside them.

"It's fortunate we're arriving in winter because I don't know whether those river boats could hold the piano box," Stan said as they glanced at slim gray boats drawn up on the riverbank.

"That's right. Thank God for this thick ice."

Now, they were across the river and standing on Chinese soil. Did they hear a fanfare in heaven? Did some of the "cloud of witnesses" rush to heaven's balustrades to watch? Disregarding the Korean cart driver's gaze, Margaret and Stan stopped and hugged each other.

"We're here!"

Again, they felt the strong hand of God on their shoulders.

Already there was a difference. Most of the people wore the indigo-blue padded cotton clothes. Some men carried baskets balanced on each end of a pole that was on their shoulders. Many horse-carts rumbled by.

"Here come some Manchurian ponies," Stan exclaimed. A team of shaggy little ponies with bright-colored bridles trotted by. They soon arrived at the Customs building. Although this was China and the Martins had Chinese visas on their passports, they were surprised to find that the Immigration and Customs officials were Japanese. It was an indication of the weakness of the Chinese government. The officials wanted to know the newcomer's destination and business, but waved their bags and baggage on without inspection. Archer was a big help as he talked to a Korean man standing nearby who interpreted for them to the Japanese officials.

It was a clear sunny day, but the Manchurian wind was bitterly cold as it blew on them. Margaret climbed gratefully into the large Russian cart with the thick Korean quilts and hot water bottles. Her heart was warm and grateful to Hazel for thinking of these gifts. After loading and tying the baggage on two flat carts, the men roped and tied down the piano, sitting in quiet dignity on a cart of its own. The horses were of normal size and they looked strong as they pawed the frozen ground with their hooves and snorted, emitting steam from their nostrils.

Finally, Stan and Archer climbed into the Russian coach with Margaret, glad to be out of the wind. They had haggled with the four cart men for the price of the trip and now they were off!

It was a twenty-three mile drive from there to Yong Jung, but as the drivers often walked beside the carts, it would be a long journey. They moved away from the village and off to the northwest on a dirt road. Because of the cold, the roads were firm. They would have been impassable in the rainy season. From time to time they had to get off the road to let other vehicles pass.

Unlike Korea with its mountains, they were now on a bare brown plain, wide open to the sweeping wind. Margaret soon fell asleep while the men chatted. (The road was not too rough at that time.) Stan had so much to learn, and asked many questions. He was glad Archer had had experience in building, because Stan knew he would be building a hospital soon.

About noon, the surroundings changed. They approached a forested area and in the distance there was a steep hill.

Archer said, "The village Tutogo is on the other side of that hill. We may have to walk beside the cart if it's too steep. We have a pretty heavy load."

When they approached the foot of the hill, Margaret asked them to stop and she jumped out to stretch her legs. The men followed and they all climbed the steep road together beside the horses. Their Russian cart was the leading cart, the other three were behind them.

The piano cart was bringing up the rear. The horses strained under the heavy loads. Suddenly there was a loud snap which meant breaking wood. The driver of the piano cart shouted as he stood by his horse. "*Aigo – Aigo – Chum*!" (Oh, my! Oh, my! Well, how about that!!!) They all froze as they saw the horseless piano cart careening down the hill and to their amazement coming smoothly to a stop on the road.

Margaret almost burst into tears of joy, "My piano! It's safe!"

Archer and Stan laughed with relief. Archer then said, "It is good that the village is just over the hill. We'll all go ahead and I know there's a Chinese inn there. We can send the piano cartman back with repair materials. He can catch up with us later."

Soon they entered the village and rolled up to the inn where the whole cavalcade stopped. Stan helped Margaret down while Archer went into the inn. Immediately, excited villagers gathered and surrounded them. Dogs barked and children came running. The Chinese innkeeper and all his family came out to see the strangers.

Margaret smiled at the little children in their bright colored trousers and jackets, different clothing from what Korean children wore. The little girls had their hair cut in bangs, with a little ponytail tied with red string at each ear. Some wore earrings. The little boys had their hair cut as if a rice bowl had been placed over their heads and the hair was cut evenly around. They chattered among themselves and ran up to touch Margaret's clothing.

At the door, a small white-haired grandmother stood with tiny bound feet. Margaret gasped as she realized what she was seeing. Unperturbed, the little lady smiled and hobbled ahead as the guests entered the inn. They were shown to a room, not like a Korean room with a hot floor, but a room with a raised platform that served as a bench or a bed. A little smoky stove was in the corner. Archer with his few words of Chinese, ordered a meal for all of them, including the cartmen. In the meantime, the piano cartman had found a Korean who showed him the shop with cart supplies. He came to report the good news, and Stan and Archer watched as he galloped off down the hill to the stranded piano.

It was nearly two hours later when the missing vehicle arrived. They made sure the driver had a good lunch, and then the party moved off. This time the villagers bowed and waved as they left. The hours went by, the peanut butter sandwiches were long gone, and their thermoses were empty. Sometimes they got out and walked. Margaret watched the sky grow darker and wondered how much longer the trip would take. Also – help! When do tigers come out? By now she was thoroughly bumped and shaken because the road had become much rougher.

"We're almost there," Archer said as he saw how tired she was getting. Stan patted her hand.

They drove up a little hill, and there at last was the Yong Jung Mission compound with four large houses looming in the darkness. One was dimly lighted.

As the carts stopped, Archer jumped out and ran to his wife standing in the lighted doorway. Stan and Margaret followed and were introduced. They entered into a beautiful warm house filled with the fragrance of familiar western food.

Stan and Archer went out again to guide the carts to House No. 4 to be unloaded. Rebecca and Margaret studied each other, and their warm smiles spoke volumes. "You have no idea how <u>happy</u> we are that you've come to be with us. You're going to have your meals with us for several days. You can sleep here too as long as you like until you get unpacked."

"Thanks so much. We're grateful beyond words. Archer has already been a tremendous help." Margaret said as she threw herself into a big armchair.

"Wait a minute. I want you to meet someone," Rebecca said as she went to the kitchen and came back with a young Korean woman. She wore the North Korean white head dress. "This is my cook Kimsi. She's my jewel. I couldn't do my teaching without her."

The young woman approached Margaret and took her hand in both of her warm hands. She spoke in a soft voice and smiled. Rebecca said, "She's welcoming you and she says she's so glad I have another Western woman to be my friend."

Kimsi bowed and went back to her work. "She teaches in our Sunday school. She's one of our few educated women."

When the men returned, Stan bounded up the steps and found his wife and Rebecca in the living room. "The house is wonderful, Margaret. I'm sure you'll love it! We unloaded all the baggage into the big sun porch for now. It's too dark to see anything tonight. We'll explore it in the morning."

Pulling Margaret to her feet, he took her in his arms. "Welcome to Yong Jung," and then he paused. "Hitherto the Lord hath helped us."

"Amen! Amen!" Archer and Rebecca chorused as they all laughed and proceeded to the supper table. Kimsi smiled from the kitchen door.

Dr. Rufus Foot setting out on an itineration trip. Dr. &
Mrs. S. H. Martin standing in doorway.

VIII

Settling In

The smell of coffee drifted up to the guest room as Stan and Margaret were waking up the next morning.

"That's coffee! We haven't had coffee for ages," Stan said as he stood up and stretched. "Just think how many miles it traveled to get here."

"Makes me tired just to think of it."

"By the way, where's our coffee?"

"It's in Crate No. 4. I packed it in Boston. I brought a lot of tea for you in my handbag to be sure and have it, but the coffee is in with the heavy stuff."

At breakfast, they found Rebecca and Archer ready for the day. The dining room was bright with sunshine. Rebecca would be leaving soon for her teaching at the Girls' Mission School, and Archer was ready to help the Martins unpack. Breakfast consisted of coffee and toast, and a mush of yellow millet served with sugar and diluted, evaporated milk. Rebecca said as she dished it out, "This is millet, one of the interesting grains they have here. They raise tons of it. We hope you like it. There are other kinds of grain that we can use for cereal, too. I'll show them to you in the market, Margaret."

As they passed the food, Archer said, "I sent Paksabang over to your house to make fires in the kitchen stove, the fireplace, and the stove in your master bedroom upstairs, so we'll be warm enough to work. We laid in a supply of firewood. He's over there now to help us."

"A good idea," said Stan. "Thanks."

"He also filled the *toks* [clay jars] with water yesterday," added Archer. "I hope they didn't freeze. With no running water, life is complicated. As you saw here in our bathroom, every drop of hot water to wash with comes from our kitchen stove. We live with buckets and basins."

"You've thought of everything," Margaret said, as she tasted the millet. It was quite good.

"On Sunday you'll meet our church people," Archer continued. "They are the nucleus of the work here. The boys and girls come from our Mission Schools, and with their parents and others, we have quite a large congregation. We'll need to look for language teachers from among them."

As Rebecca rose to leave, Margaret asked, "How far do you have to walk to your school?"

"It's only about ten minutes, but I have to dress very warmly these cold days. It's not too bad, and I need the exercise. I'll see you at lunch time." She went out the door muffled up to her eyebrows in her coat and scarf.

"Just like St. Anthony," chuckled Margaret to Stan.

After breakfast, Archer and the young couple hurried over to House No. 4. They eased their way past the trunks and boxes in the sun porch, and went into the house. Paksabang was waiting.

The stairs were to the left, and there was a small room to the right. The hallway led to a bright living room facing east and south. The fireplace was blazing with a cheerful fire. They then passed to the left, through an empty dining room, a small pantry and around to the kitchen.

Here, were the two earthenware jars – *toks*, about three feet tall, full of water. There was a large kitchen table and a western iron cook stove with a fire going. There were shelves on the wall to the right of the stove.

"We ordered our stoves from Canada when we were building these houses," said Archer. "We can't do without them, especially because we need the ovens to bake our bread. Koreans cook their food in big iron cauldrons called *sots* that are built into their kitchens, or on little charcoal braziers. They don't have ovens."

They explored an inner stairway from the kitchen to the upstairs, especially handy for carrying water, and looked down a flight of stairs from the kitchen to a full basement.

"Our cellars are for storage, but also to hold our coal supplies. We'll help you order some right away."

Upstairs, he watched as Stan and Margaret went from room to room, exclaiming with pleasure. In the master bedroom was a large wooden bed.

"We had the Chinese carpenter make that for you, and Rebecca and Kimsi made your mattress. It's filled with straw and it's covered with the heavy indigo-dyed cotton cloth that Chinese clothes are made of. You can get a better one later." Stan and Margaret were surprised and pleased.

A little Franklin stove with a metal pipe going out through a window gave warmth as they explored.

"If you keep a kettle on this, it provides warm water for the bathroom."

"Good idea," said Stan as they looked south out of the window over a broad bare field. In the distance they could see the compound gate by a large church with a steeple. Not far away, they could see the well house, and a man with a yoke on his back carrying two pails of water. Since there was a flat plain beyond, the little town of Yong Jung with its gray-tiled Chinese roofs seemed far away. From a north bedroom they looked across more fields toward a hill with sparse vegetation, not a tree in sight. There was one little Korean house and in the far corner of the compound, a tall mud and stone tower.

Archer pointed to the house and said, "That's where Kimsi and her husband Paksabang live. We'll build one or two houses for your helpers when we know what you need."

"What is that tower for?" Stan asked.

"It's a watch tower for our protection," Archer explained. "Some Chinese soldiers come to it from time to time, but they leave right away. It's just symbolic."

A road ran past the tower leading to a cemetery, and across from the tower was a completely walled-in area.

"That's the home of the British Customs official," Archer said. Only a barbed wire fence delineated the twenty-six-acre mission property.

They turned away from looking at the bare brown hill and the bare brown fields and listened to the wind blowing incessantly. There were two other empty bedrooms, one with a door to a porch with a railing around it.

"You'll enjoy that porch. We often sleep on ours in the summer, with mosquito nets of course. Believe it or not, it gets unbearably hot in July and August."

It was time to unpack. Going downstairs, they tackled the No. 4 crate first, and the four of them trekked around to the kitchen with armloads of groceries and heavy bags of sugar and flour. Then, partly because it was in the way, the men opened the piano box and trundled the precious instrument through the hall to the living room. Margaret chose a spot for it to the left of the fireplace. Then, standing, she lifted the lid and rippled off some chords to check if it was out of tune.

"Not too bad. It'll do," Margaret said, and still standing, she played the doxology. Stan and Archer stopped and listened, but Paksabang came up to have a closer look. He had never seen a piano in his life!

"We'll have to find your piano stool. Where would that be?" Stan asked as he headed for the sun porch.

"It's in the box from Maine with the things that Papa gave us," answered Margaret. "I think No. 6"

Her eyes suddenly blurred with tears as she saw her father's handwriting on the labels. I wonder when we'll get our first letters, she thought as they unpacked her treasure. It was a round, black, shiny piano stool that could be rotated to the desired height.

"Well, at least we brought <u>one</u> piece of furniture," Margaret said as Stan carried it to the piano.

They went back to work, and by noon Margaret had made up the bed upstairs and most of the food items were stored in the kitchen and pantry.

Stan claimed the room near the entrance for his study, and his precious telescope, medical books and supplies were placed in there. They would have to stay in boxes for a while.

Archer was noting their needs. "We'll send the Chinese carpenter tomorrow," he said. "I would have done more, but I wanted to see what you needed. Also, there are bits of furniture that we can buy in town, like small tables."

"Even benches will do for chairs," Margaret said. "We saw benches at the Chinese inn yesterday, didn't we?"

They returned to the Barker's for lunch, and Rebecca was back from school.

"The school girls are so excited that you've come, and want to see you," Rebecca said as she met them at the door.

"Well, we want to see them, too," Margaret said. "We <u>love</u> our house. It's far better than we ever dreamed it would be. We've made good progress in the unpacking."

"Well, sorry it's not furnished very much. It took us a few years to get where we are. It's amazing how fast we adjust to a simpler life. I'm glad you like it, though."

Kimsi had made a pheasant stew, and with her good homemade bread and Rebecca's canned applesauce, the newcomers felt they were feasting like royalty.

"I don't know what we'd do without pheasant in the winter," said Rebecca. "It's too cold to keep chickens in the henhouse in this climate. We have to wait for spring. Some hunters bring us these pheasant from time to time, frozen as hard as rocks. We just hang them up in the back porch until they're needed. Watch out for the birdshot, though. We don't have much variety, but at least we get enough to eat."

"This is delicious," Margaret said. "Remember we ate simple food at St. Anthony in north Newfoundland and in the fishing villages there."

"Right," said Stan. "Mostly fish."

By Sunday, Stan and Margaret were partially unpacked, and the Chinese carpenter had measured for shelves and was shown samples of the Barker's furniture to copy. They ordered a fine large table for the dining room.

They agreed to try Paksabang's brother Sahng Ha as "outside man," so Paksabang undertook to teach him how to make the fires in the strange foreign stoves.

Rebecca, at Kimsi's recommendation, brought a young woman with the Christian name *Tabitha* to meet Margaret. They liked each other immediately. Margaret asked Rebecca to interpret for her.

"Would you like to be my cook and learn to make Western food?"

Tabitha answered shyly, "I'll try."

Thus began a deep friendship that endured for years. Tabitha and her husband would move to compound housing when it was ready.

Stan and Margaret had their meals with the Barkers for a few more days.

"As soon as I bake my first batch of bread, I'll know we can be on our own," said Margaret. "I'll cook and Tabitha can wash dishes and do the laundry."

"You know you are welcome here as long as we can be of help for your meals," Rebecca said. Already they had had wonderful long talks, sharing the experiences of their lives. It had been so refreshing for Rebecca to talk in English to another woman.

Sunday morning, they all went down to the church by the compound gate. It was packed. All the Korean shoes were in rows in the vestibule of the church, for the congregation members always stepped in stocking feet onto the polished wooden floor inside. The four pairs of western style shoes looked strange beside the Korean shoes made of rubber or woven straw. Inside the church the people sat on the floor. Women, girls and little children sat in a group to the right, and the men and boys were seated at the left, all facing the pulpit. A bench by the little pump organ was offered to Rebecca and Margaret. Stan and Archer sat on the floor with the men.

The minister was very happy to greet the new doctor, and his wife the nurse, and he introduced them to his people. Stan and Margaret recognized the boys and girls from the mission schools by their uniforms. The women nearly all wore white, with the white *soogun* head wrap. The married ones had their hair put up into a bun, which was held at the nape of their neck with a long hair pin, made of wood, gold, silver, or jade. The young girls had braids down their backs. All eyes were frankly staring at Margaret, the new foreign woman in their midst.

Rebecca played the organ and when the people sang, they sang in the robust, sincere manner of mature Christians. The words were strange, but the hymn tunes were familiar to Margaret and Stan. Many in the congregation were Christians before they came to Manchuria. During the prayer or the reading of Scripture, they swayed as they listened, ending with a loud *Amen* in unison. The strong presence of God was in their midst.

After the service, the people crowded to greet the newcomers. Archer stood near.

"They're welcoming you and some are telling you about their sick relatives," he said. "I told them you have to learn the language first and you will care for the sick later."

That afternoon, the missionaries observed what was to be a weekly Sunday routine. They had their own English service, held at the Martins' because the piano was there. They sang hymns, Archer gave a fine message, and they all shared testimonies of answered prayer. Margaret sat on the piano stool and the others sat on boxes.

As they said goodnight after supper at the Barkers, the Martins left to sleep in their new home. The next day Margaret made her first batch of bread and took a pan of cinnamon rolls over to the Barkers. Tabitha had watched every move of the bread-making process and was fascinated to see the dough rise. She also had her first taste of this Western stuff called bread.

The next hurdle was language study. Stan had been given the strict injunction from the Mission Board to study Korean for a year before starting his medical practice. After learning polite greetings and farewell sentences, that Archer taught them, they learned the rest in any way they could. Archer recommended a teacher from the Boys' School who could give a few hours of lessons to Stan, and Margaret was learning Korean from Tabitha in the kitchen – "water, stove, dish, spoon, rice," etc. She learned fast because she had to use the words immediately. Later, a Mr. Lee was recommended for her formal studies. They didn't have the helpful textbooks that were available to students in the Language School in Seoul, explaining the difficult grammar structure.

Margaret sat with her teacher and pointed to *paper*, the calligraphy *brush*, the *clock*, a *pencil*, her *shoe*, anything they could think of. The teacher then gave her the Korean word for the object. Margaret's vocabulary grew as she wrote it down like it sounded. They laughed a lot and the time always flew. She was beginning to appreciate the Korean sense of humor.

Stan advanced to a medical vocabulary, the parts of the body and the sentences and questions that Archer had written out for him in *Romaji*, a system of writing the words as they sounded, using the English alphabet. *Odee apumnika?* "Where does it hurt?" or *Onjai su puta apoosichiyo?* "How long have you felt this pain?" Stan had given Archer the list of some questions and answers he needed for diagnosing an illness. He shared his new vocabulary with Margaret, his nurse wife.

They fell in to a happy routine for their studies, Margaret at the dining room table and Stan in his study. Both teachers brought Korean primary textbooks to introduce them to the written language. The Koreans in those days read vertically, right to left. The Korean alphabet was fairly easy to learn. It is said you can learn to read in four hours, but, of course, you don't know what you're reading until you know the vocabulary. They would study Chinese characters later because Koreans had these characters scattered throughout their literature. The Martins were quick learners. The bitter cold and constant wind helped them to be content to stay inside, in hibernation with their studies. Visits with the Barkers were always the bright spots in their lives.

Archer told them one day, as they were having afternoon tea at the Barker's, "There's another important thing we do while it's still winter. We lay in our ice supply. You saw that low thatched roof in our north garden? That's our ice house. It's a pit about 8 feet by 8 feet. We'll make one for you, too, when the ground thaws. It's as hard as a brick now. We get big square blocks of ice from the river and put them down in there, buried in sawdust or rice hulls. With the little roof over it, we can have ice all summer for making ice cream, or to use in a tin-lined ice chest. We can store your supply in with ours until your pit is dug."

Rebecca added, "Also, now's the time to order seeds for the spring planting."

Margaret smiled in eager anticipation. She had inherited the love of gardening from her father. "What kind of vegetables and flowers do well here?"

Rebecca answered, "Any of the temperate climate plants, but the season's a little short as in Toronto and Maine. We can't plant much 'til almost June. We had good success with corn, turnips, tomatoes, peas, lettuce and beets. You should have seen how excited the Koreans were when they tasted our sweet corn. We shared seed with them. They have some native corn, but it's not nearly so good."

"Every bit of the hard work is worth it, when the first fresh vegetables come in," Archer added. "We have a farmer come with his bull and plow, to plow the vegetable plots for us."

Margaret could hardly wait to dash off a letter to her father who would put in a seed order to Burpee's, their favorite place. She knew it would be a long wait for the seeds to arrive.

The days went slowly by. The first letters from home arrived, and somehow the world seemed normal again. Papa was doing well, although it was a hard winter. He was eager to receive her first letter.

The sound of the wind moaning in the eaves of the house was now familiar and they didn't notice it as much. At church they were able to greet people with their new sentences. The Koreans were delighted and answered with a flood of chatter Stan and Margaret couldn't understand, but smiles said everything.

On February 15, 1916, when it was still bitterly cold, the Martins were swept into a new chapter of their lives. That afternoon there was a pounding at the door of the sun porch. Stan jumped up from his language study to see what it was. Sahng Ha and the language teacher followed him.

There, lying on a bull-drawn cart was a pathetic figure. The young man was on a straw mat, his face contorted with pain. A man and woman standing beside him spoke in pleading tones, wringing their hands.

"Our son, he's going to die!" Stan didn't understand the Korean words, but his doctor's eyes knew what he was seeing. Even in the fresh air Stan caught a strong whiff of the deadly gangrene. They had pulled back a thin quilt revealing a black, gangrenous leg with red streaks up the bare thigh. Pointing to the Barkers' house he said, "*Sahng Ha, Barker Moksa, osipsiyo – Ba li, ba li*!" (*Sahng Ha*, ask Rev. Barker to come please. Quickly, quickly!). Sahng Ha sprinted from the door.

To the language teacher Stan said, "*Min Puin*," (Mrs. Martin), "*Osipsiyo.*" (please come.) Going down to the cart he picked up the frail form in his arms and took him around to the kitchen steps, and into the kitchen where he laid him on the table.

To Margaret, who appeared immediately, he said, "I've called Archer to explain that I have to take this man's leg or he'll lose his life. Meanwhile, you know where the chloroform, morphine and surgical instruments are in the study. We'll operate here on this table."

Margaret, used to the Newfoundland emergencies, sprang into action, running to the study.

Archer hurried to the doctor's house, puzzled by the bull cart at the porch steps. It was fortunate he happened to be at home. He found the little group in the kitchen.

"Archer, this man will die almost immediately if we don't amputate his leg today. Please explain it to his parents." These poor shivering people and the cart driver had all crowded into the kitchen. "Also, and this is very important, tell them if all goes well, he can be fitted with a prosthesis, an artificial leg, and he can walk again. I understand Koreans are deathly afraid of abnormalities of any kind. Encourage them to give their consent for the surgery."

The parents were openly weeping by now. Archer explained the desperate situation and they nodded their heads. "Yes! We give permission. *Halsoo pahkai opso.* (It can't be helped.)" They, and the other Koreans then returned to the sun porch to wait.

Margaret administered a morphine shot immediately, and the young man had his first moments with less pain in months. He contrived a distorted smile. Archer then talked gently to him, assuring him that this was a good possibility to save his life.

The kitchen stove, a few feet from them, provided hot water for sterilizing the instruments, while Margaret and Stan hurriedly went over the list of needs including tourniquets. Margaret would administer the chloroform by the method of drip inhalation on a mask while monitoring the patient's pulse and color as she had done so many times before.

When all was ready, Stan looked across the table to Margaret at the patient's head. He was glad they were together in this moment.

"Archer, please pray in Korean. Pray for this man's life." The patient noticeably relaxed as he heard the prayer. Then Stan looked at Margaret again. "Start the chloroform," he paused "now."

"For this reason we have come to this place." was the clear thought in Stan's mind as he waited for the chloroform to do its blessed work. He then proceeded with the surgery.

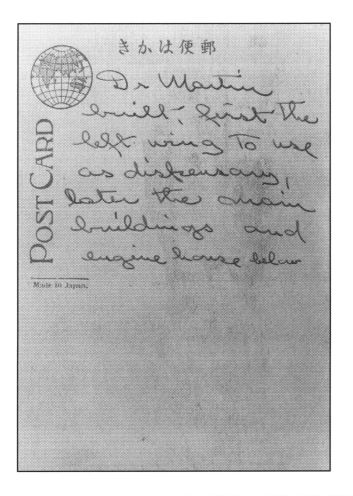

郵便はがき

POST CARD

Dr Martin
built, first the
left wing to use
as dispensary;
later the main
buildings and
engine house below

Made in Japan.

Lungchingtsun China
St. Andrew's Hospital.

룡뎡뎡
졔챵병원

龍井市 濟昌病院

(行發蜃寫崎木市井龍島)

St. Andrew's Hospital, Lungchingtsun, China

75

IX

The Flood-gates Open

S tan went to the sun porch to tell the frantic parents that the surgery was over, and their son was doing well so far. Then Sahng Ha, who was waiting there with them, stepped forward.

"Honorable doctor, since they live so far away I'll be glad to share my warm floor with the patient while he recovers." Sahng Ha had a room at his brother's house. Archer interpreted, and Stan was surprised and enormously pleased. He hadn't had time to think that far. The parents promised to bring the son's food from home, starting the next day.

Archer said as he left, "You'll have supper with us. I'll tell Rebecca. I know she'll want you to come."

After having a look at their son who was still under the anesthetic, on the kitchen table, the parents took their tearful leave.

"*Ko mop sim nida* – [Thank you]" they said over and over again, clinging to Stan's arm and hands. Stan understood those Korean words.

With the help of Sahng Ha, Stan and Margaret reclaimed their kitchen, with mop and scrub brush. The strong smell of disinfectant filled the house.

That night before retiring, Stan lighted their kerosene lantern and went to check on the patient and to administer morphine. Again, at about three in the morning, he dressed and went across the dark fields to the little impromptu hospital, to bring relief from pain.

As Stan got back into bed, Margaret said sleepily, "I'll care for him in the day time."

The next day, Sahng Ha's family watched as this young foreign lady came with the doctor to the patient, gave him his shot, and skillfully changed his dressing. She didn't seem to mind it that he was a male patient. They were amazed. As Margaret knelt on the floor to do the work, she thought, "hospital <u>beds</u> will be top priority, this is back breaking!"

Stan and Margaret hoped that their amputee would be an isolated case, and that life would become normal again, but that was not to be. The Oriental grapevine system went into full force. Word went out to Koreans and Chinese alike that a man had had his leg amputated by the doctor on English Hill, but he was now eating well and was going home soon. "This Western doctor's medicine is good."

The sick ones began to come to Stan's house. They came a few at a time at first. There, the language teacher patiently explained that the doctor couldn't help them yet. This went on until Stan could stand it no longer. The problem was, even if he started his practice, there was no place to do it. What should he do?

Rev. Foote was due back from an itinerating trip and Stan asked Archer, "When Rev. Foote gets back, do you think we could consult with him and send an urgent request to Mission Council for permission to use the empty Single Ladies' House until new missionaries come?"

Archer was very willing, and when Rev. Foote returned and saw many bull-carts and *kooroomas* (man-drawn two-wheeled carts) carrying the sick to Stan's door, he quickly agreed. Some of the pitiful patients were being carried on men's backs. Permission was granted, so now the Martins could run a small, temporary hospital even if it were a missionary residence.

Stan and Margaret hurried to look at the house. The floor plans were similar to their home, but the sun porch entrance was at the south side of the building. They decided the kitchen would be the dispensary, where medicine would be prepared and dispensed, and the dining room would be the operating theater. The other downstairs rooms would be a clinic and waiting room, with overflow into the sun porch. The rooms upstairs would be used as wards.

After preparing some minimum equipment and transferring the precious medicines over to the Ladies' Mission house, they began seeing the first patients. One nurse, one doctor. Period. Of course there was no running water, but *toks*, pails and basins, did the job. The gallant iron stove in the kitchen was there for the sterilizing. A man was hired to carry water and wood, and to keep the fires burning.

God answered prayers and met urgent needs, when a number of young Korean men and women began to be interested in what was going on in that building. Archer, Rev. Foote and the Korean pastor sought out bright and capable people they could recommend, to see if they could be trained to help.

Margaret was the only one for miles around who could handle the anesthesia, and she did so as Stan completed his first surgeries. Meanwhile, a young Korean man recommended by the pastor, stood by and watched. He seemed to be a promising candidate for the job. Another young man, Deacon Im from the church, was so quick to learn and was so helpful, Stan began to train him as his assistant. Soon, he could diagnose and treat many common medical conditions and do simple surgery. There were no formal qualifications for medical practice in Manchuria. Later a young Korean man, Lee Choon Chul, with the English name of Alexander, volunteered to help. He was a godsend, because he could speak Chinese, Japanese, and a little English. His deft fingers soon learned to dress the post-operative cases and do wound care. His knowledge of English sometimes meant the difference between life and death as Stan gave important instructions. Chinese patients came too, and Stan was picking up Mandarin, as well as the Korean language as he worked.

Margaret began to train a few women in rudimentary nursing, to take temperatures and to bathe the patients. The women were mostly young widows, because parents wouldn't allow their daughters to do that kind of work. It was a completely strange world to them. It was not many years before when Korean girls were not to be seen by men outside their family. They lived sheltered lives behind walls. If girls were walking on a country road and men approached, the girls would have to go off the road and turn their backs until the men passed. Christianity opened the doors for women when the first school for girls was started in 1886 by a Methodist missionary Mrs. Mary F. Scranton. This was the Ewha Girls' School in Seoul.

Surgery was limited to daylight hours, but if there was an extreme emergency in the night, Stan would take his Coleman lantern over to the house next door to save a life. The patient load increased. Before long, under these difficult conditions they were treating as many as sixty patients a day. Word of the good work reached Canada and a grant of one thousand dollars was sent to build a small dispensary down by the compound gate.

Margaret's Burpee seeds arrived and were carefully planted in the fields prepared by the Korean farmer. Then came a drought and they began to limit watering the crops, because water from the one well was so precious. Sahng Ha watered only the corn and tomatoes.

On June 15, 1916, 25-year old Stan wrote to his Mission Board Secretary:

Dear Mr. Mackay:

I beg to let you know of a little of our work here. Patients treated in four months, 2,885–1/3 of them Chinese. Operations with anesthesia, thirty-two, including abdominal work. This was done with a pocket set of surgical instruments given by a Dr. Scott in our Orillia church. We made 360 house visits. There was an epidemic of beri beri amongst Christians in a village sixty miles from here. It was controlled. Twenty of the one hundred with the illness died before help arrived. We want an equipped hospital as soon as possible. We can easily handle one hundred patients a day. God has been exceptionally good to us, as the foundation of our small dispensary is now complete.

Medical work continued during the early summer at the residence hospital while the dispensary was being built. Margaret and Stan often walked down at sunset to see the progress of the little building.

By July it became unbearably hot, and they slept outside on the upstairs porch, as Archer had suggested. The heat was hard on the nurse from Maine and the Newfoundland doctor. At work, someone had to keep wiping the perspiration from Stan's face as he operated. The ice they had stored in the winter was a blessing, as it provided cold drinks and preserved some food in the little zinc-lined icebox.

Fortunately, it was time for the Canadian Presbyterian Annual Mission Meeting to be held down at Wonsan in North Korea. They welcomed the chance to break up the hot summer months, and they were relieved that they would travel this time with the experienced Barkers. Also, they were happy that they didn't have the heavy baggage to worry about. When they reached the Tumen River, they crossed by boat, the kind they had seen that winter. It was a pleasant trip.

They had seen Wonsan Harbor before, but now they were introduced to Wonsan Beach, and missionary community life. The missionary families came from many stations and from many mission groups. They met their Seoul friends again. They relished the cool breeze and the joy of being by the sea. There were several little cottages and a Beach House hotel for those who needed it.

Margaret was asked to play for the Mission meetings on a little pump organ. She noticed the exuberant, cheerful nature of her fellow missionaries, and loved the way they sang the hymns and their Canadian National Anthem, while far from home. Stan gave his first report of his and Margaret's medical work, and they were encouraged by the missionaries' approval.

This strip of sand and pine trees, "Myung Sa Sim Nee" (meaning Forty *li* of Shining Sand) not only brought health, strength and spiritual refreshing to the families there, but was very important for all mission work in Korea. The denominations shared and bonded, as they played and prayed together. Sooner than they wished, it was time to go back north to their mission station. When they arrived, everything was in good order. The corn was high, and they were able to enjoy the first vegetables from the garden. Margaret was thrilled to be able to can some tomatoes. Best of all, the little dispensary was finished, and they hurried to transfer their few supplies to the new place.

Immediately, the sick came crowding to them. The building was much smaller than the missionary residence, so before long, a number of patients were lying on benches or on the floor. The small clinic had only four beds. The staff members in training were becoming more capable, and they all did the best they could. But in September, disaster struck.

Stan wrote to Rev. Armstrong on Sept. 2, 1916:

> A short note to say we are all well. Rev. and Mrs. Barker are not back from Annual Meeting so we are alone on the station.
>
> Our dispensary building was finished and plastered, but a typhoon blew all the roofing off, and to-day's rain brought all the plaster down. I've heard of captains being fond of their ships, but no one was more interested in a building so much as I have been in the building of this one.
>
> Every day at 2 p.m. we hold services in this building for the heathen, and I don't know of any service I enjoy more. We have had about 60 operations all together so far and we're seeing 40-50 patients here daily. I study the Korean language every morning. This country is like Labrador except you don't get the pleasure of the sea.
>
> All the crops have been blighted this year because of drought, and now the rain has come, I fear too late, as most things are lying down.
>
> It's interesting to see new patients in church for the first time, and to hear reports of serious cases becoming quite well.
>
> Mrs. Archer Barker needs rest. The rest of us are happy since we are all busy.
>
> Best respects to you and Dr. Mackay.
>
> Sincerely,
> S. H. Martin

The roofing was replaced, and the walls were replastered as soon as possible. Life resumed its busy schedule.

As Stan and Margaret walked past the fields to the dispensary every day, they were aware that another bitter winter was approaching. The wind was getting colder. It would be a hard winter for everyone, because of poor crops. Another concern was a growing fear of Chinese bandits. Rumors of their activities came to the hospital from time to time. These lawless groups would sweep down on unsuspecting villages, steal the grain, burn and pillage, then take off to their hiding places in the hills. One of the patients, a woman from Tutogo, told of hearing the thunder of hooves in the night, as a band of them swept through her village. Providentially, that group was only passing through. Other news was that the Chinese government was cracking down on the opium trade, and dealers who were caught would be summarily executed.

Of particular concern as they heard of danger, was the fact that they were expecting their first child in the spring. Fortunately, Margaret felt very well and continued her training of the nurses. The young Korean man learning to do the anesthesia was doing a good job under careful supervision. Stan and Margaret's language ability was improving each day as they heard Korean spoken constantly. There was little time for Stan to write letters, but by November 1916, Stan's family in Newfoundland had heard from him. His father, the Sunday school superintendent at George St. Methodist Church, hurried to share the news with Rev. Armstrong in Toronto.

Cashiers Office
General P.O.
St. John's NFLD
November 4, 1916

Rev. and Dear Sir:

Your very kind letter saying that the lantern and books for Stanley were safe with you, and going forward by one of the missionaries, has been received, and I thank you for your kind words of appreciation of his work. Since his last report he has performed some very serious operations, such as mastectomy and the removing of a cataract growth from the eye of an official. The operations promise to be quite successful.

It would have interested us to be in the background, to witness the taking of several vessels full of fluid from the abdomen of a prominent Manchurian with dropsy. He had been brought many miles in a sedan chair, held by poles on the shoulders of men, changing by relays every two miles. Having no hospital, it was done on a table of a large inn with Chinamen looking on with staring eyes and open mouths, curiously wondering, "what next?"

He speaks with much praise for all his coworkers. He has always been a good son. We knew all along God would lead him. Revd. Dr. Bond, a life-long friend of mine is sorry the Methodist Church lost him. Still, it's God's way and he best follow his leading.

Yrs. Respectfully,

Arthur W. Martin

Assistant Secretary Armstrong wrote Stan Nov. 14, 1916:

What a great misfortune you had in losing the roof of your dispensary! I can quite understand how it would seem like losing a pet.

I do not understand how you manage to do so much medical work and at the same time study the language. In our Board it was a mystery and we would be glad to have a letter from you explaining how you have succeeded, if you have, in doing more than one man's work, in addition to several hours a day in language study. An Edison who requires only four hours of sleep might manage it, but I presume you are not so abnormal as that. If you have found some strange secret of getting up the language while asleep there are many others who are undergoing the monotony and strain of getting a new tongue who would be delighted to share your secret with you.

I tried to vote the money for a hospital at Yong Jung but we are cutting down building estimates from various fields $98,000 to $28,000. Deficits are stubborn facts. We only hope that when the war is over, people will give more liberally.

With kind regards,
A.E. Armstrong

That first Christmas was a very simple, but joyous one. At dawn on Christmas morning they heard carols sung by the Mission School children outside their home – sweet, happy voices out in the bitter cold. At the dispensary they gave Korean candy to the in-patients and staff, then joined in the Christmas services at the church.

Margaret had saved her spices and raisins for a mince pie for their Christmas dinner with the Barkers, and singing carols around the piano made the day complete.

By December 27, 1916, the dispensary felt the full crush of the work. The now 26-year old doctor wrote again to Rev. Armstrong, this time it was on stationery printed with "Canadian Presbyterian Hospital, Manchuria" across the top, and with Stan's name and mailing address.

I am in receipt of your letter Nov. 10th and have noted the fact that Dr. Menzies is to communicate with me re medical needs of the fields here.

I shall endeavor to do what I can to help along this good plan.

We have treated 7,700 in our nine months of work here. (When I was at Annual Meeting the work had to be closed for a month and a half.) 120 operations under anaesthetic.

We were discussing tonight the advisability of continuing medical work here – as only $250 was given for it in 1916, and only the Korean Dr.'s salary granted for 1917.

Needs

In our small dispensary last month we had a bad typhoid case in our mens' waiting room. Two eye operative cases were in our womens' waiting room, six other cases, mostly Chinese, in a room 8 x 12 feet. (very bad medical practice) and besides this, three patients are in one of our servants' houses on the compound. We need somewhere to put patients after operations.

We have had, and expect to have, some seven obstetrical cases amongst missionaries and their servants. There is no equipment for them in case of emergency. This is not fair to young missionaries coming to the field, or to other women out here who need this help. This dispensary is without any proper accommodations for in-patients, and has never been equipped or granted any running expenses.

My language study was interrupted in the first half of the year, but with my assistant's aid, the proper amount of time is being put on the language and I expect to write my first exams very soon with the others.

We are discouraged this Christmas that we are not getting our hospital, but are hoping to get a temporary place built to house patients after operations – the work here must go on, or stop. The dispensary is proving its great worth to the whole community. It seems a pity to see four fine looking gray brick buildings out here and only two occupied, and when the Barkers go, only ours will be occupied. I hope this war shall soon be over, for while medical work is needed, there's a greater need for more ministers and single ladies, this section of the work here is just longing for helpers, the phrase, "white unto harvest," expresses it well. Now is the time to work this great area of 500,000 people.

I have a Korean assistant now, who takes care of the clinic and gives me time to study the language every morning. One naturally longs for a western doctor as a friend, and someone to talk over serious cases with, but while there are only three missionary doctors in the field, it's a sin to look forward to anyone coming away up here to work.

With regards to Dr. Mackay,

Sincerely yours,
S.H. Martin

Although letters and newspapers came long after the events occurred, the Yong Jung missionaries followed news of the war's progress in Europe with intense interest. The war not only affected the finances for mission work throughout Asia, but some of the men missionaries were leaving the field to volunteer for military service. A directive came from the Presbyterian Mission Board, "Missionaries are not to leave their fields for war duty. They are needed far more on the mission field." Even Stan, who once had been in uniform to go to Egypt with the RAMC, was restless as he read the news. Immediate, urgent needs at hand always drew his mind back to his work in Yong Jung, much to Margaret's relief!

He sent sketch plans for a 50-bed hospital to the Mission Board, hoping and praying for the time when the world situation would improve.

The coldest winter months brought a slight drop in the number of patients, so Stan found time to write of his new and strange experiences. His comprehension of all he saw and heard had grown, because of his greater understanding of the Korean and Chinese languages.

He had come face to face with many diseases; some that most Western doctors only read about. Typhoid, typhus, leprosy, diphtheria, malaria and many types of tuberculosis affecting different parts of the body. To complicate the medical problems, he had to deal with severe damage done to patients because of the results of native medical practices. He wrote a report to Newfoundland to his family and churches.

> From a hill behind our compound can be seen *Pak-to-Shan*, (*Paek To San* or *Paekto* Mountain), nine thousand feet high, an extinct volcano, with now a large lake in the former crater. To the south of us lie the *Chang Paek Shan* range or the "Ever White Mountains" from which wolves sometimes come to the villages, carry off pigs, destroy the dogs, and sometimes bite the men who attack them. Some wolves have rabies. I had my first case of hydrophobia in March. Poor fellow, it was a sad affair.

> It was at the base of one of these mountains that the first Manchu Chief was born, and his descendants have been the rulers of all China up to the abdication of the late Empress Dowager of China.

> Manchuria has a population of about twenty million, is very rich in minerals, grows millions of bushels of wheat, beans, etc. which are shipped constantly to Japan and thence to other countries. Opium is grown in distant places, far from police surveillance, and indigo is so plentiful that all the Chinese of the middle and farming classes, exclusively and always, dress in blue cloth.

Camels are used in Northern Manchuria, and there are many donkeys. The first time I saw our friend Archer Barker he was riding a donkey.

This land is full of peculiar customs. For example, when about to buy a cow, we asked the man if she gave much milk, and on going out to see him milk her, we found the cow on its back with the four legs tied, and three men trying to milk the poor animal. "Surely working against gravity."

The Koreans cook the cows' food and serve it to them warm. When traveling in the country I have often found it hard to sleep, because of the noise of horses fighting only a few feet away from me in the same house.

Shamanism is one of the religions of Korea. This religion causes them to fear the thousands of spirits, which they believe to be all around them. They live in terror of displeasing a spirit and earning its hatred and vengeance. Shrines at which offerings are placed are found everywhere, particularly at road crossings.

But things are changing fast. A new order of things is coming about, and the transition to a brighter, higher life is very rapid.

In medical work we see the strangest things. The Korean custom of treating pain is to drive hot needles into various parts of the anatomy. Scores of cases are brought to me, marked with a large scar which has been caused by burning with an instrument called a "*Doom*" or red hot brand. Ironically this hole is burnt into the hand to relieve pain. Frequently these burns are on the stomach, as big and round as a fifty-cent piece. Imagine how this hurts the sufferer, especially if it's a few months old baby. We have heard the most terrible screaming from victims of this fearful practice.

I have just received a dozen artificial eyes which will be placed in sockets once occupied by normal eyes, ruined beyond repair by those dirty, rusty, awful needles. The old gentlemen practitioners have their long hair done up in a top-knot, and it is the favorite place for "sterilizing?" the acupuncture needle, by thrusting it through his top-knot before sticking it into some poor creature's joints.

On one of our itinerating trips, Rev. Mr. Barker and I while riding through completely deserted country, were caught in one of those eastern cyclonic hailstorms. We put on speed to get shelter for the horses and reached a dirty old inn. News soon spread that an English doctor had come, and the cases gathered in. After the storm cleared, some patients were brought from quite a distance. We were discouraged because of the delay in our trip – only half our distance was covered, but when a poor girl was brought in with a large abscess, shocking to see, we opened it, giving her relief. Then I knew why the Lord had sent us there.

We have to treat many cases of eye trouble. Cataracts and eye infections are common. A deaf man aged 26, blind from birth in the left eye, went to a Korean medicine man for some small trouble with his right eye. This quack put some very strong corrosive on the lids so that they swelled up and were burnt, so the good eye completely closed and he was totally blind. We did an operation and made him new eyelids so that he can see now.

Last week a man who had been blind for eight years, came in for treatment. Having gone into the history of the case I found that his eyes had been treated for a long time with bile obtained from a bear's liver.

We went to see a case of a woman about forty who had inflammation over the stomach due to repeated punctures of the abominable needle. We found her in bad shape, and I told the husband who was a great drinker of Chinese wine to keep that needle doctor away! He replied he didn't care if the woman died, as she was his middle wife and was already too old. However we saw that she would be properly looked after, by visits from our hospital-trained Christian nurses. The other day she came to the dispensary, and I didn't know her she looked so well.

Last September when at Kookjaga, while in church and listening to a scholarly Chinese minister explaining the details of one of the gospel incidents, the solemnity was marred by much noise from a passing Chinese funeral procession with its weird music, something like bag pipes, and the furious beatings of gongs and copper tom-toms. This particular funeral was for an ancestor who had died some years before, and they were carrying stretchers to his grave. These stretchers were decorated with flowers, a live sheep, and a dead pig propped up on his legs with an orange in his mouth. These animals were for the departed man's spirit to eat. The church service was resumed, and the hearty manner with which seven hundred people sang, "Oh happy day that fixed my choice on thee my Savior and my God," was thrilling to hear. They swayed as they sang. Thus you will see it was interesting to have Christianity and heathenism pass each other "as ships in the night" and to be there to see it.

When riding past a Chinese grave-yard a doctor can often see the coffins of his former patients, as they are made of four inch hard plank, and kept above ground for up to a year after the person dies.

One of these people while asleep in a field, a certain species of gadfly deposited its eggs in one of his nostrils. The larvae produced, burrowed upwards into his brain and just after we called in to see him he died of meningitis. This man's coffin is behind our compound in sight of everybody. Hard on doctors!

Another peculiar case was a Chinese man with a bad headache. When I was probing through his nose yesterday, a large (butterfly like) insect flew out of his nose and his pain stopped immediately. The eggs had been put there by another fly during warm weather, and probably while the man slept in the fields.

On my trips with our ministers we often meet with some bad cases, for which I am scarcely prepared. For instance a small boy, three years of age, had diphtheria and when I got there, he was almost dead. Without waiting for sterilizing instruments, by feeling with my left fingers, and with the aid of a sharp pen knife I opened the wind pipe and put in a tracheotomy tube. They were very poor people but so grateful for his recovery. When I saw him later in a little new coat, I was glad to have saved his life.

Riding home on horseback one day, we found a woman who seemed to be weeping bitterly by a grave. We dismounted and tried to cheer her up, giving her some apples. She forgot her sorrow in three minutes. Asking what was troubling her, she said her husband was dead. We were sorry, and inquired when he had died. She answered <u>fifteen years ago</u>. We smiled and rode on. The Koreans pay people to come and wail for them when a death occurs, and before a funeral.

Last April 2nd all of the Koreans of this place who are not Christians, carried food to the graves of their relatives. The graves are mounds of earth five-feet high with a trench around them. There they wail for about twenty minutes at a time, saying "*Ai go! Ai go!*" and then they offer food to their ancestors. On the way home they have a jolly time, and seem more like a party returning from an outing. Some funerals are held at night, and coolies act as carriers of the dead. As they often are needy poor fellows, they are paid well.

Returning recently from a journey I found a man on the road who had been run over by a heavy cart. He was too far from my hospital to have the needed surgery. I tried to get him into ten different farmhouses, but the people there were afraid he would die and his spirit would haunt them ever afterwards. So I was forced at last to get help and carry him off the road to a bypath. I stayed with him alone until he died, sixty miles from my house. I could only give him morphine to ease his passing. Later we heard that if that poor fellow had not given his life in stopping a runaway horse, two Canadians and their little boy would have been thrown into a ravine sixty feet deep. They would certainly have been killed.

A boy went home yesterday across the Russian border. He came in here with seven inches of one of his leg bones protruding. He had walked one hundred miles in that condition, limping with a stick. He is now returning well.

Many of our patients have to lie around on benches, or on the floor as we have only four beds in the dispensary. We are longing for the time we'll have our hospital.

Our staff now consists of the lady superintendent Mrs. Martin; three nurses she has trained, a good dresser, a secretary for patients records and finance, an anesthetist, and a coolie for attending to fires and bringing water etc. I am hoping shortly to have an assistant doctor, a graduate from the Severance Medical School in Seoul.

We had a smallpox epidemic here last year, but it is nearly all stamped out now. I vaccinated 60 people one morning, five hundred in one week. They are learning to appreciate its benefits. The people did not take enough precaution to prevent smallpox from spreading in all directions during the last epidemic, and the same ignorance and carelessness is displayed in the treatment of other complaints such as cholera infantum, etc., etc.

We shall use our present dispensary as an isolation ward after we get our hospital. Last August in my report for the preceding twelve months the following figures will be found: -- Outpatients: Medical cases, 6,882; surgical cases, 3,459; total 10,341. In patients: Operations under anesthetic, 231; discharged well, 145; improved 50; unrelieved, 30; died 6. Total number of treatments 12,428. Seventy percent of cases were Korean, twenty five percent Chinese and the rest were English, Russian and Japanese.

My Alma Mater, Queen's Medical School has given a large sum for missionary work, one half was sent to me, and one half to a friend who is now in India fighting against the plague which is now raging there.

****

As the time grew near for Margaret to give birth to their first child, she no longer worked at the hospital, but turned the nursing services over to three of the best of her students and two capable women assistants. These women were impressed by the results of the work, the many people who had regained their health. They were also encouraged by the approval of the Christian community.

Spring came again, and Margaret found wild flowers on their hill. Lilies of the valley, as fine as any found in the Boston florist shops, little wild iris and pasque flowers, that the Koreans call "grandmother flowers" because of their shaggy white heads when they go to seed. Later there were wild day lilies, rugosa roses, bluebells and tiger lilies. New to her, were flowering cherry bushes that produced red, tart fruit, wonderful for pies and jam. The Koreans called them *"aengdoo"* bushes. She had ordered seeds again, and hoped for a good crop as she watched the Korean farmer prepare her vegetable garden. He dug flowerbeds around the house, for the asters, nasturtiums and mignonette seeds to come.

Tabitha helped Margaret find some white silk in the market, and she lined a Japanese *"corey"* basket for a little crib. She was glad she had brought some baby clothes, as Aunt Addie had suggested. Luckily, some precious parcels of baby gifts also came from home, sent by the Barnes and Rogers family to welcome the little one to come.

Ruth Ann was born May 3, 1917, and soon became the darling of the community. The Koreans crowded around her, on her first day at church. It was their first time to see a little Western child. Later, "Her smiles did an untold amount of good mission work," her mother, Margaret said.

Another great joy to them that spring was the news of an $8,000 gift promised for building the hospital. Stan was especially moved to hear that a Presbyterian farmer in Canada had sold his farm and given $4,000 of the gift, practically all he had. The other $4,000 was from Montreal. Another gift, small but tremendous in value, was $100 from a Canadian black man in Orillia who had heard of the project.

The Barkers were to leave for furlough in August, so every minute of Archer's and Stan's spare time in the evening was spent poring over the hospital plans. The Chinese contractor who had built the Mission houses was hired again, and with Stan's and Archer's meager Chinese vocabulary and Alexander's interpreting, the plans were made clear. When the first money came in, they began to order building supplies, and had the groundbreaking ceremony. This was a solemn but joyful occasion for the church members, and they eagerly crowded to the site. They felt that this was their hospital, for many new members had come to God through the medical work. The hospital was to be built to the east of the dispensary a beautiful location on the brow of the hill. When word reached Stan's church in Newfoundland, the people there were amazed that the hospital could be built for $8,000. They said such a building would cost $16,000 in St. John's. Stan explained that the low cost of labor (fifty cents a day) and the presence of a good grade of clay nearby, for brick-making, and a fine quality of granite and other stone on the hill a short distance away, brought the cost of construction within the lower figure.

In August 1917, Stan and Margaret stood and watched as the Barkers put the last of their baggage into a horse-cart, and climbed in, waving goodbye as they started their long journey to Canada for their furlough. Stan was holding little Ruthie. A sense of loneliness swept over them as they turned to pick up their tasks again. They would miss those dear friends. Their new Korean friends would mean more than ever to them. To be sure there was Rev. Foote in House No. 2 but he was gone most of the time. For Margaret, it was the season of canning precious fruits and vegetables for the winter. Stan returned to the dispensary for morning clinic.

Besides the clinic hours, the surgery, and language study there were the many letters Stan had to write to the Board and supporting churches. Sometimes the missionaries used the Japanese postal system with letters coming through Korea, other times they were advised to use the Chinese postal system. Sometimes the letters were lost. One letter brought the good news of $12,000 from their Orillia, Canada church, a gift for the hospital heating, plumbing and water system. Another brought approval for the building of a Boys' Academy by the Martin's home. Dr. William Foote had urged this important project. The little settlement would be growing. Some letters from the Board told of the cutback of funds, because of the war. It would take reams of paper to report Stan's orders for equipment or news of delays, disappointments or exciting news of successes.

At last they were encouraged to hear that two ministers and their families, the Scotts and Frasers, and one nurse, Maud Mackinnon were appointed to Yong Jung. They arrived in the fall and were warmly welcomed. Stan was especially happy to have Maud Mackinnon join the hospital staff.

The weeks flew by as everyone settled in, and soon it was Christmas again. Margaret wrote home to her father about their second Christmas in Yong Jung. She had invited their Russian friends the Nadarovs for Christmas Eve. Part of the letter is missing. It started from:

… and peas, tomato bisque to start and finished with tea and candy. From then until six we had music and a social time. Mrs. Nadarov played our piano beautifully. Then at 6:30 we went to the Christmas concert at the church. It was great, a fine cold moonlight night, and a big crowd about 800, many heathen among the number.

I could not help wishing that our people at home could have seen and heard the program as the Christmas story was told and sung by the little girls and boys of the Sunday School. To the many heathen in the crowd it was all new and strange. And how they did sing! It was an inspiring chorus. "Hark the herald angels sing, Glory to the Newborn King!" One of the first and most impressive things which strikes the foreigner on coming to a new land is hearing the old familiar hymns sung in an unknown tongue. And last night it again impressed me greatly to hear the Christmas joy in the voices of the Korean children, though as yet I understand the language so imperfectly.

A group of little girls sang a Christmas lullaby to the baby Jesus, kneeling around an imaginary cradle, and as they sang *"Chamnita, chamnita,"* ("He sleeps, He sleeps"). I could see my own wee baby sleeping so peacefully at home in her basket.

Some of the older boys carried in the Christmas tree, and after a little march about, each one placed something on the tree. One, a little white angel, which he explained was the Christmas messenger, another some stars, telling of the star in the East, another, gifts for the poor, in this way showing to the people the meaning of the Christmas tree. It was rather pathetic in a way, for they had such poor little things to trim it. Yet they thought it very fine. No doubt there was quite as much of the true spirit of Christmas there, as at many more richly laden trees at home.

After the concert, there were gifts and candy for the Sunday School children, all arranged by the Koreans themselves. Our new foreign pastor Dr. William

Scott and his wife drilled the children for the concert and it certainly was a great success.

Time to go to bed with my little Ruthie who sends a great big kiss to dear Grandpa.

Lovingly,
Margaret

The next year with the first signs of spring the hospital builders could work out of doors again and the first supplies began to arrive at the site. Men were seen toiling up the little hill, pulling two wheeled carts through the compound gate, bringing large stones and stacks of gray bricks. Also, great logs were brought to be prepared into suitable beams and boards. They were so big, that one end of the log was placed on a horse-cart, and the other end just dragged on the ground as they came up the hill. The work was done on the premises with a system the Martins had not seen before. The log was propped on a high wooden frame, with two men working a two-handled saw. The man on top would pull the saw up and the man below would pull it down, sawing back and forth until the board was formed. It was slow, tedious, and dangerous work.

Stan wrote to Rev. Armstrong, March 27, 1918:

"Your letter to us advising the Mission station of $3,000 towards the Boys' Academy was received with much joy. I'm sure Mr. Barker was especially pleased. We hope to start building the hospital next month, and to be in our new plant by November 15th. In the meantime I am trying to collect equipment both for the present dispensary, and for the new building, so that we can use it when the building is finished. On account of the great cost of freight, I think it would be wise to buy most of our beds, fittings etc. in Japan. There were several reliable houses there, and I have been dealing with the Medical Supply Co. of Tokyo, and have obtained both American and Japanese made goods from them.

Would you please then, advise the treasurer to advance to Mr. Fraser, money given for my equipment so that I can have it on hand, so such things as sinks, W. C.'s [Water Closets] etc. can be fitted into place as the building is finished. I am charging higher this year for operations. Got 22 yuan in one day, for operations, and we're also trying to save on the running expenses to help buy beds, etc.

Yesterday, a completely blind boy got sight, a fifty year old Chinese man who had a compound fracture of his leg was put in plaster splints, and the wife of one of our most promising preachers was successfully operated for two abdominal tumors."

Sincerely yours,
Martin

When the ground began to thaw in April, the lines for the foundation of the hospital were indicated, and the digging began. After hours, some of his staff members often changed their clothes into old cast-off Chinese soldier uniforms and helped to dig. Partly it was for sheer joy, but also they were learning that it was not degrading but noble, to work at manual labor.

All summer the sound of building construction was heard outside, as Stan and his staff worked in the dispensary. The hospital was taking shape, and when the walls were up, the builders raced to get the roof on before the rainy season set in.

Stan had eagerly described and sketched the plan of it in his letters. "Our new hospital will be the pavilion style, and will be attached to the existing dispensary. It will have fifty beds, operating room, dressing rooms, nurses' rooms and all necessaries."

In the fall, Margaret got out the little silk-lined baby basket and prepared for their second child due early in January.

Then came the day in November when Stan and his staff moved into the new hospital. There was a great celebration as the first sections of the building were dedicated to the service of God. Stan chose the name St. Andrew's for the hospital, to honor a church in his homeland, and also because the disciple Andrew "brought others to Jesus."

On November 23, 1918 Stan wrote to Dr. Mackay who had commissioned him just three years before.

Your letter October 10th regarding the special gift from Orillia has been noted and I have already written to the six who donated the $132. Thank you. Our hospital is now going along very well, all the mens' ward being complete, and the new operating room is daily called into use. Our increasing number of patients has made it necessary to take on more assistants. We are still doing without a native doctor to save the valuable 60 Yuan a month and house rent, which he would take. We are all very busy and therefore happy. Owing to the great cost of fuel we are using a small ward this year, heated with a good Russian stove which needs firing only once in several hours.

The Spanish influenza has swept its path through our valleys, but strange to say there has hardly been a death amongst our Christians, while very many unbelievers have passed beyond, and many of them without getting a word of Christian witness to them before they went.

They say a hospital with a death roll is a working hospital. We have had a hard fight with "The Reaper whose name is death." Three this week have been saved just at the moment of being cut down. Three Chinese brothers, shot by policemen for opium dealing, have been in our hospital, one died, shot through the lung. The second one died after surgery to sew up the gun shot in his abdomen. The third one, also shot through his lung is still alive, and will be all right. He certainly has a good mind towards Christianity so far. His father died from a broken heart after hearing that two of his sons had died from the shooting.

Another man, 70 years old, blind over a year, after cataract surgery can see to read with strong glasses and to work around the house. His first words after surgery were "That young man is my son!" My assistant Deacon Lim, right there and then, while the patient was full of joy at again seeing his son, directed his eyes to the Son of God to whom he has been blind until recently.

Space and time prohibit mentioning more about these many interesting cases.

Sincerely,
S. H. Martin

Stan thanked God daily for his Christian staff working beside him. Their prayers and skill added greatly to the healing of the patients.

The next month, on December 5, 1918 as the cold winter winds swept over the compound, Stan wrote to a Dr. Stewart in Halifax, Nova Scotia, Canada.

My Dear Doctor,

Please convey to your friends, and the different good people who have donated sums towards our hospital equipment, our heartfelt and sincere thanks for the gifts.

Enclosed you will see a snapshot of our 50 bed hospital. We expect to open all our big wards in the spring and will then be seeing about 100 patients a day. Now that the winter has set in here, we have about 40-50 per day. My main aim out here is to get Christians through up-to-date surgery. I'm trying especially to get up an ideal technique for tuberculosis bone lesions. I have some cases here that would improve on Albee's spine splint etc. We have quite a little spontaneous gangrene out here, the cause of which is at present unknown. I am keeping specimens from many of our amputations to study when I can raise enough money to buy a decent microtome [An instrument for cutting organic tissues for examination under the microscope].

The gangrene may be due to certain Korean drugs which produce endarteritis. They have been known to eat copper dust. I opened an abscess the other day and lots of free mercury ran out.

We are aiming to do decent surgery. That is one thing the Japanese here cannot do.

Today I amputated for gangrene in a boy who was seven years old. His father said he would rather the son died than lose his hand. "What's the use of a boy without a left hand, he had better die." Along with medical help we try to teach the value of human life and concern and love for the handicapped.

We also did a double cataract for a man who can read his Bible again with 10+D glasses.

Ever so many thanks to you,
In the Work,
S. H. Martin

To add to the excitement of that momentous year, the welcome news of the signing of the Armistice ending World War I reached the little group in Yong Jung. Margaret wrote again to her family in Houlton, Maine.

Yong Jung, Manchuria
December 8,1918
Dear Aunt Addie,

We are so very sorry to hear of Dr. Baker's death. [Margaret had worked with her in Newfoundland.] I wrote at once to the family to express my sorrow as well as I could.

We have been well this winter, I am thankful to say, except for a short run of the "influenza" in October. Miss Mackinnon is a great help in the hospital, tho' she is far from well. We hope that our bracing winter will put her on her feet again after the malaria, which troubled her so much in the south.

All the mission babies are well. Mrs. Scott came to our Sunday service at our house with her four months old Lornie. Our Ruthie (19 months) kissed him and patted him and said "Baby" a great number of times during the service.

She is so funny, when she wakens in the night, she sits right up and says "*So chut*," Korean for milk, and as soon as she has a drink she says, "Bye Bye" and drops down on the pillow fast asleep. When she is perfectly well she is a good little sleeper, so my rest is not broken into very much.

We are having some of our first zero weather with high wind today. The Russian stove in the dining room works very well. We have closed off the dining room with big double doors, and it makes a cozy warm living room. I have my sewing machine there, which Stan gave me for my birthday, and some growing plants, big chairs and a couch.

You asked about our season. It is much like New England with the first zero weather coming in December, rather colder than Boston I should say, and usually winters are dry with little snow fall, but what does come, stays on the mountain tops a long time it's so cold. We have high winds, frozen rivers and dust from the Gobi desert, although not so much dust as the Honan area west of us.

We have been reading last week the account of the German fleet on November 23rd. What a spectacle of triumph and humiliation. Not a salute fired, the surrender received by the British and American fleet in absolute silence, with decks cleared for action.

Mr. and Mrs. Nadarov our White Russian friends are as usual. They have been very sad at the shocking state of their home country. They haven't heard from relatives in Petrograd since July 17, with cholera and the Bolshevik revolution raging around. But since the Armistice was declared, they seem more cheerful.

When we heard of the armistice had a bonfire and celebration in front of our houses the other night, flags of all nations flying all day, and lanterns and candles illuminating the hospital and our houses at night. All of us foreigners gathered around, and sang national anthems around the bonfire.

Rev. Scott who has been several weeks itinerating in the country wrote to ask of the "war news." He has not yet heard the good "peace news." He will be in by Christmas.

This is a long letter and I must go to bed. Sending a lock of Ruthie's hair from her first haircut. She looks like a little boy now.

Lots of love from,
Margaret

Soon there were preparations for Christmas. Margaret and Tabitha wrapped large packages of candy for the hospital patients, – barley candy sticks; *yut*, rolled in sesame seeds, and clear round hard candies. Margaret didn't take part in the church program as she was expecting their second child early the next month.

When Christmas and the New Year 1919 came to the little Mission station, the beautiful hospital, St. Andrew's, could be seen from a great distance, a beacon of hope and healing to many. God's plan would reveal that it was ready just in time for crucial events to come. On the fourth day of the new year their second daughter Margaret Evangeline was born.

St. Andrew's Hospital staff with Dr. Martin and nurse Lenora Armstrong

X

"Go! Die for your country!"

It was the year 1905 in a small village near the city of Seoul, Korea. A little Korean boy peeked around the corner of his family's front gate. Their servant girl, Oksooni, was doing laundry in the courtyard, slapping wet clothes with a broad wooden paddle. Was his mother there? He slipped forward timidly so he could see better. Yes, there she was sitting quietly at the doorway of the women's quarters with her cream colored silk skirt billowing around her. It was a beautiful scene with the curved tile roofs of the wealthy home, a ginkgo tree shining golden in the sun, but Kap Sungi's heart was pounding with fear.

He waited for his mother's signal. For days now he had been creeping back home for a few minutes with her. His father had banished him from home because he had been attending Sunday school at the Christian church in the village. If his father were there she would wave him away. If the father had gone to market she would beckon the little fellow to come to her.

Today she caught sight of him, and her hand made the Korean gesture to come to her – palm down, fingers beckoning. Running to her he put his head on her shoulder while she held him and rocked him back and forth.

"How are you? Is Cousin Soon Hi feeding you well?"

"Yes."

"Is Cousin Yongsuni going to school now?"

"Yes, but I can't because no one will register me." The tears were streaming down his face. She held him and rocked him some more.

"*Omah* [mother], I think I'll have to go away. I'm going to walk to Seoul. I can't stay near here. What if father catches me?"

The mother hesitated, overwhelmed by the thought. A feeling of helplessness came over her. She knew her husband's stern, autocratic, cruel ways. She had heard of other fathers who had killed their children for becoming Christians. She was quiet for a moment. She too, had been thinking of the danger.

"Yes. It's the only choice." Reaching under her skirts, she pulled out her embroidered silk money pouch.

"Here, take this." She gave him a ten-yen bill. It was the most money he had ever seen in his life. Sniffling he put it in his little money pouch at his belt.

"Yes, go – but when you find a place – a family or an orphanage where you can stay – come tell me where you'll be." Her hands dropped down.

"*Halsoo paki opso*," [It can't be helped] she said.

Kap Sungi hugged her and ran to the gate. After looking to the left and right to see if the coast was clear, he turned and waved and was gone.

Late that afternoon, tired and thirsty, Kap Sungi approached the massive West Gate of Seoul. He was confused by the crowds of people everywhere. He entered the gate and walked slowly up a long hill, bewildered by everything he was seeing. He saw a foreign man and woman walking just ahead of him. Curious, he hurried his steps so he was right behind them. He heard them laughing and talking to each other. Strange, he thought, maybe they're a man and wife, but I never saw a man and wife talking and laughing and enjoying each other like that. Then, as young as he was, he said to himself, "*when I get married I want to have a happy time like that with my wife.*" They were approaching a gate with a large foreign-style house beyond. Suddenly, realizing they were being followed, the couple turned to the little boy. "What do you want?," the man asked in Korean. Kap Sungi was startled, but he said. "I was just curious about you."

"Oh!" The man looked down at the tired little boy – something strangely attracted him.

"Where were you going?"

"Nowhere, I've just run away from home."

"What?"

"Let's at least give him something to drink," Mrs. Miller said as they led him through their gate.

"It's so hot today."

In a few minutes he was sitting on a western chair, dangling his legs, drinking cold tea and having some cake. It was the first time he had ever sat on a chair.

The couple learned that his name was Yi Kap Song and they listened to his story. When they realized that the little fellow had been banished from home, and was being persecuted for being a Christian, they were touched and their hearts opened to him. After conferring for a while they decided to take him into their home, to see what should be done. He had no other place to go. Thus began the care and education of one who was to become the Honorable Dr. Yi Kap Song one of Korea's greatest patriots.

The couple who took him in that day were Mr. and Mrs. Hugh Miller missionaries of the British and Foreign Bible Society. They sent him to school and took him to church where he happily attended Sunday school again. He helped with the chores, weeding the strawberry bed, washing dishes, or helping around the house.

One day when he was washing the dishes, he broke the gravy boat, and he came trembling to Mrs. Miller with the broken pieces in his hands. To his surprise she burst into tears.

Most kids would have just hidden the pieces, she thought. She hugged him and said, "That's all right." She knew this was a very special young man sent to them from God.

They bought him an English typewriter and he eagerly learned to type. Of course he was learning English while he lived there. The years went by.

They continued supporting him through high school and then medical school at Severance Union Medical College in Seoul. He was brilliant in his studies and became a fine doctor.

All during his schooling he was aware of the humiliation of his people under Japanese rule. The dream of independence for his country burned in his heart.

It was at the end of World War I and the Armistice had been signed November 11, 1918. Now the Peace Conference was being held in Paris and everywhere there was talk of peace and liberty.

The Koreans were thrilled to hear the American President Woodrow Wilson say in his famous speech, "Every nation should have the right to self-determination." The Koreans responded with, "That's us! He's talking about us!"

Encouraged by this, thirty-three ardent patriots secretly organized an Independence Movement. Dr. Yi Kap Song was a member of this group. They made plans to hold peaceful demonstrations all over Korea to call the world's attention to their suffering, and to proclaim their independence from Japan. The plan was to gather in large groups only to wave their Korean flags and shout "Mansei!" meaning "Korea live 10,000 years!"

On March 1, 1919, at twelve noon, the thirty-three patriots were to gather in Pagoda Park in the heart of Seoul, and read a Korean Declaration of Independence. At that time all church bells were to ring, and the people were to swarm into the streets and shout, as planned.

Fifteen members of the group were Christians, and their boldness encouraged the others. Another fifteen were leaders of the Chundo Kyo (a native religion associated with the Tonghaks) and three were Buddhists. "Let there be no violence" read their manifesto. Although the organization centered in the capital, it had branches in every province, city, town, and village. Young people traveled secretly, carrying instructions, information and pamphlets to prepare for March first. Some of them were high school girls, and they were terrified of "body searches" by Japanese policemen, if they were apprehended. Any stranger who approached a village was apt to be checked.

In the meantime Dr. Yi Kap Song had a thriving medical practice on the first floor of a building on the Severance Hospital compound. All day patients were seen coming and going. The Japanese authorities were unaware that one of the headquarters for the Independence Movement was in the basement of the building. Dr. Yi was the leader there.

He was in touch with what was known as the Korean Provisional Government in Shanghai, the Korean government in exile led by the patriots Kim Koo and Syng Man Rhee. By disguising telegram messages pertaining to the needs of the Independence Movement, as if they were medical needs for the hospital, telegrams were sent back and forth between Seoul and Shanghai. The Japanese didn't know what was going on.

For example they wired "We need medicine. Please send medicine," which meant, "We need money. Please send money." The answer would come back. "The medicine isn't ready yet." Or "It will be there in two weeks." etc.

At last the crucial time approached. It was the night before March 1, 1919. Dr. Yi was in the basement of his clinic with about twenty of his young people responsible for his area. They were all to return there by midnight. All but one of the couriers, a high school girl, were back safely. The group sat on the floor watching and waiting. Dr. Yi stood by the door. All of a sudden, just before the clock struck twelve, the door opened and the missing girl flew in and fell full length on the floor shouting, "Mission accomplished!" Then she fainted. Dr. Yi rushed to feel her pulse. She was all right. While she was recovering, he turned and looked down at the faces of the young boys and girls. His heart was wrenched with anxiety for what the next day might bring.

"I might die," he said.

"All of you might die." He paused.

All of a sudden a voice rang out.

"What if we die a hundred times? So what!!!"

It was one of the high school girls. Her voice was so strong and confident that the atmosphere changed instantly and they all regained courage.

Many years later Dr. Yi, in telling of that night said, "Korean men are taught that women and girls should be kept down; let them learn to sew, keep house, take care of the children, but don't give them prominent positions. But I want to say that the women and girls who took part in the Independence Movement were some of the strongest and most courageous women in the world! I have nothing but admiration for our girls and women and what they can do!"

"That night the little group scattered to go home, being careful to leave at intervals one by one, so the night watchmen wouldn't be suspicious. They would be ready the next day with their little flags at their designated places, to listen for the church bells at noon. Dr. Yi returned to his home to a sleepless night. He would join the other patriots for the reading of the Declaration of Independence the next day." [This story was told by Yi Kap Song to the writer.]

In the meantime, as at schools all across the country, the girls at the Methodist Ewha High School in Seoul were preparing for the big day. They knew the plans for the demonstrations because some of their classmates were couriers. Also they would get news from the *Yut Changsa*, the barley-candy man. When he clanked his great candy-cutting scissors near the school gate, one or more of the girls would run to the gate, open it a crack and get further information.

March 1, 1919, dawned, a chilly but sunny day. The students at Ewha were seated in the various classrooms pretending to listen to their teachers. Each girl had laboriously drawn her beloved Korean flag on a small oblong piece of paper. She had pasted it onto a little bamboo stick, and had rolled it up and tucked it into her voluminous *choguri* [jacket] sleeve.

Suh Myung Hak, who later became principal of the Methodist Ewha High School, was one of the girls in class that day. She told this story:

> On March 1, 1919, we were sitting there in school trying to pay attention as the
> hours dragged by. As it grew time for action, all eyes were on the big clock on
> the classroom wall. The teachers watched us. We were restless. The big hand was
> getting closer to twelve. At twelve, we jumped out of our seats and ran to the front
> gate. Miss Lulu Frey, our principal, ran after us.
>
> By that time all of Seoul had erupted into a roar of sound, people were shouting
> and now we heard the sound of gunfire. Through it all we heard the nearby Chung

Dong Methodist Church bells ringing. Miss Frey stood facing us with her back to the closed gate.

"Don't go out there!" she shouted. "You'll be killed! Your lives are precious! You are the future of Korea!"

She was crying. For a moment we hesitated, held back by the strong respect we had for her.

But I had another idea.

"Come on – follow me to the back wall!" I turned and ran away. Like a flock of startled birds, all the girls rushed after me. We ran to the back of the schoolyard. Part of the school wall joined the ancient broken city wall, but I knew the place where we could get through. I was a big husky girl from the country and I said to them as I bent over, "Here! Step up on my back, then you can jump over the wall!" One by one I felt the heavy pressure of their rubber shoes, but felt no pain, as girl after girl stepped up and jumped.

As they landed about six feet below, with their skirts billowing, Soon Hi, one of the classmate leaders had a big piece of red cloth in her hands. She was tearing off strips of the cloth, and giving a strip to each girl as she landed. She shouted.

"Here! Red! – the color of blood! Go die for your country!"

As the girls clustered below me, I was able to jump and join them. We didn't know which way to run, but the sounds of the loudest shouting attracted us to the street near West Gate. We were supposed to hide the red cloth strips in our sleeves but we ran with them fluttering over our shoulders. Then we saw an unforgettable scene. Hundreds of people were milling about. They were shouting "*Mansei!*" and waving their little flags, then we heard screams of agony and the sound of gunfire. Our Korean men were trying to join hands and make circles around the women and girls to protect them from the Japanese advancing with their slashing swords. That day, no matter who it was who came running to them housewife or schoolgirl, the men would bravely grab them and thrust them behind them. We were all pulled into the circles. <u>The men who had no weapons bore the brunt of the attacks.</u>

This scene was being repeated all over Korea. The Japanese military, police and civilians were attacking the innocent demonstrators, thousands dying with their little Korean flags clutched in their hands. Tens of thousands were imprisoned and many were executed. I lived through that day, but so many didn't.

The furious response of the Japanese to what were to be peaceful demonstrations lay like a black cloud over the land. Later there were photographs of blindfolded Koreans standing before big wooden posts, waiting to be executed. Their crime? Loving their country. They were the lucky ones. Thousands of others were being tortured in prison. Dr. Yi Kap Song and the other famous thirty-two patriots were among those in prison. His skillful doctor's hands were scarred when he was hung by his thumbs and tortured. But he lived to tell the story. [Told to the writer by Dr. Yi.]

In the midst of the horror, some of the Korean Independence leaders in Seoul realized that the thousands of Koreans in Manchuria were unaware of what had happened. There was no radio and there were very few newspapers. Two young Christian ministers and an Ewha High School girl volunteered to walk to Manchuria to tell the news. The girl put her hair up, and wrapped her head in the North Korean *soogun* so people would think she was married. They started out, walking night and day going north. In the night they sometimes saw the glow of animal eyes watching them.

"Do you know what those are?" one of the men asked the girl.

"Yes! T-t-t-tigers!" she said.

She was right. But they walked on, unharmed, crossed the Tumen River by boat and came to Yong Jung, Manchuria, with its large Korean population. There they shared the news. When the Yong Jung people heard what happened, they decided to hold a demonstration too, in the area near St. Andrews Hospital. It would take place March 13, 1919, at twelve noon when the church bells rang. Volunteer young people hurried to nearby towns to tell of the plans. They would follow the same program as in Korea – the people simply gathering and shouting *Mansei* with their flags. It was to be peaceful.

They chose a market day, so that the Japanese garrison and Chinese soldiers wouldn't be suspicious of crowds coming in to town. The churches and schools were ready, and other individuals gladly prepared too.

That day, people came down the mountain paths like swarms of ants, as if they were on their way to market. Some carried various goods on their heads or shoulders. All seemed quiet and peaceful.

That same day March 13, at the Canadian Mission "Myung Shin" Girl's School, the students sat at their desks with their small Korean flags hidden in their sleeves, and their eyes on the clock. Then a scene took place exactly as it did at the Ewha High School in Seoul. When the clock began to strike, the girls jumped out of their seats and raced to the gate. The Canadian missionary teacher ran to stop them, but the girls climbed over the school wall and escaped. They ran to join the great crowd that was near their school.

One of the student survivors told the story.

> There were mostly school children near us, but men, women and children were everywhere, shouting and waving their flags. Then we saw a group of Chinese soldiers approaching, and we saw a glint of guns. Immediately shots rang out and I fell to my knees. *"Aigo-mana! Chooguta!"* (Oh mother, I'm dead!) I cried out. I was covered with blood. I struggled to my feet, felt myself all over and realized I

wasn't hurt at all. I was drenched with the blood of my classmate, Poksuni, who was killed instantly. She had fallen on top of me.

A few days before this, the missionaries on English Hill had heard of the tragedy in Korea and the planned events for Yong Jung. They wondered what would happen.

At noon on March 13, Margaret was in their mission home bedroom, rocking two-month-old baby Margaret Evangeline, while Ruthie played at her feet. Stan was at the hospital with his staff members who were fully alert for trouble. Margaret sat and rocked and prayed. Then she heard the church bells and the distant sound of shouting. She stood with the baby in her arms and looked out of the window, but there was nothing unusual to see. Then she heard gunfire. Where is Stan? What's going on? Her nurse's instinct to go and help gripped her – but no, the children come first, she thought. She paced the floor and waited. She heard a commotion down in the kitchen, and then Sahng Ha raced up the stairs to the bedroom.

"*Pween! Pween!* The soldiers are shooting at the crowds and they're bringing the wounded into the hospital basement. The doctor and the staff are separating them out for treatment. Doctor told me to tell you."

"Go back and tell Doctor we're all right here, but to let me know when it's safe to come and help."

Sahng Ha bowed to her, then raced down the stairs and back to the hospital.

Margaret called down to the kitchen to Tabitha, asking her to prepare a thermos of hot tea, then she changed into her nurse's uniform. All the while she agonized as she heard sporadic gunfire. At last, all was quiet.

After about an hour Sahng Ha came running back with a message.

"The honorable doctor says its safe for you to come now, if you can, to help."

In an instant Margaret called Tabitha to watch the children. Then she put on her coat, grabbed the thermos from the kitchen table, and was almost running as she and Sahng Ha went past the fields to the hospital. There she went straight to the basement.

Stan, his white coat red with blood, looked up at her with a look of relief. He and the other staff members were binding wounds. There were moans and occasional screams from the men lying there.

"Give morphine shots to the six over there. The others are dead."

Margaret gasped as she looked over to the rows of silent bodies.

"The equipment is on the table behind you. After you give the shots, they'll need you upstairs. Most of the wounded are up there now."

Margaret was speechless, as she walked on the bloody cement floor to get the morphine and syringes. She was used to blood, but this was horror unlike anything she had ever seen.

A little later, she went upstairs to the large men's ward. Every bed was filled with bandaged figures. When the Korean nurses saw her they ran to hug her, casting aside all formality.

"Oh *Pween!* Something terrible has happened! What shall we do?!!"

Margaret answered calmly as she looked around.

"You already know what to do, and you're doing it."

But they took courage at her presence, as she began to work with them. Nurse Maud Mackinnon at the far end of the ward came toward Margaret with a sober expression on her face. Maud was usually so bright and cheerful.

"This is unbelievable. It's like a bad dream and they're all so innocent."

Maud went on to point out the condition of the most seriously wounded. Stopping further hemorrhaging, and plying those who were awake with liquids to counteract their loss of blood, were the most urgent needs. There was no intravenous equipment. All the nurses helped, as the last of the wounded were carried up from the basement. Stan came up with them, and pointed out which patients were to be brought to the operating room.

In the meantime, the Koreans were storming the hospital to know the condition of friends and family members. So the hospital gate was closed, and the known names of the victims were hastily posted there on large sheets of paper until things settled down.

As soon as he could, Stan wrote of that day.

St. Andrew's Hospital
Yong Jung, Manchuria
March 30, 1919

Dear Ones at Home:

You will no doubt wonder why I have not written to you for some time, and I'm just getting these lines off tonight (Sunday) after making hospital rounds.

As you know, the Koreans have declared their independence of Japanese rule and are demonstrating in tens of thousands throughout Korea and Manchuria.

Well, on March 13th, thousands gathered outside of our town in the long, broad valley in front of the east hill on which is situated our compound. There, in the cold Manchurian gale, they listened with tense excitement to the stimulating speeches of their ringleaders. We, the missionaries, watched the proceedings from our houses with the aid of powerful field glasses.

The Koreans in the main, decided not to enter the city, but others on the outside of the crowd did not hear the orders and advanced, led by school boys and girls. They were fired on by a company of crude, undisciplined soldiers under the control of Japanese indirectly, but who were really Chinese troops.

About ten were killed outright; some were shot through both lungs, but most of the dead were shot through the brain. There were over 40 wounded seriously, all of whom were brought in on roughly-made stretchers to the hospital, where a quickly organized team busied themselves with sterilizing wounds, stopping hemorrhages, and setting compound fractures. Each case received morphine on admission and was put to bed immediately in our large ward.

The brain and lung cases died within the hour, and others wounded in other vital places, very soon afterwards. The bullet being of an old German make, Mauser type, 45, flattened on impact with bone, the result being a gaping wound, which in case of the skull wounds, resulted in extrusion of portions of the brain.

One man of 53 was shot through both thighbones, and died from sudden bleeding on the way to the hospital. A boy of 15, in his school uniform, with his little homemade Korean flag, was shot exactly through the heart and died with a smile on his face.

So that the reaper whose name was death,
*   Armed with his sickle keen,*
Gathered the bearded grain at a breath,
*   And the flowers that grow between.*

Fourteen died that day, the 13ᵗʰ of March, others died later, and surely it was a slaughter of innocents, for the Koreans did nothing that would necessitate for a minute such cruel treatment.

There was not an armed Korean in the whole 10,000 and it's a horrible feature that although in Korea, the Japanese use the Koreans very brutally and cut off arms, etc., and shoot scores, the Koreans have never once retaliated.

Many of our Christians, being mostly among the educated classes, have been arrested and it remains to be seen whether Japan will be foolish enough to torture these people in this time of world justice. This they did ten years ago, when they dishonorably annexed this country of 20,000,000 of Koreans and were compelled to stop as Great Britain and America became wise to the facts.

Yours truly,
Stan

Korean Christian women who were in Yong Jung at that time gave this report.

"There were 22 dead, five of the bodies were taken home to their villages to be buried there, but 17 were buried at the same time. The women needed time to prepare the funeral clothing according to their custom, and ten days after the tragedy they were ready for the burial service March 23, 1919."

Stan wrote of the tragedy in another letter repeating some of the information but adding more news. He said, "except those who died immediately that day others were healed and returned home, good earnest Christians." He also wrote of the outdoor funeral service.

> "At the burial of the dead, from our hospital were seen thousands of people with heads bared, most of them listening for the first time to the words of a Christian burial service. More than half of the dead had died non-Christian, yet all their friends asked for the Christian service, which was conducted by our pastors and elders. Where could one find a better opportunity than this to sow the seed?"

The Korean Christian women's report continues:

> "The long line of coffins borne on men's shoulders, moved out from the hospital area and started on the long march to a cemetery 20 li (7 miles) away. About 10,000 people joined the procession. They shouted *Mansei!* again, other times they were singing "*There's a land that is fairer than day.*" At the head of the procession marched a well-known little grandmother beating a drum. One of the women telling the story ended by saying bitterly, "Even in our grief the Japanese cavalry followed us all the way to the cemetery!"

XI

Life Goes On

An uneasy peace settled over the land. Grieving friends and families heard the names of the dead read at the churches around the area, and prayers were offered to comfort the people. The churches and hospital took on new significance as symbols of hope and strength for all who suffered. The Korean Provisional Government in Shanghai, and the people of Korea gradually heard the news of the Manchurian demonstrations.

Full reports of the atrocities were sent from the missionaries to the Canadian Foreign Mission Board of the Presbyterian Church and the Canadian government. Dr. Armstrong wrote to Stan's father in Newfoundland on August 22, 1919:

> You will be glad to know that in Britain everything is being done to give publicity to the Korean cause. The matter has been discussed in the House of Commons. The British Foreign Office knows all about the situation. Dr. Gale of Seoul is now in Britain and is a friend of Lord Bryce. He had sent Lord Bryce a long statement in March. The Conference of Federated Missions in Japan came out with its report. Part of it said, "We found it exceedingly difficult to believe the stories of inhumane cruelty and outrages committed on the people of Korea by the Japanese government in the suppression of the recent uprising. We were shocked inexpressibly, and amazed at these reports. We have been forced to believe that the reports are substantially true and that the people of Korea have endured sufferings which are unjust and unnecessary."

Although the demonstrations in Yong Jung had been cruelly stopped by the Chinese soldiers, Margaret reported later that the Chinese had been urged on by the Japanese, who had said, "These demonstrations are very dangerous. Do something about it."

Now, the Japanese were aware more than ever of the Manchurian Koreans strong desire for independence. They became watchful with a simmering anger and made plans for reprisal. They declared, "The Koreans in Manchuria are our citizens, we have the right to control them."

They had already built and controlled the South Manchurian Railway and posted garrisons along the route. They had established a consulate in Yong Jung under pretext of protecting the Koreans. They also stationed a garrison there. They built Japanese schools and tried to force the Koreans to attend them.

It irritated the Japanese that the missionaries always seemed to side with the Koreans. At one time a Japanese officer made an appointment to see Stan. They were in Stan's living room seated before the fireplace. The officer sat in a chair opposite the doctor with his big sword between his knees. He was gesticulating and laying down the law about some problem concerning the Koreans.

Stan said later, "Just to put us on an even footing, I reached over and got our long handled corn popper and held it between my knees, as we continued the conversation. It went very well."

The work of the mission compound continued. This work included teaching, healing, and traveling to encourage the churches in the rural areas. Much of Stan's thoughts focused upon improving the hospital facilities. Again he wrote to Mr. Armstrong:

> We find our biggest problem is a lack of good heating. As you know, we need some heat especially in the operating rooms, for eight months of the year here where the wind is so cold. Out of our building money, with care, we can save $2000. This we wish you to use to the best advantage to get us a serviceable heating plant.
>
> You will notice that we are dividing the women's ward up into men's and women's wards for winter only, so that if it comes to the pinch we will only heat the dispensary and women's ward. If the $2000 is not sufficient, we shall have to do without heating the men's ward at all. The number of our patients is much smaller in the winter.
>
> I have visited Pyeng Yang and Songdo (Ivy) mission hospitals to see their heating plants. Dr. Falwell's hospital in Pyeng Yang is very well heated with a Montgomery Ward plant. The Songdo steam plant is very good, too. We use a lot of fuel here with wood and coal stoves that are dirty and dangerous.
>
> I prefer steam. (a) It heats the building quicker, especially the operating room. (b) It's cheaper to install, as it's only one pipe to each radiator. (c) If the water pipes freeze it's impossible to mend them here in this isolated place. (d) We can sterilize with steam from the boiler. (e) Water holds heat and can be used for bathrooms, etc.
>
> Mr. Scott and our Station advised me to send this plan to you, to have you get an expert to look it over and advise us as to the best plan to have for our money, and cheaper if possible. Please send to Montgomery Ward for an estimate, and if possible, have pipes cut the proper length so we can put the outfit in ourselves as they did in Pyeng Yang.

Please correspond with Montgomery Ward so as to save time as we would like very much to have a heating system, or part of one, by next fall or winter.

Patients are increasing rapidly and many are becoming Christians from results of the work. I saw forty this morning and performed two operations.

If the money is not sufficient, I would like to put, say, four radiators only in the men's ward so we could use it in the spring and autumn.

Please do what you can in this direction, and so help out a work which is almost running away with us, we are kept so busy.

Kind regards to Dr. MacKay.

Ever sincerely yours,
Martin

After all the tragedy and turmoil, it was a great relief for the little family to get away to Mission Meeting and a vacation that summer. Margaret wrote:

June 29, 1919
Wonsan Beach, Korea

Dear Papa,

Here we are in Wonsan. We left home a week ago Friday and reached here the following Thursday morning, in a pouring rain. The babies (Ruthie two, Margaret five months) are fine little travelers, did not get sick at all. We had two days cart journey to Hoiryung, one night there at the Mission station and then took the train to Chongjin. There we stayed one night in a Japanese inn. On Monday, Tuesday and Wednesday we were on a small coastal steamer on which we had first class cabins and were very comfortable. We called in to many pretty little Korean harbors, and made long stops. Rev. Foote met us in Wonsan and took us to the Beach. I brought Lydia (the Korean amah) to help with the babies. Our cottage is a little box of a place, front porch, middle room, back porch and latticed outer kitchen. Every afternoon about five, there is a lovely cool breeze that comes up, so we manage to get through the heat of the day. Baby is kicking up her heels in the basket, and Ruthie has been asleep on a mattress on the floor.

Rev. Cornelius Patton of the American Board was our speaker at church. He gave us a fine world view of missions with special reference to the war, and their Red Cross relief work in Armenia and Bible lands.

The change is doing us good and we are eating like everything, enjoying strawberries, fresh fruit and vegetables. We take meals at the beach house.

The Japanese didn't bother us a bit on the journey – were quite nice to us.

Love,
Margaret

She also wrote more about their beach vacation to Aunt Addie:

We have been attending language school one hour in the morning, but not doing outside studying. We have one more week of language study, and then one week of Bible Conference that begins August 4 led by a Mr. Wilkey of Japan. We expect to go home about August 10th or 14th. We heard that it was 106º-112º for ten days in Yong Jung.

We have been able to spend an hour or two in the salt water every day. That has helped a lot. Even Ruthie goes in and gets wet and plays around in the sand.

August 7. We are in the midst of a revival meeting. Yes, even missionaries have to have revivals now and then to wake them up and keep them going, the dear saints! (I don't include myself with the saints!) This is led by Dr. Wilkey who has been in Japan for twenty-five years, a marvelous leader of men. He is speaking to the younger missionaries especially, and has stories of conversions in Japan through prayer and the power of God, that were nothing short of miracles. I must confess I cannot follow all these dear missionaries in their deepest religious experiences. But they are certainly God's saints on earth.

[Margaret had been on the mission field about three and a half years.]

When they returned from Wonsan, Stan had a reply from Armstrong. He reported that Montgomery Ward was executing the order for the heating plant. The Board would cover the excess amount of $300, which was over the allotted sum. This included packing, transportation and insurance. Stan was relieved to hear this. Stan answered this letter repeating the urgent need.

We received your letter OK, and were more than glad to know you had received the hospital plan and order for the heating plant. There is no station in our mission I think needs heating so badly, as you know the need of heating an operating room for an abdominal operation, and the impossibility of being able to keep that room clean with a coal stove going at the same time.

Mr. Hylton put in one of the heating plants at Pyeng Yang. He is an English Customs man, married to one of our Canadian missionaries here and is on our station. He will no doubt be glad to help us out, as he is keen on that sort of work.

Our one big trouble is lack of staff. Please note the great increase in our work as last reported, over 7000 cases in six months and seeing patients only in the mornings.

I am still tired from the work and until we get either another nurse or foreign doctor, we must keep down our cases in order to keep in fairly good condition. I am just learning to type as you can see.

With all good wishes to yourself and Dr. MacKay.

Sincerely yours,
S. H. Martin

On another day a very tired doctor wrote:

I have just finished my fifth operation and am fed up. –6pm. We had over 100 patients today. This afternoon, a Chinese woman went home able to see – a boy, the only son of an old man, went home cured from Bright's disease (nephritis) with uraemic convulsion, and a little school girl age 15 went home cured of pneumonia.

So we have just seen as the British Commissioner of Customs for this district, who is visiting, said. "It's certainly great to be able to make people happy."

I am in communication with the electrical engineer of the Rockefeller

Board regarding the lighting of our hospital and compound with electric light. At present we have only cheap Japanese lamps, a great source of danger at night with irresponsible patients. As our plant now is quite worthwhile, I'd hate to see it go up in smoke. I think we shall be able to light the Boys' Academy and our mission houses off our hospital lighting plant as well. Our pumping and water system works extremely well.

Best regards and thanks to all the members of the Board.

With best wishes,
S H M

P.S. The Korean Provisional Government in Shanghai presented Mrs. Martin, Miss Mackinnon and me with gold medals for treating 45 wounded cases March 13, 1919.

Winter closed in, and with it came reports of the increased activity of bandits and opium sellers. The bandits were raiding villages on the plain surrounding Yong Jung. If the people tried to save their crops, their houses were burned.

One day at the hospital, Stan was called from his clinic office into the hallway where there was a great commotion. Patients, staff and visitors quickly gathered around. A group of Chinese soldiers with their fur caps, ragged uniforms and padded boots were standing over two men writhing on the floor. The men were bound with their hands tied behind their backs. Their faces were scratched and bruised, and blood seeped from their clothing on to the floor.

The soldiers spoke in Chinese, hastily bowing to Stan as he approached. "*Min Dai Foo,*" (Honorable Dr. Min) one said. "These are opium sellers. They are criminals. They are to be executed, but they are badly wounded now. We leave them in your care. Please tend to them and we'll be back for them later."

The absurdity of their logic, healed to be executed, flashed through Stan's mind, but without hesitation, he said to the soldiers, "I'll be glad to take care of them, while they're in my hospital. Please unbind them."

The soldiers did so and left. The crowd dispersed and the men were hastily carried on stretchers to the operating room.

Stan was glad he could speak in Chinese to the terrified wounded men. They were suffering from bullet wounds, but fortunately not in vital places. Soon they were sedated, their bleeding stopped, and they were resting in hospital beds.

The days went by, but there were no signs of the soldiers coming back for the men. One night as Stan was making his rounds he said to the two Chinese patients, who were ambulatory now and sitting in their beds, "I recommend for you fresh air and exercise."

The men understood immediately what he meant.

The next morning the two men had escaped, but in their beds were gifts – bolts of silk and some frozen tangerines, precious as gold in these days because they had been imported from Japan.

When the soldiers came back to the hospital and found that the men were gone, they were complacent about it. The hospital, after all, was not a prison and they hadn't left a guard.

Some months went by before alarming news came to the compound. A large group of bandits was terrorizing the villages to the north, and there was no way of knowing where they would strike next. The missionaries gathered at the Scotts' house to discuss the situation. There was nothing to do but pray and wait. Faithful Korean friends brought any small bit of news. Life had to go on, and each family continued in their duties.

Then one afternoon, a large group of *keesaeng*, dancing girls from the wine shops, crowded through the hospital gate and into the hospital. They were terrified. When Stan and the Korean staff faced them to inquire what was going on, they wailed, "Save us! Hide us! We've just heard that the bandits are on the edge of town coming this way!"

Stan understood the situation immediately and said, "Of course, you may stay here."

To the nurses he said, "Take them to the basement. They'll be safe there. Also tell the cook to prepare soup and rice for many people."

To Chungsi, the hospital water carrier, he said, "Go to Mrs. Martin and the children and the single ladies and tell them all to gather at the Scott's house. Quickly! Quickly!"

Stan told the story of the next events.

I went down to the gate with my faithful staff members to see what would happen. We were standing under the flagpole with the British flag, symbol of Great Britain's protection, but my heart and mind were praying for the greater protection of God. There was no sign of danger yet but I knew the bandits were primarily thieves, and the temptation would be great for them to loot the homes of the 'foreign devils.' I thought of Margaret and my little girls. I hoped the doors and locks of the Scott's house were strong. I wondered what the families were doing just then. Praying, like I am I'm sure.

We didn't have long to wait. At the far edge of the plain in front of the hospital, a large group of about forty men became visible. They were marching, marching straight towards us. The dust was rising from their tramping feet and as they approached we could see they were heavily armed. They had guns and some had two or three bandoliers of cartridges around their waists. Frankly, we froze with terror as we watched. They came closer and closer.

Suddenly, one of the men broke rank and rushed up to a man who seemed to be the leader. This man was shouting and pointing toward our little group at the gate. Faintly, we heard his shouts in the distance, 'Min Dai Foo, Min Dai Foo!' He was calling my name.

Then to our amazement, the leader raised his arm and the marchers stopped. After a pause, he took out a little tin whistle, ridiculous in contrast to the ferocious looks of the men. He blew it, and the men turned and began to march again, this time across the plain and away from the town. We learned later that the man who had persuaded the bandit leader to spare our compound was one of my former patients – one of the opium sellers.

As the eventful year 1919 closed, Stan wrote his annual report. Besides the news of the March tragedy, he added:

The new hospital, over 200 feet long with its 60 foot Women's Ward in the rear and adjacent native doctor's house, is practically all completed and represents a plant of which our church may be very proud. The inpatient capacity is about fifty beds. The new large operating room is practically ideal and since we have been working in it we have had the best results.

The work during the last part of the year was the same as usual, except that the new inpatient department was more fully organized and the two wards of the rear wing were kept full almost all the time.

This year, over 800 people have been inoculated against typhoid, cholera and smallpox, thus helping to keep down epidemic spread of these diseases. The dreaded Spanish influenza has at last arrived here, and already almost fifty cases have proven fatal as a result of secondary pneumonia. There is nothing so discouraging to an isolated medical missionary, with no one with whom to consult, to have to deal with such virulent and fateful cases.

The object of a report seems to be to make the readers feel happy, but a real report includes many discouragements and disappointments in the work. However, every now and then, one of the "cleansed lepers" returns with a heart full of gratitude and becomes a Christian. Recently a man whose wife had been cured came back to say, 'Although I have no money to pay my bill, I couldn't help coming back to say thank you for saving her life.'

During the nine months the hospital was open, 12,089 patients were seen amongst whom were 6,935 unbelievers and to whom 4300 tracts were distributed, and all these patients with the 4,202 friends who came with them heard the Gospel from our hospital evangelist and Bible Women.

217 operations were performed under anesthesia, many of them of a serious nature. 1,181 outcalls were attended. The patient aggregate days in the hospital was approximately 3,985. The total surgical treatments given were 31,200 and of those who came in contact with hospital influence, 150 have decided to live 'Christian lives.' Much of this is the result of the Bible Women's' visits to the sick in their homes and during the year over ninety such visits were made. The Canadian missionaries Miss Cass and Miss Palethorpe have also, as time permitted, visited the sick in the hospital, telling the old, old story.

In closing, our work this year, with all its joys and sorrows, we believe that we can truthfully say that many have not been left hungry, thirsty, sick or in need of the cup of cold water or the touch of a gentle hand. We only hope for continued health and strength in order to help, physically and spiritually, the least of His brethren.

The British flag that flew at the Canadian Mission compound gate
at Lungchingtsun, China, indicating extraterritoriality.

XII

The Pot Simmers

The next year, 1920, many were still concerned with the aftermath of the demonstrations. The Japanese were watching for further disturbances. The Koreans were still grieving, but a change came over the Korean independence fighters. The peaceful demonstrations had been put down so cruelly that their patience turned to anger. Now they watched for every opportunity to fight the Japanese. Rumors came in to the hospital about their exploits. They heard of a young patriot who could approach a wall or building at a fast run, and be up and over it, as agile as a cat. In the spring the patriots burned the Japanese Consulate building in Yong Jung. Later in June Stan wrote, "Three hundred Japanese were ambushed by Koreans not far from here. One hundred and seventy were killed, and only four of the Korean independence soldiers were killed or wounded. The Japanese in revenge used machine guns on a village and school, killing seventy Koreans, mostly women and children."

Tensions were heightened, but the mission work went on. Word came that the Orillia church had subscribed $18,000 to improve the hospital water system and sanitation etc. The furnace was on its way. During the war the Canadian Presbyterian Church, was low on funds but since the Armistice, the financial situation improved, and there was a greater interest in missions. A campaign called The Forward Movement brought increased financial support to missions.

Mr. Armstrong in Canada reported to F. A. Mackenzie in London at the House of Commons:

January 3, 1920

I am sending documents from our missionaries in Manchuria. Tens of thousands of Koreans have migrated there, upwards of 300,000 scattered through to the Trans-Siberian Railroad over to Vladivostok. We are the only mission in that area. We have approximately eighty churches together with a fairly equipped station at Yong Jung.

I enclose clippings from Toronto papers, which is our own Executive statement of defense, along with the statement by Rev. W. Scott to the Toronto Globe. We believe wide publicity should be given to atrocities and treatment of Koreans. We shall keep out of political controversy. We are having an interesting correspondence with the Japanese Consul in Ottawa over the *Kando* situation. *Chientao* is the Chinese word for *Kando*.

The Japanese Colonel Midzumachi in charge of their forces in Manchuria has sent a letter to Rev. Foote the head of the Yong Jung Mission charging complicity in the Korean opposition to the Chosen (Japanese) government. This gives us the opportunity for flat denial at the same time emphasizing the right of vigorous protest when troops conduct a campaign of fire and sword on innocents.

Please send news regarding discussion of the Anglo-Japanese Alliance.

With the flurry of diplomatic letters going back and forth between Japan, Canada, England and the embattled missionaries in Manchuria, Stan's family had a more immediate concern right in his own home. Margaret wrote of it to her father.

Yong Jung, Manchuria
February 11, '20

Dear Papa,

Our poor baby Margaret, age thirteen months, has just had a bad attack of pneumonia, but she is convalescing now and begins to play again, tho' still thin and white. We had a desperate time with her – Doctor and I, Mrs. Hilton and Korean nurses working day and night. Everyday for a week we thought we would lose her. But dear friends far and near were praying for us, and God in His mercy spared her to be the light of our eyes. She was so good all through it – let us do any medical procedure we needed to do.

I will never forget that week of agony! Every time the sun set we wondered if we would still have her in the morning.

Chulsi, our *amah* (nurse maid) spent many hours with her tied to her back the way Korean mothers carry their babies – "piggy-back." This helped keep little Margaret's lungs in an upright position.

We have a new missionary; a Scotch trained nurse, Miss Jessie Whitelaw with us now. She happened to be visiting at Hoiryung and has come up to help us and is going to stay awhile. We may get her for the hospital. I think she likes it up here.

I have been laid up ever since she came and she is taking care of me [She was expecting their third child due in July].

116

I seem to have a low form of "sub-acute" rheumatic fever with the general played-outness after such a strain. We hardly knew if we ate or slept there for awhile. Sufficient rest in bed, with freedom from care, will fix me up all right.

I have been hoping so much that you will come out this year. Please give the news in this letter to the family as I am not able to write any more just now.

Cheer up and don't worry. I am so thankful to have a live, happy baby, that I don't care about anything else.

Ruth and Stan are well.

Lovingly,
Margaret

P.S. Stan's record for the past year was 22,000 patients including outpatients. We see nothing of the famine that is in other parts of China. We see heaps of rice and grain in the market here. Our winter has been mild. No snow.

On March 15th, '20 Stan wrote to Armstrong.

I have just returned from Peking to see their medical work and consult with the Rockefeller people. After seeing so much heathenism in China, I felt like asking to be sent to Honan, especially where there might be a chance of a "two man" (two doctors) work. But since coming back I see its up to me to stick by the Koreans, although I have no missionary nurse to supervise our nurses, and we are overworked.

I hope to put in our heating plant when it comes, and hope to order a water system for our hospital. We are also going to put in a septic tank, buy more beds, and open up the new men's ward.

Dr. Mansfield has gone to Severance Hospital in Seoul to stay, and at present Miss Whitelaw is up here from Hoiryung helping with Mrs. Scott who has just had a son named Keith. Miss Whitelaw is going back to Seoul at the end of this month. We asked the executive to let us have her work here, since Severance has two of our missionary doctors.

The Songjin hospital is a wreck inside -- good apparatus rusting, windows broken etc. I wouldn't mention it but when I saw it last Sunday, not a bit of the heating or lighting or water system was being used, I thought of the use I could make of it here. I'm glad to hear however that the clinic outside of Songjin is improving.

We are in a critical stage in our Mission just at present. The Japanese have closed up our Boys' Academy in town. The boys had shouted *"Mansei"* (Korea live 10,000 years) again. However the Bible and the use of the Korean language has been allowed again in private schools. Mr. Scott will probably go to Seoul when he gets back from furlough. Miss Roger's heart is worse, and she will have to go home on furlough soon. The McRaes are going home, and it's a question whether Dr. Schofield will be able to come out again.

At Medical Meeting I got a resolution through by which we hope to get rid of smaller hospitals and dispensaries, and have strong centers throughout Korea, well manned and efficient, as at present we are all spread out too thin, and overworked. Men are going home, and not coming out again.

As I look out the window I see fifteen people on the hill, coming to the dispensary. We have already had fifty-six this morning.

The competition is getting strong now from three government hospitals, Japanese, Chinese and Korean. There are also three native doctors, but there will be a lot of emigration this year from Korea, so there's a lot of work to do.

We hope that you can get us another doctor. Ask my chum Sellery at Western Hospital, Toronto to come out with me. We could also use a nurse or a business lady. We hope the Forward Movement will help us to install the water and heating plants.

More later
Regards,
Martin

The next month in April Stan wrote again.

Dear Mr. Armstrong,

Everything is going very well with us. This month we have had over 2000 cases, and over 500 yuan to the good, one day. We had 120 outpatients and all our beds are full and we have ordered twenty new beds.

Last week we did a strangulated hernia that gave back to the church a young Christian man of thirty. Sunday last I heard another man Lee Moksa preach. He is considered the best preacher in *Kando* – a man who is out for soul winning. He spoke of how he was saved from death in the hospital. He had acute Bright's disease. We successfully removed a bladder stone from a Chinese boy. It weighed

37 grams. The boy is thirteen and has had this stone growing for eight years. He now calls me "father."

I study the Chinese language every morning from eight to nine. I found that when treating Chinese cases in a village the other day, that I could get along quite well with the Chinese I have gotten so far. It seems much easier than Korean. I am using materials from the Peking Language School and I have a good teacher. I have only missed one lesson since March 15. The teacher speaks English well.

A woman with two sons came to our hospital. One of her boys had erysipelas and is now recovered. Now all three of them are believers. I have also received a letter from a man saying that since he has left the hospital he has decided to believe, and is attending a nearby church.

As you know we wish to have the heating and water systems put in together this fall. I have ordered a complete hot and cold water system, which has been approved by the station. The engine and pump will be powerful enough to supply the houses with water and fire protection. I am planning to have a hose faucet lead to the houses from the hospital this year.

The new Boys' Academy (Eun Jin) is being built in our field just across from our houses. It will cost 30,000 yuan.

Please have the treasurer deduct from our Orillia donation of $14,000:

1. The heating plant
2. The water supply system
3. Two telephones [He planned phone service between the hospital and the Martin house for emergencies] Blinds etc.
4. The operating room equipment
5. The Bramhall Dean Sterilizer

The town of Yong Jung is growing. There is a 200,000-yuan bank going up here, also a huge Oriental Development Co. Building and hundreds of new Korean and Chinese houses. So it looks bright for the future.

I am aiming to get the hospital completely equipped before I go home on furlough, so that when we come back we will be able to go right ahead. I expect to spend vacation this year putting in our heating plant. It will be a real pleasure. Tell any Doctors you see, that it's "Sure some fun building up your own hospital plant from the good of others."

Best regards to Dr. Mackay and thanks very much for your continued goodness,
Martin

June 13, 1920

Dear Papa,

"My Burpee seeds didn't arrive until May 25th and as I superintend all the
gardening we had a big hustle to get them in. However by the 28th they were
in, except some I have saved for a second planting.Baby Margaret is quite well
again and runs all around talking mostly Korean. She started yesterday trying
to call Ruth by name, the best she can do is "Bad Bootie!" "Bad" has no special
significance as they are very fond of each other, but little David Hylton our
neighbor child uses it. "Bad Billy (the dog) etc. and Margaret caught it.

Stan had to go to Hoiryung for over Sunday. There's a smallpox case there on
the mission compound. I had a pleasant birthday yesterday, June 12, tho' Doctor
was away he sent me a telegram. The girls, Miss Cass, Palethorpe and Whitelaw
invited Ruthie and me over to dinner at their house, and Mrs. Hylton made me
a birthday cake. We all had supper together. With Mr. Foote there were six. Mr.
Hylton is away and the Scotts have gone to Canada. My third year language exam
would not be so difficult, if I had the time to do the required reading, but I don't
expect to have the time! So I have given up all thoughts of it at present.

I'm sorry I didn't write you for so long but with sewing, house cleaning and
gardening I have had a busy spring.

I have a bunch of wild roses, another of yellow lilies and wild peonies, on the
mantle. We have had lovely lilies of the valley, from our hills. My acacia has
bloomed and morning glories, sweet peas, cabbage, turnips, radishes and lima
beans are sprouting now after some welcome rain. We have had no severe heat yet.

The foundation for a new Boys' Academy is going up; just outside our dining
room window, on our mission property. Mr. Barker was instrumental in getting
the money for it when on furlough. Our hospital heating plant is on its way. Wish
we had one for our house.

Baby's awake,
Lovingly,
Margaret

[Margaret is expecting a child the very next month but doesn't mention it.]

Stan wrote to Mr. Armstrong on May 7ᵗʰ, '20:

My Dear Mr. Armstrong,

Just before I received your letter of March 18ᵗʰ with the encouraging news of Dr. Florence Murray coming to our station I said to myself, "Things can't go along like this. I'll have to get more help or give it up." I suppose it's because one gets tired, but today I have had an extra dose of trouble.

1. The Japanese want 200 Yuan before they will forward twenty boxes of my heating plant from Hoiryung – It's too much.
2. My bladder case from whom we removed a large stone, has developed peritonitis.
3. We have a smallpox case in a private room. Looks bad.
4. We have a woman case with Spanish influenza
5. A baby with a bad heart who was cured of a very bad septic throat died unexpectedly from an embolism this AM.
6. A man who came in last night can hardly breathe and cannot swallow water. Diphtheria, and I have no more vaccine. I used it all on our Korean nurse and the parcel post is suspended.
7. Mrs. Martin is not well, and daughter Ruthie has a high fever.

We all have our little troubles, but I am lucky so far not to get infected.

I have no trouble in speaking and preaching to the Koreans. My vocabulary is short on sermonizing.

It seems almost a sin to wave before my eyes the possibility of having someone to help take some of the worry and responsibility. Rev. Foote here is a great friend of Dr. Florence Murray's father, Rev. Mr. Murray. All I can say is that any lady; doctor or nurse would soon have her hands full. Miss Jessie Whitelaw has only been here a month and women have been coming in large numbers for female troubles.

I am sending a set of pictures which I should like you to please use with our annual report, and in the "Presbyterian Record," thanking all the many kind friends for their help, and to show them what grand results have come from the use of their money.

We on this station can never fully thank you for your practical love and continuous kind thoughts toward us.

Yours in the Work,
Stan H. Martin

On June 12, '20 Stan wrote again to Armstrong,

> Your letter of May 25th has arrived, and I am taking this chance of thanking you for the most excellent slides of the "Life of Christ." They are beauties.
>
> I am down at Hoiryung looking after a smallpox case on the mission compound. The foreigners are all OK.
>
> All of the heating plant except the furnace doors have arrived. Some of it is broken, so I have sent immediately for new parts. Please advise Fraser to let us have money for our new isolation wards, engine house etc. and let him know what bills have been paid for our hospital.
>
> We have a new Chinese pastor at the Yong Jung Chinese Church and had sixty Christians attend last Sunday. The only unbeliever there was a well educated man who has been blind for ten years. He is now able to see as a result of an operation at our hospital.
>
> The Chinese pastor's son, an excellent Christian who studied in the Mukden hospital is one of our assistants now.
>
> We removed a thirty pound tumor (carefully weighed) from a woman last week. People came from the town asking to see it. The woman and her husband have become believers and there's a good chance of their whole village becoming Christian.
>
> Regards,
> SHM

When he returned to Yong Jung he wrote again.

> I used the lovely slides of the "Life of Christ" which you sent, last Sunday in a new church that has been started here. The church was crowded, and after dark the people looked into the building from the outside. The Koreans of this church have asked me to preach next Sunday. I gave my first address in Hoiryung, two Sundays ago. I told them of a man in Canada who sent ten dollars towards a wooden leg for one of our patients. The ten dollars was saved from his poor apple crop.
>
> For the last six months we have had 9,561 outpatients, 215 operations under anesthetic and 199 inpatients. This is almost twice as much as last year and from our outpatient department we have one hundred and ninety-six decisions for Christ. What's more important, more than half of these cases are attending church. Almost every Sunday in the local church a new believer stands up who has

come via the hospital. We have in this town, two government hospitals, (Japanese and Chinese) and one Korean hospital, yet we get practically all the work.

I am not at annual meeting this year. First, because the medical work would be without a doctor or nurse. Second, we are superintending the building of the academy and the isolation wards. Third, Mrs. Martin and Mrs. Hylton are both due to have babies soon. Also there is the hospital heating plant which must be put in by our staff, as expert help from Seoul would be too expensive.

The Japanese have no right to close some of our schools as they have, or to bring in 120 new Japanese police here (soldiers in police uniforms) – or to examine British passports on the Chinese side of the Tumen.

Yesterday we operated on a man from Siberia, who walked all the way from there. He had cancer. It took four hours working fast to clean it completely out. We didn't want to operate but he said he would commit suicide, for "if the mission doctor couldn't cure him he was sure to die," etc.

We have a sign in our hospital in Chinese saying, "The head of this hospital is Jesus Christ."

Best regards and thanks for all you do for us,
S H M

In May, Stan had written that he was lucky so far that he had not been infected. But unfortunately just before his third daughter was born, a severe infection occurred in one of his fingers. In a time before antibiotics this was extremely serious. His hand was heavily bandaged, so his assistant, Deacon Lim was the one who received Edna Kathleen into the world on July 13th, with father Stan supervising. Edna was later known as Nanoo, named thus by her sister Margaret in their early childhood days. All was well, and the summer passed peacefully. Margaret wrote to Aunt Addie – "I have an amah, one who was a nurse at the hospital helping me with the babies for the summer. She is a dear woman who has been studying in Wonsan at the Bible Women's Institute last winter and plans eventually to be a Bible Woman. It is a course of five years study, though she knows her Bible better than I do now! We have had hot days, alternating with heavy rains.

In September she wrote to Papa.

Just a line as I am in the midst of canning beautiful fat tomatoes, and bathing babies. (Ruthie three years, Margie twenty months, and Edna three months) Ruthie is better; her eardrum broke, it has been running for ten days, with great relief to the poor kiddie. She was so sick with it and we couldn't be sure what was the matter. Stan arrived from a three-week vacation in Wonsan. He was very homesick for us

Edna Kathleen weighs 10 lb. at seven weeks, and mother is gaining.

Last week a Korean musician Mr. Kim gave a "musicale" (!) in the church with the foreigners to help him. He had trained a band and some boys to play violin, so there were several band pieces and a string quartet. We had drilled a girls' chorus to sing an English hymn. Miss Whitelaw dressed in a Scottish costume with kilted skirts and tam o' shanter and sang "My Ain (Own) Countrie." It was very sweet and nearly made some of us cry. Then Mr. Kim played some violin solos really very well. One was the "La Cinquantaine" that you are so fond of. He also sang in a well-trained clear, sweet baritone voice. It was the first event of this kind in our *Kando* province, and everyone seemed to enjoy it.

I played Chopin's "Fifth Nocturne" and sang "Mighty Lak a Rose." They were good enough to encore me. They made three hundred yen ($150) on tickets for the benefit of the "Heathen Sunday School," a S.S. conducted on Sunday afternoons for children off the street, which has had an attendance as high as 600 sometimes this summer.

Well, I had to take all the babies to this concert including little Edna, as the amahs and the cook wanted to go. They were very good and seemed to enjoy it, only were a little afraid of the noise of the band!

Love from us all, Ruthie asks, "Is this Auntie-Grandpa's letter?"

Lovingly,
Margaret

That same month word came from fellow missionary, E. J. O. Fraser in Wonsan, Korea, that a wave of demonstrations calling for Independence had occurred on September 23rd involving the Canadian Mission Boy's Academy. The whole town was under armed police guard. Scores of people including teachers and students were arrested. Mr. Fraser had gone to the police station to protest that students who had not even left the dormitory were also arrested. The answer always was "upon examination all the innocent would be set free." While there he heard sounds of beating and groaning. Later he learned that even women and little boys and girls were subjected to the beatings. Days later, several students were still being held, including the known innocent ones.

In spite of the unrest, Margaret's next letter to her father was from Wonsan!

October 1, '20

This letter was begun last week when I was sick in bed with a cold, and I had not much notion of coming to Wonsan then! But Mrs. Barker was coming out from Yong Jung to meet her husband in Seoul, and they were to go to the World's Sunday School Convention in Tokyo. I could travel with her as far as Wonsan. So I got ready in twenty-four hours notice, and took little Edna and came with her.

I have just had a telegram from home saying, "Children well and happy, have a good rest," which I needed much. I am here at the Frasers with my amah in the lovely spot where we stayed when we first arrived in Korea five years ago. It was the Robb's house then. It's on a high hillside overlooking Wonsan harbor. Without question, to my mind, this is the most beautiful place I know in Korea.

Mrs. Fraser's Jean and little Clarence here are good little kiddies. It was hard to leave my babies, but I felt that it would be for their good in the end for me to take a vacation.

Stan is taking care of Ruthie at night, and Miss Whitelaw the Scotch nurse has taken Margaret's little crib over to her house and is taking care of her for me. She is very fond of Margaret, having taken care of her when she had pneumonia. Then there is Tabitha the cook, and another good amah Chulsi to watch them during the day, so I hope they will be safe until I get back.

It is quite like summer here in the south – beautiful weather, but the mountain pass from Yong Jung was splendid in autumn colors. There is a railroad now from here to Ham Heung. It takes about four and a half hours, and I think I shall go there for a little visit to the missionaries.

The Robbs are there now, and a lady doctor, Dr. Kate MacMillan whom I admire very much, and a Miss Fingland who is a Toronto University girl, I think.

Stan has been much better for his vacation in August, the infected hand and finger all healed, and he's busy as usual in the hospital.

I am sending you a cosmos flower, the first flower my baby Edna grasped and held in her hand. Little Jean Fraser here, brings her bunches of flowers and puts them in her baby hands. It's very cunning. How much I want to see my other babies, but I must rest as hard and fast as I can now while I'm down here. Miss McCully is giving me the "rest cure."

There is a Japanese battle cruiser in the harbor tonight and they have been playing three big searchlights all over Wonsan. It was a great *koo-kyung* (spectacle).

Margaret made her trip to Ham Heung, with baby Edna, Miss McCully, and Miss Elizabeth Keith, the famous English artist. Margaret wrote, "Miss Keith and I will amuse ourselves seeing the town of Ham Heung while the rest are at class. Miss Keith has been traveling around Korea making sketches and preparing to do block prints of Korea and its people. She did an exquisite block print of stars, and the harbor through pine trees, at the village of Too Nam Nee near Wonsan while she was here.

Hope you are well and comfortable for the winter.

Lovingly,
Margaret

After the trip to Ham Heung, Margaret returned safely to Yong Jung with baby Edna and the missionaries returning from the Convention in Tokyo. Although it was peaceful in Yong Jung, she learned that bandits had burned the Japanese Consulate in Hoonchun. The country was tense and bracing for trouble. The children were well, and they settled into their routine. It was good that Margaret was well-rested because rough times were ahead.

The Martin house in Lungchingtsun, China

XIII

The Punitive Expedition

In October of 1920 the Japanese struck. They used the burning of their Consulate by bandits in Hoonchun as an excuse, but they had been preparing for this time.

Thousands of their soldiers marched into the *Kando* Province. However, instead of concentrating on bandit and Independence Fighter strongholds, they punished the Korean population as a whole.

Exasperated and worked to exhaustion, Stan wrote a hurried letter to Mr. Armstrong Oct. 26th, 1920.

> Please report to some one in authority both in USA and Canada, that the Japanese Military Party is carrying out exactly the same tactics as regards Koreans in this part of China, as they did when they annexed Korea.
>
> There are now over 8,000 soldiers in this district, with 4,000 at Ninguta on the way here from Siberia. Koreans are daily being shot, and whole villages are being burned. We have many Korean wounded men here in the hospital. Japanese wounded and dead are being brought here to Yong Jung too, this adding to the extreme hatred the Japanese have for Koreans or anything or anyone connected with them – missionaries.

These are the first reports.

> Myung Tong Academy that had 300 students, has only its brick walls standing like the Lovain in Europe, or the Cloth Hall at Ypres
>
> The Elder's House there is now in ashes, and all the young men in the whole district have fled

<u>Chong Tong Academy</u> Burnt. Twelve people shot (Christians).

<u>Sorangtong</u>, thirty li from Hoiryung. Seventeen shot, ten were Christian. A village five li from there, fourteen shot for giving food to the compatriots.

<u>Kilseidong</u> where the people had built their church before building any of their own houses. The school and houses were burnt. The fires were put out by the women after the soldiers left. Only one house burnt that was not Christian.

<u>Namkoa</u> school and houses burnt.

<u>Chankol</u> the same.

<u>Yangmunchuncha</u> School burnt. Besides this, all families connected with the Independence soldiers had their houses and crops burnt.

The Japanese control the whole *Kando* Province, thus linking up with Siberia, and controlling everything from Sakhalin to Formosa, Shantung etc.

Our whole province is connected up with Japanese telephone and telegraph lines. Koreans are not allowed to travel.

The Japanese are now shelling the Koreans, whom the Lord seems to be helping as Japanese casualties are high – 300 in one day. Japanese aeroplanes and motor cars have gone to the seat of the action.

I am in daily touch with the British Consul General in Mukden who is watching the Japanese movements. If this wholesale eating up of Chinese territory doesn't start either the U.S. or Britain on the warpath, then life won't be worth living. We know of over one hundred Korean deaths now. I'll send more details later as the news becomes more accurate.

Our heating plant is working fine. The staff helped me put the whole thing in.

Best regards
Sincerely,
SHM

Slowly more news crossed the Pacific. Emma Palethorpe's letter took a month and arrived at Mr. Armstrong's office Dec. 6, 1920.

I am enclosing some articles which we thought may be of interest to you. We fear the Chinese P.O. here may be taken over, so we are anxious to get this to you before that happens.

We are living through a reign of terror. Everyday we see fires in the nearer or further distance, and know only too well what that means of sorrow and bloodshed.

Shocking stories come in from every side, of deeds one could scarce credit to a human being. We now have a list of thirty-three villages which we know to have been in whole, or in part, destroyed by fire, and in nearly all, if not all, people killed at the same time. A large number of these, particularly those burned during the past few days have been non-Christian.

We look to you to do what you can to stir up public opinion in the defense of the defenseless and unoffending Korean.

Yours truly,
Emma M. Palethorpe

[Miss Palethorpe was an evangelistic missionary stationed at Yong Jung. She arrived on the field in 1916.]

This was only the beginning of weeks of tragedy. The missionary children on the compound were too small to realize what was happening, and the parents tried to give them a normal happy life. Often, when Stan dragged himself home in the evenings, he would hear the piano and come into a little island of comfort – Margaret playing and singing to the little ones.

Since Stan was in constant touch with the Consul in Mukden, he felt he could not rely only on the reports that came in with the wounded at his hospital, but felt the need to go and investigate the situation. He wrote further news to Armstrong.

Dec. 6, 1920

I have been so rushed that I haven't written anyone for months, but have been busy itinerating and investigating atrocities. Our report on the high handed methods used by Japanese soldiery in this part of China is not yet complete. But on the arrival of Mr. Barker from one of the worst districts, we shall report completely.

Enclosed, you will find another copy of the "Norupawi" massacre concerning which I wish to add the following:

Miss Palethorpe, Miss Whitelaw and I went out the following day, and had worship service to comfort the remaining few people there. We distributed 100 yuan and a lot of American Red Cross material, mostly flannelette and clothing.

At this time I saw an old man aged 62 years, who had been quietly walking down a valley road when he was shot by some Japanese troops encamped on the hillside. He was shot in two places, but an operation later at our hospital saved his life.

Two days later on Nov. 5th, seventeen Japanese soldiers and three policemen (one a Korean) arrived at the village of Norupawi and began pulling down the walls of the burned houses and covering up as much as possible the hideousness of the place. All men of this village being dead, men from neighboring villages were ordered to gather in thirty-one of the victims from their temporary graves.

The day was so cold and the ground was covered with snow. Many of the bodies had been carried to distant family burial grounds, so that only thirteen bodies were recovered. The villagers were then forced to gather the remaining wood in the village, and the remaining sticks from the ruins of the houses, and pile the bodies on it. After which, the women and children looking on, the bodies were once more committed to the flames. (There's nothing more repulsive to Koreans than having their dead treated with disrespect.) The widows were then called into a room and rigorously questioned regarding their dead, after which they received a portion of ashes of the bodies. They were made to sign a paper stating that they would never again disturb the ashes of the dead.

The Koreans were warned that they must confess their sins to the Japanese. About a week ago a special Commission from Tokyo visited the spot, and at this time an old man stating that he was the principal leader of the Independence Movement in the district, presented the Colonel in charge with three banners and an ox. On the banners were inscribed the words, "Thanking the Japanese soldiers for the peace they have brought to our village, in protecting them against Independence soldiers."

After careful investigation, the only sin committed by the village was that several men from there helped to beat a Japanese spy who had been the cause of the death of several innocent Koreans the year before.

Our list of burnt villages now number over sixty, and it includes over 800 killed and over one thousand houses burnt. The majority of these people are innocent of any crime worthy of death, as most of them are accused of giving food to Independence soldiers, and then under force in many cases. At Chungsan, through clever tactics on the part of the Independence army, the Japanese in a heavily wooded area and during heavy fog, fired on each other killing 260, and wounding a great number.

The Japanese being so enraged at this untoward result, destroyed the whole of four villages, including men, women and children. Over one hundred are dead. How many more we cannot tell accurately.

I have a five-year-old boy from there, shot through the arm. His father is dead – shot. In one village there were only two women and two children left. There are several true reports of raping at this village. Fifteen churches and schools have been burnt. I have just visited a place where for ten li along the road there are the ruins of twenty-seven houses, ending in the Christian church. The oxen were burnt in three of the houses. All the people were robbed by soldiers previously, of money, watches, women's rings, and cloth in great rolls, also dishes, spoons etc.

At Sorangtong, 14 men were stood up in a trench, shot, and their bodies were piled on wood and kerosene, supplied by force from the relatives of the victims. The bodies were burned and the ashes were buried.

At Meridon now you will see another "Cloth Hall at Ypres" as the Korean Louvain stands with its tower a jumble of blackened plaster and bricks. The Academy, our Boy's school is just burned enough to look ghastly. I have photos of it. The old elder of the church there with tears in his eyes, said to me when I visited them, "The Lord stopped the wind from blowing, and thus saved the whole village."

The elder's house is a pile of ashes now. Excuse this attempt to put feeling to words.

"Sweet simple village by the plain,
Where oft at evening rose from scholars' games
The shouts of youth and energy.
But now, although you listen,
'Tis in vain,
For many who have shouted are now dead
And all the blooming flush of life has fled."

Thousands of Koreans have come in now and had their photos taken, and have sworn at the point of the bayonet to be loyal Japanese citizens. One village refused to come, and all the houses in that district were burned. A colporteur [Bible seller] from there, says he saw where nineteen bodies were chopped up like beef, beneath the trees on the mountainside.

A girl gathering potatoes, fled at the approach of soldiers and was shot. (Age 18) You have the copy of the murder of Lee Kun Sik one of our colporteurs.

The Japanese have wireless stations here, and aeroplanes to impress the Koreans. On Sunday, they shelled the hill behind our house from 10am to 1pm to show the Koreans how the guns work. We are fed right up with the injustice.

Mrs. Martin is going home in the spring.

Writing more later,
Regards,
SHM

That Sunday morning had been a terrifying time for Margaret and her crying, frightened children, but fortunately there were no more loud explosions near their house, after that day.

The missionaries kept sending a steady stream of information about the atrocities to the outside world.

A long report including Stan's and the other missionaries' eyewitness accounts appeared in *The Daily News* St. John's, Newfoundland.

Tokyo, Dec. 20, 1920

Details of alleged massacres of Koreans by Japanese troops, the burning of Korean villages and the destruction of native crops are given in statements from Canadian missionaries in the Chientao district of China, supplementing previous reports on this subject heretofore received.

One of the missionaries, Dr. S. H. Martin, of Newfoundland, a physician attached to the Canadian Presbyterian Mission at Yong Jung, who visited the village of Norupawi, on October 31, two days after the Japanese went through that district, states: The facts recorded below apply to the whole district of *Kando* or Chientao, in the southern part of the province of Kirin, China.

Japan, under the strongest protest from China has sent 15,000 men into this part of China with the seeming intention of wiping out of existence, if possible, the whole Christian community especially all young men.

Village after village is daily being methodically burned, and the young men shot, so that at present we have a ring of villages surrounding this city that have suffered from fire, or wholesale murder, or both. The facts below are absolutely accurate:

At daybreak a complete cordon of Japanese infantry surrounded the main Christian village of "Norupawi," and, starting from the top of the valley, set fire to the immense stocks of unthreshed millet, barley and straw, and then ordered the occupants of the house outside. In each case, as the father or son stepped forth, he was shot on sight, and as he fell on his face, perhaps only half dead, great piles of burning straw were thrown on top of him.

Bayonets Follow Bullets

I was shown the blood marks on the ground caused by the bayonet thrusts inflicted on the men as they strove to rise from the flames, in spite of the fact that they had been shot three times at close range. The bodies were soon charred beyond recognition. The mothers, wives and even the children were forced spectators of this treatment of all the grown males of the village. Houses were set on fire, and soon the whole country was full of smoke, which was plainly visible from this town. The Japanese soldiers then spread out and burned the houses of Christian believers in other villages all the way down the valley to the main road. Then they returned to their camp to celebrate the Emperor's birthday.

As we approached the nearby villages we found only women and children and some white-haired men. The women with young babies on their backs were walking up and down wailing.

I photographed ruins of nineteen buildings, among which were old men tearing their hair and raving, while mothers and daughters were recovering bodies or unburned treasures from the burning ruins. So many women were crying, and I was so angry at what I had seen, that I could not hold my camera steady enough to take a time exposure.

We have names and accurate reports of thirty-two villages where murder and fire have been used. One village had as many as 145 inhabitants killed. Houses have been burned with women and children in them. At Sorangtong fourteen men were shot, and their bodies destroyed with burning wood and oil. This is typical.

Rev. W. H. Foote, Canadian Presbyterian missionary at Yong Jung, names several villages in which the homes, schools or churches of Christian natives were burned. He said that in one of the churches, twenty-five persons were shot and the bodies burned. Those cases, he declares, are "absolutely authentic," the premises having been inspected by four missionaries and a customs official.

Quoting Koreans as his authority, he says that twenty-three persons were shot, and seven burned to death in their own houses, at Chen San, that eighty were shot at Tong Ja, and that these were all Christian villages.

"The soldiers and commanding officer who go to these places," asserted Mr. Foote, "as a general thing, have no conversation whatever with the people, but do their diabolical deeds and pass on. Ku Sei Tong is the only place where any reason was given to the people at all, for the action. A Korean accompanied the soldiers, and told the people that the officer said he had evidence that the owner of the house had collected money for patriotic purposes. If only the offenders suffered, even the Koreans would not seriously object; but it is because the perfectly innocent and helpless are done to death without even an opportunity to say a word in their own behalf, that the injustice and hardship appear.

Herded and Shot Down

Describing the action of the Japanese soldiers at Kan Chang, Rev. Foote said that the young men of that village were "herded in front of a Korean house, and without even a form of examination, shot down, twenty-five in all. Then the bodies were heaped together in two piles and covered with wood and burned. While the fuel was being placed on them, some of the wounded still were able to rise, but were bayoneted to the ground, and met their fate in the flames.

"I know these people well." Mr. Foote continued. "They live in an out-of-the-way glen. The land is not fertile, and firewood is scarce. They were a quiet hard working people, who struggled hard to make a living. Their church and school, their Bible and hymn books, their Sunday worship and above all their Saviour, were their joy. They were not patriotic soldiers and disapproved of the church taking part in politics."

Miss Emma M. Palethorpe of Ontario, a member of the Canadian Presbyterian Mission at Yong Jung tells in her statement of the execution of five men from the village of Suchilgo who, she says were led by the Japanese soldiers to the top of a hill, about three miles from Yong Jung and there put to death.

"In the top of the hill," she declares, "there is quite a large hollow, not visible from the road or village. The victims were made to sit at the bottom of this, where they were slashed with swords. It is reported by an eyewitness that two swords were broken and then the work was finished with bayonets. Then the loose earth was pulled down from the sides of the hollow to cover the mutilated bodies.

Japanese War Office Explanation

In answering inquiries at the Japanese War Office, Lieutenant Colonel Hata told an Associated Press correspondent that the number of Japanese troops employed in the Chientao affair was 5,000, not 15,000. Villages had been burned he said, but only in cases where the majority of inhabitants were known to be in league with the outlaws.

Referring to the charge that an organized attempt was made "to wipe out the whole Christian community," Colonel Hata said that it was possible that a majority of those who had been executed were Christians, but they were not punished for their religion, but for banditry and rebellion. No charge was made against the missionaries.

Colonel Hata, while admitting that harsh measures had been adopted, said bad conditions had existed in that district for a long time, owing to the unchecked activities of Chinese bandits, Korean outlaws, and Russian Bolsheviki. He said he was confident that the Japanese soldiers had not been guilty of the barbarities with which they had been charged.

About a month after the punitive expedition began, Margaret was at last able to write more news to her father.

Ruth 3 yrs. 6 mo.
Margie 1 yr. 10 mo.
Edna 4 mo.

Yong Jung, Manchuria
Nov. 20, 1920

Dear Papa:

I have had it on my mind to write Christmas letters and to get off a Christmas parcel to you, but have been so busy. This week we have had a shocking experience. One of our young nurses took bichloride, thinking it was aspirin for a headache, and died after four days of dreadful suffering. Stan was in the country at the time and I had the responsibility of the case for two days till he got back. It was the worst case I ever had. Then after he returned and took charge, when this girl was at her worst, one of our young married women came in labor, and I had an obstetric case too, as Doctor couldn't leave poor Songja for long at a time. It is the most nursing that I have done since little Margaret was sick. (She nearly died of pneumonia when she was 13 months old).

O, except Mrs. Hylton's baby. He is a fine fat boy now, and his name is Robert. Ruthie says our baby's name is "Enna Klakleen" – which is the nearest she can get to Edna Kathleen!

I have not had a letter from you for a long time. The mails are very poor. The "Good Housekeeping" and "Outlook" are coming to the correct address now. Mr. Hylton sent me a beautiful cloisonné bowl from Tientsin. I suppose as a reward for my services! But Mrs. H. has done so much for me. I think we are quite even.

I lose a good deal of sleep with the babies, so I don't feel like writing letters in the evenings, which is my only quiet time. I try to get a nap in the afternoon. Last week, of course our time was all broken up. I had to leave the children with the Koreans entirely and go on that poison case and to make matters worse, Miss Whitelaw (Head nurse) got sick the second day!

I am quite touched by the trust that the Koreans put in me when "Min Weesa" (Dr. Martin) is away. Our first medical assistant "Im" is one of the finest Christian men here, and the girl who took poison by mistake was his niece, and he was just heart-broken over her. She was conscious to the last, and he brought the Bible and held it for her to read, "For God so loved the world that He gave His only begotten Son that whosoever believeth on Him should not perish but have everlasting life. "Now," he said, "put away every other thought, and just think about Jesus and pray to Him," and then he prayed with her and his voice was choking with sobs. Their faith is so earnest and real, those who have a deeper knowledge of Christianity as he does. This is a sad Christmas letter, but it is just about our life this week.

The Japanese are evacuating this district by degrees. As public opinion in this country and fear of their standing with the foreign powers was too much for them. They have terrorized this district for a month now, and killed the Christians by scores, and burned their homes, churches and schools. Every night for a while we could see the light of burning villages on the horizon.

We feel that the crisis is over now. We see long columns of Japanese soldiers marching out towards the frontier. The Chinese are waking up to the situation and are undertaking to police the district, and are sending their own troops from Mukden now, so we are hoping for better times for our poor Koreans.

Mr. Barker and one of the lady missionaries [probably Emma Palethorpe] started out for a place 40 li [3 li to the mile] in the country yesterday to visit the Koreans and see what they could do to comfort them. Of course all class work and regular itinerating has been broken up on account of this trouble. They don't dare bother us. We have British extraterritorial rights here. They did arrest one foreigner, an American in Korea, named Shaw, but they let him go again in a hurry, also due to pressure from public opinion. Japan is finding that she must walk more warily as the eyes of the world are upon her.

My babies are well. Margaret is beginning to put words together, mostly in Korean. She said this morning, "All gone, pin: also "mama," "butter," "bad baby." Meaning Ruthie usually!

I can get passage for home in May if I want it, but cannot yet decide whether it is right to break up the home here. I am tired, of course, but would I be any better off in America is the question.

I went over across the river to see my obstetric case today as they took her home. There was a tremendous market today and I had to thread my way between bullock carts, loads of wood, piles of beans, bags of millet, peas and wheat, a great sight. I also called on Lydia Pak, my former amah, and saw her darling baby. It is kept beautifully clean. If I haven't done anything else, I taught one girl to take proper care of her children.

Must go to bed.
Lovingly,
Margaret

PS Stan is well; he went out with Mr. Barker for three days to a place 70 li away.

The closing month of the year had happier news for her father. Her letters tell the story.

Dec. 5, 1920

Dear Papa,

Please make this a family letter as I have been too rushed and too tired to write individual ones. Also please send it to St. John's. Stan says he hasn't written home for three months! They will be anxious, hearing how disturbed things are out here.

I have some quite interesting news to write. We have had a visitor in our home for the past ten days, a newspaperman from Chicago. I shall repeat this in several letters, in case some of my letters are lost. The visitor has been investigating conditions in *Kando* pretty thoroughly and is telegraphing reports to his paper, the *Chicago Daily News*, also writing articles for it. Now he says if you want to get hold of these articles (and he cannot tell exactly what date they will come out from this distance) to write the *Chicago Daily News* for the papers in which are Mr. Junius B. Wood's articles on Korea and Japan especially Chientao, which is the Chinese word for *Kando*. Mr. Wood is a very delightful man to meet, he has a magnificent head on his shoulders. He is a friend of Gregory Mason, the *Outlook's* around the world correspondent, so you can imagine the type of man Mr. Wood is, and our friends the Japanese can't "put anything over" on him. In fact I think they are rather afraid of him, and also they are afraid because the missionaries have been exposing their cruel treatment of the Koreans. Mr. Wood came in with a number of high officials from Tokyo who formed a committee to investigate the high-handed methods of the Japanese military in Chientao (*Kando*). Though Mr. W. was quite independent of said committee. According to Mr. W.'s investigations, and according to Stan's which were carried on quite separately, and tallied when compared, there have been 800 Koreans killed up here in the *Kando* district, and 1300 buildings, including schools and churches, burnt. At the beginning of the savage north *Kando* winter, some poor people are left without clothes or food. At this time of year, the great piles of grain representing the years labor and the winter food, are stacked about the houses, and in most cases these were all burned. You can get lots of details from the Chicago paper, which I haven't time to write. The native pastor of our church in this town was arrested last week and I think beaten, and asked many questions before he was finally released.

To come to family affairs, little "Edna Klakleen" (Kathleen) as Ruth calls her, is well and fat, weighs over twelve pounds, and is so happy and good. She knows me now, and wriggles with delight, and laughs when she sees me coming. She rides around on the amah's back wrapped up in blankets, Korean style. Margaret (23 mos.) cut a new tooth this week, the last but one of her baby teeth to come. She seems quite well of her cold now, though I shall have to watch her carefully this winter on account of her pneumonia last year. She talks a lot now, mostly Korean, and tries to say little funny sentences. The shoes Mr. Hylton got for us in Tientsin, she calls "Mary's papa shoes!" and pats them fondly. They are beautiful little shoes, nice leather.

Poor little Ruthie (3 yrs. 7 mos.) had another abscess in her ear, which broke this morning Dec. 5th. The last one was Aug. 22. She has been sick all this week. I hope she will be much relieved now, as it is draining freely.

Now don't bank on this too much as I said before, in fact I probably couldn't get across the Pacific alone with three babies, but I can get passage in May on a bat (yes bat is a good word) boat for Vancouver if I want it, and have reserved it for the present. On the other hand we are to have furnaces and steam heat in our houses next winter, so the chances are about even that I stay, and come with Stan in the spring of 1921.

Stan has been out in the country villages itinerating, and is also busy in the hospital. Rev. Foote is leaving Yong Jung for Canada in two weeks. He boarded with us for two years you know.

Dr. Grierson came up with me when I came from Wonsan, as far as Songjin. He is just back from California where he left his wife and children. [Mrs. Grierson died just fifteen days after this was written.]

Must stop now.
Love to all,
Margaret

Dec. 23, 1920

Dear Papa,

You can't imagine who we have as a guest in our house tonight! Last time I wrote you about Mr. Wood from *Chicago Daily News*. This time it is a Major Philoon from Auburn, Maine. Class of 1905, Bowdoin College! He is sent on a tour of investigation from the American Legation in Peking (Military Attaché). He was tickled to death when he discovered some Bowdoin College pictures in his room. So far, that is all I know about him. He knows some of our Putnam cousins who were with him in college.

Just a line tonight, for Christmas Eve is tomorrow night, and Christmas night I am playing for the Sunday School concerts in the two local churches. Mrs. Barker has translated and arranged for the Koreans to give a pageant, "The Light of the World from Bethlehem's Manger," which she says was given at the great Tokyo SS Convention. So tomorrow, and next day will be very full. I am having the Christmas tree for the foreign children at our house Christmas afternoon, before the evening concert.

Stan's father will be sending you some newspaper accounts of things out here. Ask him for them. Without fail, write to *Chicago Daily News* and ask them to send you all copies containing anything by Mr. Junius B. Wood who was here two weeks ago.

This Major Philoon from Auburn knows Dr. Lincoln of Shanghai.

Babies pretty well now. Margaret has cut her last double tooth and the little one (Edna 5 mos.) has not started in cutting yet! Ruth (3 yrs 7 mos) is much better but her poor ear is still running. She knows most of her letters and with assistance can spell 'dog'.

Mr. Joly the Customs man is having a party for us on Monday evening the 27th. Our guest is to be here until the 28th.

Lots of love from,
Margaret

The Night After Christmas, 1920

Dear Papa,

I was made very happy yesterday by the arrival of three home letters, one from Cousin Anna, one from Aunt Addie and one from you. So you see if you write on our wedding anniversary it reaches me in time for Christmas (Nov. 4 – Dec. 25) The mails are late this year.

Major Philoon is still with us. We had a very jolly Christmas party at our house yesterday, with guests who would otherwise have had no Christmas celebration. Besides Major Philoon, there was his Chinese friend Mr. Tao, a very intelligent, educated man. There was Mr. Joly the British Customs man who is to be married in the spring, and a nice young Russian girl who has recently come to town. Her brother is also a Customs officer.

We had a tree, and Mr. Barker was Santa Claus for the little ones – Mrs. Hylton's and mine. They were made happy with some nice dolls and blocks. We had a sandwich and coffee supper, and hurried down to the church for the concert. But there was such a crush of people in the church, and the crowd surged from the back down on the children packed like sardines on the floor at the front of the church. There was a danger of someone getting hurt and we had to give it up. There were hundreds of people in the church! The school teachers ordered the boys out by one of the doors at the side of the pulpit, which relieved the congestion, and then the girls were dismissed in order. They were awfully disappointed. We had given a very successful concert in the little church across the valley Christmas Eve, and had hoped to do even better in the big church in Yong Jung. The Major and Mr. Joly went down with us for a "sight see." As we were in the very front facing the great congregation, it gave them an idea of our people that we have to work with. Mrs. Barker and the ladies worked so hard training them for the concert it was too bad! Poor Mrs. Barker is in bed today with a cold and fatigue. You will be sorry to hear of the death of Mrs. Grierson in California on Dec. 20th. A cable came and we heard on the 26th. Now he has to go back again to his four motherless girls in Los Angeles. Poor man! We are all so sorry for them all. Mrs. Grierson had expected to return to Korea in May.

Major Philoon's visit has been a great treat to us. He knows the Rileys, Sue Winchell and some Houlton boys, also Dr. Lincoln of Shanghai. He says there are a lot of Bowdoin men in banking business in the Orient, due to General Hubbard. He was head of the International Bank you know. The Major must be a very capable officer as he has had important missions here in the East, and during the war he was Provost Marshal of the city of Washington DC – had charge of guarding all the great public buildings! With all his honors, he is a very modest and charming gentleman, and quite young. Stan is greatly taken with him. You may be proud to know that it is largely through my husband's efforts that news of these Japanese atrocities has been published in the papers and the world had come to know of it, and these various commissions have been sent in to investigate. Also, to a certain extent, the burning and murdering of the Koreans has been stopped. We are in communication with the British Consul at Mukden and with various papers in the Orient.

The better class of Japanese repudiate the action of the military here.

Must stop and write a Christmas note to Aunt Addie and Cousin Anna. You notice I'm sending this by Chinese post, as they say the Japanese censor all our mail.

The babies are feeling much better from their colds. We have two more Russian stoves built this winter, and hope to keep warm. We had many lovely Christmas gifts, and so did the babies.

Be sure to write the *Chicago Daily News* for Mr. Wood's accounts of the events here.

Lovingly,
Margaret

At last the tumultuous year 1920 was over. Now the little settlement on English Hill faced the future wondering what the New Year would bring.

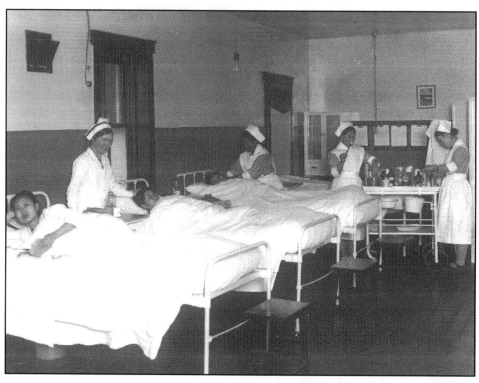

Lenora Armstrong with Korean nurses. Women's Ward in St. Andrew's Hospital in Lungchingtsun, China.

XIV

Aftermath

It was late on a winter evening in 1921, when the phone rang at No. 4 house, the doctor's home.

"*Min Uisa*, we have an emergency here in the hospital. It's the little five-year-old you admitted today. We think he is dying. Will you come quickly?"

The man who called was his chief assistant, one of the staff members on night duty. Throwing on his clothes, Stan raced out into the dark, and down to the hospital. Here he continues the story:

> "I found the child in a private room properly isolated, breathing his last, with long gasps that sucked in it's little ribs with each inspiration, as the larynx was occluded because of the diphtheria. I simply mentioned the word "intubation;" the two doctors disappeared, and came back in less than five minutes with all the necessary instruments, sterile gowns, masks etc. Each man knew his own position and his own work. In another five minutes, the almost dead baby took a long sweet breath through a silver tube in its larynx, and after coughing up some membrane, fell into a refreshing sleep, and slept all night. This child is now at home and is the delight of a young Christian couple.
>
> Ten years ago, these doctors as heathen, might have put "the needle" into the child's throat, or burned it with hot irons to let out the evil spirits, whereas now, each man knowing his work and doing it quickly, a child with but a few minutes to live, is saved by a simple but delicate operation. Certainly if there's anything worth while it is the training of a young Christian Korean or Chinese person to be able to help his own people with modern medicine.
>
> While I am proud of our hospital, I am more than pleased with the transformation of long-haired heathen boys into bright, clever young doctors and assistants, whose movements express kindness, and from whose faces one can easily see that

they know Christ. The example of the diphtheria case shows this well." [Although customs were changing rapidly, there were still some boys and young men with long hair which they wore in a braid down their back.]

Early in the year 1921, all was quiet although there were over a thousand Japanese soldiers in the district. They were gradually being replaced by Japanese military police stationed in fifteen garrisons.

A revival swept through the area with hundreds of new believers coming in to the churches. In the town of Yong Jung, a town of eight to ten thousand, there were about a thousand Christians. On Sunday mornings about five hundred of them attended the church by the Mission Compound.

The new Eunjin Boys' Academy was almost completed and was to open in April. It was a two-story building with a fine, bright basement just across from the Mission houses. The missionary children would later have a school room there. Stan was concerned that coal stoves would ruin the inner walls of the school, so he wrote to the Mission Board requesting steam heat for the building.

He worked steadily on improving the hospital. He supervised putting in the hot water heating system, and the hot and cold water plumbing system. He added electric bells and a telephone between his house and the hospital. An operating table and instrument cases, sterilizer and pump were ordered to be paid for out of the $14,000 gift from the Orillia Church in Canada and the St. John's church in Newfoundland. The equipment was nearly all in place. Stan made the dispensary into an isolation ward and planned for a septic tank at once. There was a plan to repair and put up a better fence and do some grading.

In the meantime two of the barns for the missionary families' cows were burned and had to be replaced.

In February news came to Lincoln Rogers, Margaret's father in Maine, from Rev. Foote in Canada.

My dear Mr. Rogers,

I just reached home after leaving Yong Jung December 16th. I know you are anxious for news.

I have not received any letters from Dr. Martin, or others in Yong Jung, since I came away, but do not think they are in any personal danger. The itinerating missionaries on the station were visiting country and village congregations without any inconvenience.

Through all the unrest in Korea during the last ten years, the Christian church has certainly shown a splendid spirit and has made remarkable progress. This progress has been not only in increased numbers, but also in a higher Christian life, and in following loftier ideals. I have never heard it hinted that the work of the missionaries and the Korean leaders might be retarded by the action of the Japanese – rather there is an impelling power in just the opposite direction.

Your good and much loved daughter, Mrs. Martin was in good health when I left. You quite understand that with three little tots, that she has not the strength and energy she had when she first went out to engage in mission work

Mrs. Martin is very wise and steady, and so does not have the worries that shake the nerves of some people in trying or lonely surroundings.

I hope to hear from you again. I found my wife and the five children quite well. I hope to be home nearly a year.

With kindest regards,
W. R. Foote

While on furlough Rev. Foote gave a report of the Japanese atrocities in Manchuria, to the Federal Council of Churches in New York. Mr. Armstrong wrote of it to Margaret's father, on March 11, 1921.

Rev. Foote's report called forth expressions of indignation and horror from many present, and questions were asked. "We are following up the matter and though we do not know what will be the result of our dealing with the Japanese government, yet Japan is very anxious to have the Anglo-Japanese Alliance renewed. What we want is assurance that there will be no more interference with peaceful religious work by missionaries, nor with Koreans becoming Christians and practicing their Christian faith, unhampered by the antagonism of police and soldiers."

Rev. Foote had quite another session with some Federal Council leaders and Consul General Kumasoki and Mr. Shirakami, Secretary to Governor General Saito in Korea, who was visiting New York.

Here, they incorrectly told the godly white-haired pioneer missionary, Rev. Foote, that the crimes were committed by "bandits and disaffected Koreans," and the churches and schools were used by Korean "rebels" as centers from which to carry on their anti-Japanese belligerent campaign.

They also asked Rev. Foote if he had himself seen the shootings and the cremations of the killed, and of the still-living wounded Koreans. He acknowledged that he had not, that he had relied upon Korean statements. To this, the Japanese replied that Korean statements are proverbially unreliable and cannot be accepted without further investigation.

In answer to the request for steam heating for the Eunjin academy Stan received an alarming suggestion, "We have received your request but cannot vote any more money at present for the academy. We suggest you pay for it with the money from Orillia and the St. John's NFLD churches."

This money was designated and already spent for the hospital. The remaining $5,000 Stan had planned to use for his greatly needed X-ray machine he planned to purchase on furlough. This problem would have to be worked out, but added anxiety to Stan as he faced life and death situations daily in the hospital.

Stan wrote to Armstrong:

I have just returned from Hoiryung where I have been doing a medical examination of the staff, which together with that of the station I will soon send to the Board for consultation. We are in pretty good shape. Miss Cass is doing too much night work and I am reducing it. The Hoiryung nurse, Miss Miriam Fox and I spent most of Sunday seeing patients. One afternoon I saw 35 patients. There is a well-equipped Japanese hospital there, but somehow they want to see the Christian doctor or go to the English hospital at Yong Jung.

I have been so busy writing to the Peking and Tientsin Times and the Kobe Chronicle that I didn't get time to write home. At the time of the Punitive Expedition I spent hours every day informing the newspapers and the British Minister at Peking by letter and telegram, of the happenings here. When Norupawie was burning I sent a telegram to the Consul at Mukden "Japanese troops burning churches, schools, houses advise Tokyo." This message was sent to our Minister there, and was the beginning of British protests.

I am out of printing paper else I should send you some snaps of the village of Norupawie while it was still burning.

Our mails are censored to pieces by the Japanese. We rarely get anything. It takes months for a note to get from here to Hoiryung, one day's trip. Four important registered letters in the Hoiryung P.O. were held for two months. All our mail is sent to Seoul or Anam, a military station near Hoiryung, for censorship. I received a letter from Montgomery Ward, one with a tissue paper window in it. Through the window only a blank could be seen. On opening it up, it was addressed to me. I sent my assistant to the P.O. and told him to tell the Postmaster General that when he censors our letters to please put the contents back as he found them.

Mr. Barker, sending an important letter, showed the Postmaster the contents before he sealed it, and told him to send it through and not keep it for ages. Please report this to the Ottawa Minister of Foreign Affairs. We are fed up with being treated like enemy subjects when Japan and Britain are supposed to be allies. One would think we are at war.

When news of the atrocities became widely known, the force of world opinion on Japan caused a marked change of attitude in members of the Japanese military in Manchuria.
Stan's letter to Armstrong continues.

Although there is no one they hate like your humble servant, I have been wined and dined for the last two months at intervals. General Higashi sent me an elaborate telegram from Hoiryung thanking me for all my kindness to him. We were dined twice by Col. Midzumachi, the one who wrote the letter accusing the missionaries of complicity in the Korean Independence Movement.

We were invited to dinner with the Japanese Consul and General Higashi. I just got out of a dinner by the commanding General Ishobayashi yesterday, by going off to Hoiryung.

Colonel Komimura came up from Seoul and presented us with a tin of biscuits and Cadbury's chocolates, which the Korean children on the compound appreciated. Colonel Saito, a Japanese attached to the Kirin government (forced upon it) gave us all very expensive presents. "Old Michumachi gave us 100 yuan for the hospital which was promptly used to relieve survivors of Imperial Japanese slaughter at the hands of his own troops. I received a post card from Washington from the former Japanese Consul General here, sending best wishes.

They all know they are in the wrong, and they try in this way to be friendly, while the Japanese local press has us all crawling on our "tummies," and living out here because of the great wealth we can get out of our mission work, etc.

The Japanese have done quite a lot here, which will add to the laurels of their Imperial army, but the most dastardly of all was the murder of a Korean reporter who came in here from Seoul with a proper passport from the Korean government.

He passed through Norupawie on his way. What he saw there made him weep. He paid a visit to me – a young man of twenty-eight, dressed well in a blue serge suit. I told him to be careful. He, speaking perfect Japanese went to the Consulate and protested against what he had seen. The military told him to get out!

Saturday night at 8pm, Japanese cavalry called at his hotel, and took him off in the direction of Kookjaga 40 li away. He never reached this place. The Japanese Captain in charge of the escorts said, "He was killed by Hunghutze" (Chinese bandits). He of course was quietly murdered as he knew too much and loved his country.

Oh! Weep for those who weep beside the Tumen's frozen stream.
Whose homes are desolate, whose land a dream.
Weep for the sacred church, a gutted shell now where their God has dwelt, the godless dwell.
Men of the wandering feet and weary breasts,
Where can your spirits find a rest?
Your women true, and men as brave.

Mankind has a country, Korea the grave.

It's pathetic to meet these poor people wandering over these cold bleak hills, and plains, persecuted and beaten, worried and slaughtered like helpless sheep. Certainly outside of Christian pastors they have no leaders at all.

By the way my father has been speaking a lot about our work in the Presbyterian church in St. John's, NFLD, and I think it was due to this that they gave such a good donation. My father will be an "elder" yet if he's not careful.

I hope to go on furlough next year, and as our hospital is now quite well equipped, I wish very much to study if possible. I am anxious to see good up-to-date surgery of all sorts, but am specializing in tubercular bone work with radiography connected with it. As a doctor in China I have a very good chance of getting one of the Rockefeller fellowships. I am writing to Peking regarding it.

Mrs. Martin is pretty well worn out with three years of Japanese aggression in this part of the world. She may go on early furlough. Her father is over seventy and is anxious to see her and is much worried. She wishes to spend more than a year with him. He has seen very little of her since she was a child. She is the only child, her mother having died when she was six years old.

With best wishes to Dr. Mackay and yourself,

Sincerely yours,
SHM

In that winter of 1921 more illness came to the doctor's household. Margaret wrote to her father:

We can't get through January without sickness it seems. Little Edna, six months old, is very ill with erysipelas. No one knows where she got such an infection. She has been sick a week. She's running a high fever and is very weak. I will write again as soon as she is better. I have not had any mail from you for a long time. We have good proof that the Japanese are holding up our mail lately. I haven't written you since Major Philoon of Bowdoin College made his welcome visit.

I'm sending all mail now via Chinese post. It will take a little longer but is safer.

Margaret's dear friend Rebecca Barker added to the letter.

Dear Mr. Rogers,

I am going to finish this letter for Margaret while she has a little rest, and I watch by the baby a little while, while the baby is sleeping. We are all hoping she is over the worst and on the road to recovery.

We have had a lovely mild winter. There has been a lot of sickness however, and Dr. Martin is certainly kept busy. Ruthie (3 ½) and little Margaret (age 2) both had colds, but are better now. They are dear little girlies and you will greatly enjoy them when you see them. Ruthie is as active as a butterfly almost, and talks Korean better than we grown-ups do, I fear. Dr. and big Margaret are well and have done lots of good since coming to this far off land. Many of the new believers come in through the hospital. I hope you are well and that 1921 will bring you much of joy and peace.

Yours sincerely,
Rebecca Barker

Another letter from Margaret to Aunt Addie that winter was more cheerful.

Ruthie has gone to church with Stan, and Margaret age two is sitting on the floor beside me, looking at pictures in the Mother Goose book. She pointed to Jack and Jill and said "Dat's Wootie" "Dats Margie" "Dats Kitty." Then she saw the beautiful baby "on the tree top" in a little birdies nest with two wee birdies sitting on the edge, and said in Korean that the baby's hand was *apoo* meaning hurt. I think she thought the birdie had bitten it. Then she laid herself down on top of the book to comfort the baby! This morning little Edna was asleep in her basket, and the room was very quiet. When I came in, I found Margaret sitting beside her so still, and smiling at her.

I try to write down the funniest little things they say and do. It is so easy to forget, and much of it is in their funny baby Korean talk.

The executive decided that it would be most unwise for me to attempt the journey home alone this year with three babies, so we are planning to come as early next year as possible.

I am planning for my garden. I'm going to try currants and raspberry bushes this year. I get them from a Yokohama nursery.

You asked if my <u>courage</u> was getting low! Well when it does, I just have a spell of loving my three precious babies, and get cheered up pretty quick. I work to the limit of my strength, but if I were home I should probably have to work beyond my limit with no servants. I have some good ones now, only four!

My good cook Tabitha runs the kitchen and pretty nearly runs me too! She helps oversee the new amahs and the man of all work, (the outside man) who tends the cow, and builds the fires, scrubs and washes. I have two good amahs at last, one a young married woman whose husband is a political exile –"Oksuni." She is as smart and clean as Lydia used to be. The other is a nice young girl of sixteen who is good with baby Edna – her name is Sungsiri.

We still have our graduate nurse Miss Lee, and Miss Jessie Whitelaw for the hospital. Stan is proud of the fine operating room with the big handsome sterilizer, and table, as good as any in a hospital at home.

The political situation is more quiet here now. The Koreans suffered so badly last fall. They have no desire to start any more demonstrations at present. They are beginning bravely to try and rebuild their burned churches already.

With much love,
From Margaret

On February 4th, Margaret wrote to her father:

Dear Papa,

Your letters of Nov. 24th, Dec. 13th and 20th all came in a bunch last week. Hereafter write to our Chinese address.

As for any personal danger to us, you need not worry, the Japanese are too careful of their British Alliance to do any harm to British subjects. The Associated Press clipping which you sent, dated Tokyo Dec. 3rd, is entirely distorted, and you have doubtless by this time heard from Mr. Armstrong, of the repudiation by the Board of the charges against the missionaries. We had nothing to do with the political movement, and we only protested against the atrocities and wholesale slaughter of innocent persons. Mr. Junius B. Wood you remember was here and gave a full report of it in the *Chicago Daily News*. That Associated Press article you sent was pure "camouflage" lies from one end to another. Mr. Barker and Stan have been all over the district and have seen and heard from the Koreans their story, and have given out facts the Japanese are only too anxious to deny and hush up.

I am sorry you are anxious about us, but there is really no need, for the Board would recall us if there was any danger. There are now nineteen foreigners here including women and six children. We are all perfectly well and happy. Little Edna is very much better, though she had a hard time, poor lamb.

This week we have had as guests, two ladies from Hoiryung, new missionaries just out from Canada. So you see the country is quite safe when ladies can travel around like that.

I am wondering about our furlough, what kind of help can I have with the children? I don't want you to be all worn out looking after us. It is one strenuous job especially watching Ruthie.

Please tell Mrs. Minot we make more of her sponge cake in our house than any other kind! She gave me her recipe long ago.

I think you are standing 'life's knocks' very bravely dear, from your good letters. Only you mustn't get excited about us. Stan has a "long head" on him and will look out for us.

We have steam heat and plumbing installed for most of the hospital, and hope to have steam heat for our houses by another year. Our Russian stoves give even heat.

I have a handsome set of flower stands for my bay window in the dining room. There, I have geraniums, parsley, a cactus, and three rose bushes. One rose I had before, but now I have a crimson one from the missionaries in Hamheung and a yellow one from Wonsan.

I bought soft coal yesterday, 5,000 lbs. for 14 yen -- $7.00 – soft coal we burn in the Russian stoves. You remember we store the coal in our big cellar.

Must go to bed.
Lovingly,
Margaret

Mr. Armstrong in Toronto, and Mr. S. Shimizu the Japanese Consul General in Ottawa, exchanged a steady stream of correspondence. Armstrong sent all the reports that came from the missionaries, and the Consul sent them to Japan. Although Mr. Armstrong was grieved by the atrocities, he was mindful that he had to keep a civil tone, because the future of the mission work depended on it. The Japanese could shut down all the mission schools in Korea and Manchuria if they wished to. They did shut down the Boys' Academy in Yong Jung for a short while.

The thorniest problem was when Col. Midzumachi wrote the letter accusing the missionaries of complicity in the Korean Independence Movement. The Japanese finally responded that the letter was merely the man's personal opinion.

Stan's next letter to Armstrong in March 1921 concerned hot water furnaces for the three missionary houses there. The single ladies' house plan had already been sent to their Board. He gave the many reasons in favor of hot water systems including the need for hot water for baths.

At Hoiryung because of the lack of proper bath facilities, three missionaries have been without a real good bath in six months. Good sanitation will reduce our "going home for treatment." The great advantage of a furnace here is the help against fire. For example today it's blowing clouds of dust and is very cold. A fire in the Scott house would probably take the four houses, and we haven't our "worldly goods" insured. We have five extinguishers in all the buildings, and have a hose in the hospital. I'm making a hydrant for the four houses this spring. If we're not able to obtain an expert to put in the furnaces I could superintend putting them in myself. I have sent the plan for the Academy steam plant to Mr. Scott.

Everything is quiet. There are about fifteen hundred Japanese soldiers in this district, a hundred new ones last week. The Japanese residents are increasing. There is a new three hundred thousand yuan bank, and a new Oriental Development Building this year. The Japanese are certainly not going to give up this province of Chientao unless they must.

I turned five armed Japanese signalmen off the compound Monday. They were insolent. They entered through a gate, which has in Chinese characters "No admittance except on business." I reported them to the Japanese Consul. The soldiers were reproved. They said they "didn't know."

In March of 1921 Stan sent a pamphlet to his supporters summarizing the work at that time. He starts it with: "Does this interest you?"

The writer wishes to take this opportunity of expressing on behalf of the Canadian Presbyterian Mission of Korea his heartfelt thanks for the many gifts for our work and for prayer, without which we could not do the little we have tried to do.

How the work is done.

This year the work of the hospital has almost doubled. The opening up of a new dispensary in the city proper, has added a thousand more outpatients per month to our total outpatient department, and we are now having an average of ninety patients per day in both outpatient departments.

Because of disturbed conditions, it was natural that the hospital, which supplies the needs of the Chientao, (*Kando*) district, should have amongst its patients many gunshot cases. This being a Christian hospital we take in and treat all sufferers, irrespective of their nationality or political views. We have wounded Chinese and

Korean soldiers now, together with a sick Japanese policeman in the hospital at the same time.

A great joy to the work, is the way our young Korean and Chinese assistants have developed into quite capable workers. These men have studied English textbooks on medicine and surgery with me, and this, with continuous practical training daily, has made them quite efficient.

One of the Korean assistants runs the city dispensary with the assistance of a dresser, and a graduate nurse. A Bible woman is also there. The other Korean assistant takes charge of the hospital in the doctor's absence, and sees and treats many of the outpatients. These men can treat all minor cases, and do all of the simple operative work, such as small amputations, etc.

Equipment

This year we have installed our hospital heating plant, and the hot and cold water system is complete. This work has been done by the surgical dressers and assistants under the doctor's direction, and in this way we have saved quite a little money, as to get experts from Seoul would be quite expensive.

After the last patients are seen in the afternoon, the assistants get into some cast-off Chinese uniforms sent us by the American Red Cross, and are soon busy connecting up pipes or digging for a septic tank. Koreans need to be taught the dignity of labor, but no one on our staff so far has been trouble with a "high collar" (Too proud for manual labor)

Results

One of our best mechanics came to us, a Chinese cancer patient, having walked from Siberia, begging as he came. At first he seemed inoperable and I told him so. My Korean assistant came later and said, "If he doesn't get his operation, he says he will commit suicide." I said, "Better die on the table than that." After the operation, he recovered rapidly and is quite well. He is now, as I write, working underneath the women's ward section, connecting up a bath with hot water. He is well educated and has become a good Christian.

It would take too much time to tell of many cases that became Christians, but as I have said before, "Our VITAL statistics are registered in heaven."

Statistics
Outpatients during the year   22,000
Inpatients   380

Operations under chloroform	418
Operations under local anesthetic including eye operations	100
Number of visitors to the sick	2,584
Out-calls to city and villages	1,496
Tracts and gospels sold and distributed	6,000
Definite decisions for Christ, many of whom are now in the churches	196

Stan closed with sincere thanks to the St. Andrew's Presbyterian Church in Orillia, Canada, and the St. Andrew's Presbyterian Church of St. John's, Newfoundland.

As plans were being made for the next year's furlough, Stan applied for a Rockefeller fellowship to study at that time.

The China Medical Board wrote to the Presbyterian Mission Board in Canada regarding this, to which, Dr. R. P. Mackay responded.

> We have no more ardent and successful missionary than Dr. Martin in Korea, China or any other country. He is altogether a rare man, and I am delighted to think that such help as the China Medical Board gives is possible.

A three hundred-dollar scholarship was granted him.

In the mean time, Rev. Foote on furlough was having important consultations with the Consul General of Japan at Ottawa. He spent some two hours with him. He was able to give a full report of the atrocities in Manchuria. The consul seemed to be surprised that the Korean pastors, elders and many leaders have always been opposed to violence. He had been told just the opposite was true.

The Consul asked about the report that the Presbyterians and Methodists gave the Japanese government much more trouble than the Baptists. Rev. Foote explained that Mr. Fenwick had been the only Baptist missionary working in Korea, and had not been there for several years.

He continued. "The English Church Mission is a small mission with headquarters at Seoul. The Catholic Mission goes quietly, is opposed to schools and has developed no strong leaders. The Methodist and Presbyterian churches are energetic and have spread all over Korea. Most of the private schools are in these missions, and as lawyers, doctors, and especially as teachers and ministers there are many who are able leaders."

When the Consul General asked what Rev. Foote would advise, Rev. Foote said, "Here I was careful and told him I took no part in the political issue. However I said that if Baron Saito's promised reforms were made good in both letter and spirit, I thought it would do something to relieve the situation. Then I added that the Japanese police should take a different attitude to the Koreans, and that the Japanese should not discriminate against them but treat the Koreans as Japanese. I advised freedom of worship, of speech, of the press and some share in the government of their own country."

Rev. Foote was asked many questions which he answered as diplomatically as possible, and he came away hoping that the consultation would lead to a better understanding of the difficult situation.

The courtesy with which Rev. Foote was received by the Japanese Consul General at Ottawa was indicative of Japan's change of attitude in the Korean situation. Also, there was new hope for Koreans and the missionary body alike, that Baron (or Admiral) Saito the new Governor General, would bring about change for the good.

At Yong Jung, the Mission Station was pleased to have a visit from the British Consul stationed at Mukden. He came to check on the Japanese doings. Stan gave him a tour of the hospital. The medical work impressed him greatly and he gave twenty yuan as a gift towards it.

The weather was improving with the approach of spring, and the children were able to spend more time out-of-doors. Margaret had minor surgery, and while recovering wrote more letters. She was so pleased that the journey they would be taking to Wonsan in July, would be so much easier this year.

She wrote to her Aunt Addie:

> I expect to ride in a sedan chair in state to the railroad this year. It is only a day's journey by road, now the railroad has come half way from Hoiryung on the Korean side of the Tumen river. It used to be two days by cart, an awful trip. So we are very thankful that it is so near. From there on it is easy, with a good railway and steamers. We shall have quite a large group with all the Yong Jung folks and all the Hoiryung missionaries. The next time after that, when we cover the road we shall be going on furlough!!
>
> You say that far away calamities don't affect you, and you are more touched by my personal troubles, my sick baby. Thank you dear for your kind sympathy.
>
> I don't know why I should wish to make the Korean problems too real to you, but just suppose for instance that your Katie's husband was bayoneted to death without trial, and for no reason save that he was the chief man of the village. Suppose Katie was beaten and her clothes torn from her, and she was put in prison, wouldn't you feel it? That has happened to our people, and if the missionaries had not protested and brought things to the notice of the outside world, worse things might have happened. The world is watching now. We had a visit from the British Consul of Mukden, and two weeks ago the British Vice Consul from Dairen (Port Arthur) was here to see what the Japanese were up to. He said in a frank talk to the Japanese Consul in this town that the missionaries could not do work with the Koreans unless they were friendly and sympathetic with them, but we did nothing to encourage them politically.
>
> We have appreciated our fellow missionaries the Barkers so much. Their one great sorrow is that they have no children. Dear Mrs. Barker, her eyes fill with tears sometimes. My little Margaret told her she was "Margie Barka," much to Mrs. Barker's delight though there was a "tug at the heart strings" too.

Stan continued his correspondence with the Mission Board concerning the order for hot water furnaces for the compound houses and the Boys' Academy.

> You have suggested using some of the hospital money for the Academy furnace. Mr. Fraser, while here, added up approximately the amounts of money used from the Orillia grant, and we find that practically all of it has been used up, both here and at home leaving only St. John's money, which is not enough to buy and install the hospital lighting and x-ray. This St. John's money was sent us mainly as the result of lectures etc. by my father and I have thanked the church for the money and their good will. The roof of the hospital, which is cheap Montgomery Ward material should be renewed. It now leaks in twenty places.
>
> We should like to have an asbestos tile roof rather than have to replace the roof every five or six years. The isolation ward has to be equipped and heated, and our Bacteria Lab has no equipment but a microscope. Our septic tank works well, so does the water system.
>
> At present I teach Physical Drill, Chemistry, and Physics in the Academy, and am most anxious to help it, but I feel until we have had the very necessary work done for the hospital that it would be better for the Academy to wait.
>
> All of the missionaries of Yong Jung and Hoiryung have been medically examined. Mrs. Barker is now quite well.
>
> I see that Mr. Scott (on furlough) has his MA. Now, Mr. Armstrong, I think it's nothing short of madness for men whose constitutions are so far below par as his was, to do extra study, when he should have spent most of his time in recuperating. I had him with me for two years, and its not an MA he needs as much as a good talking to, followed by six months in a sanatorium. (Not as a result of the talking).
>
> I know a Queen's man who got the gold medal in Philosophy, and died a year later from pulmonary tuberculosis.

The welcome summer came, and Margaret and the children made the trip to Wonsan for the Mission Council and vacation. This time it was easier in every way. Stan used some of his vacation time for a special tour. Margaret wrote of it to her father, from Wonsan August 24th.

> Stan has been away over two weeks. He had a fine time in Vladivostok. The city is a great sight – cathedrals, warships, and a Korean, Japanese and Russian population. The ladies of the party were staying in a house recently vacated by an Admiral, and are having meals with the YMCA workers.

Before Stan had been gone a week, the Koreans at Yong Jung began telegraphing for him to come back to *Kando*. It seems, as we learned afterwards, that our best Korean nurse has been arrested in connection with the death of that nurse last fall. (She took the wrong medicine.) I had a telegram from Hoiryung saying he expected to arrive there that night. So he is safely home from Russia. The children and I will stay here a little longer.

We had a visit to France a couple of weeks ago. A French warship was in the Wonsan harbor for ten days, and two boatloads of us went off to see her. We left the Wonsan Beach shore and went around the point to the Wonsan harbor. You know it's the third largest natural harbor in the world.

As we approached the ship we sang the "Marseillaise":

Allons enfants de la patrie, la jour de gloire est arrive! Marchons, marchons! etc. and the sailors lined the railings and applauded.

It was almost like a visit home, to see so many foreign faces. The officers were most courteous, and showed us all about. We saw the great guns, and anti-aircraft guns and the solid steel turret from which the ship is controlled during gun engagement. She was an old cruiser, but had acted as convoy to merchant ships from New York during World War I. She had 150 Alsace Lorrainers on board who spoke mostly German.

I am feeling very well indeed, and the daily sea bathing is doing me so much good. I don't go in when it is rough or <u>alone</u> at any time, as we have had a sad lesson this summer, a missionary child, Marjorie Robb had drowned. In the mornings, sometimes it is perfectly calm and we can swim or float as much as we like. My swimming is improving, and I have learned to float and try swimming under water. Also since my operation I can walk long distances and do all sorts of things.

Miss Elizabeth Keith the English artist has come for a visit, and I must stop now. She is as dear as ever.

Lovingly,
Margaret

In the fall of 1921, Stan was still concerned about the funds he had raised for his X-ray machine. As Mission Secretary, Margaret wrote to the Mission Board.

Regarding the use of $4,000 Hospital Funds of the grant of $5,000 from St. John's, NFLD for the use of the academy at Yong Jung; we should like you to notice in the enclosed statement passed by the station and the mission in March, that the grant from the Orillia Church has been used or is being used at the present time. This leaves only the $5,000 out of the $19,000 and this was appealed for and granted especially for x-ray purposes. Dr. Martin has had five years experience installing and operating x-ray machines before going to the mission field. He has been looking forward to having it installed in our hospital, as 50% of his cases are tubercular bone cases in which he is specializing in his studies at home next year, and he intended bringing this outfit out with him on his return to the field.

The use of this x-ray money while so necessary to the academy at this time should be considered as a loan from Hospital Funds, as otherwise Dr. Martin's scope of appeal will be removed. The enclosed church bulletin shows that it is being used for this purpose.

After consultation with the engineering staff of the Rockefeller Plant and Dr. Hodges in charge of the X-ray Department when Dr. Martin was in Peking, the type of apparatus was agreed upon and a generator sufficient to light the whole station at the same cost as it would light the hospital alone is being installed this year by Dr. Martin. The engine of the lighting plant has been obtained at 25% discount because of its being used for Mission purposes. While on vacation this year Stan installed the x-ray apparatus of the Ivey Songdo Hospital in Korea for Dr. Reid of the American Methodist Mission.

Sincerely yours,
Margaret Martin
Station Secretary

Dr. Mackey responded with a very kind letter.

By Sept. 18th, 1921, Margaret and the children had returned from Wonsan. She wrote of her trip to her father.

Dear Papa,

We arrived home the 9th of September after a safe and comfortable journey. We spent the 6th in Songjin as the steamer lay there all day, and the children all had naps and three square meals. We had a nice visit with our missionaries there. We went to the Grierson home for a few minutes where Dorothy, age 21 is so bravely taking the place of the dear lost mother.

Mr. McMullin of Hoiryung met us the next day at Seishin (Chongjin) and took us to Hoiryung, and Stan arrived that evening from Yong Jung. The next day was Bruce Macdonald's birthday and they persuaded us to stay over. The children had "high jinks" all day, they play together very nicely.

Next week the Frasers are coming to Yong Jung with their three children, just the age of ours. They will be here for the year. So with the Hylton's three and ours we shall have quite a kindergarten. The Frasers are to go on furlough in the spring and we hope to all travel together.

Since our return, Stan has had a mild run of dysentery, something we never had in our family before. I was rather anxious about him, but he is improving nicely now, is getting up today. Stan says I look much better for my summer at the beach, and I certainly am feeling much stronger than I have for some time.

Stan continued the letter at this point. I am anxious to get up, begin working on my electric light plant. This will light the whole compound and The Boys Academy and will provide power for a future x-ray. This x-ray I will bring out with me from home when I come back. We plan to come on furlough by one of the Empress boats leaving here in March or April. We will stop off at Orillia our supporting church, as it's on the way, and then go on to Mere Point for the summer.

We should like to have a cottage, house or apartment say at Portland or Boston, so that you could stay with us, so that Margaret might be able to go to shows etc. – music, so that I might be able to study at Harvard, or Massachusetts General, or work with some busy surgeon and Ruth could go to kindergarten.

You might think up a plan that might help us do these things. We are allowed $30 per month for house rent during furlough.

SHM

Margaret continues the letter.

Please let Aunt Addie and Cousin Anna know we arrived in Yong Jung safely. (don't mention the dysentery) I think Stan will be all right now if he is careful.

Must send this to mail –
With love,
Margaret

In November of that year something occurred which would have made an hilarious farce on stage if it were not for the danger. Stan wrote of it to the British Consul at Mukden.

Yong Jung
November 15, 1921

I wish to inform you of the following incident, so that you may know what our relations with the Japanese officials are at the present time. On Friday, Nov. 12th at 11:00pm, I was aroused from sleep, and found a person asking in Chinese for the doctor. He was accompanied by our hospital secretary, who said in Korean that the man was Japanese. I told the secretary to take him to Mr. Barker's house, so that I might gain time, and so that two foreigners would see him. Having dressed, I proceeded to Mr. Barker's home and found the Japanese man, dressed in foreign clothes (overcoat, soft hat, large muffler around his neck), sitting in Mr. Barker's study. The man would speak only Chinese. Seeing he was Japanese, I called in my assistant who speaks perfect Japanese and asked him to ask this man what he wanted.

The Japanese man then ordered my assistant out of the room, speaking in Chinese, at the same time muffling his face completely and pulling his hat down over his eyes. Seeing the state of affairs, I sent for Mr. Joly the British Commissioner of Customs here. His home is near our compound about a five-minute walk from our house. He came immediately, and taking in the situation, sent his "*ma fu*" for four Chinese police who quickly arrived and were kept waiting outside, out of sight. As the Japanese man persisted in talking only in Chinese, Mr. Joly who spoke Chinese engaged him in conversation. Before Mr. Joly arrived, we had searched him carefully looking for arms, after which he tried many times to leave the study where he was being detained. When Mr. Joly arrived, the visitor took him to be the doctor, calling him repeatedly the *Dai Foo,* and endeavored as before to leave the room. Seeing that the tables were turned on him to all appearances, he gave in, and wrote his name and the name of the Korean inn at which he was staying. He also wrote in characters that he was a Chinaman, and gave us a name which was probably not his own.

He then asked Mr. Joly many questions; such as "Are you a friend of the Japanese Consul?" "What do Britishers think of the Japanese invasion of Chinese territory?," and various questions which were palpably made up on the spur of the moment. Mr. Joly gave evasive replies, and in turn questioned the Japanese man, trying to get as much information out of him as possible, without allowing him to realize he was being pumped. Nothing of any importance however was obtained. He emphasized the fact that he had come to tell us something, and that since he had been searched and had found himself in an unfriendly atmosphere he would come the next day and inform us.

Mr. Joly and I then saw him off the compound, and found that outside the gate three Japanese soldiers were patrolling. They looked at us most intently, but on a command from our visitor, the three soldiers disappeared. As we were walking up the path, he came back and shouted out, "Have you telephoned the Japanese Consulate, since there are soldiers here?" We replied that we had no telephone. [I only have a line between the hospital and my home.]

The Chinese Chief of Police and the Chief of Chinese Gendarmes arrived then, to whom we gave the story. They in turn, communicated with Mr. Kao, the *Shang-Fu Ju Chang*. Mr. Kao the following day visited the Japanese Consulate and protested. The Japanese informed Mr. Kao that this man was one of the Consular police and was drunk (not true) and partially insane, and apologized, asking Mr. Kao to act as mediator in the present case. They apparently wished to localize the incident. The same morning two Japanese gendarmes arrived at the hospital asking information about "The drunken policeman and two soldiers" who were on our compound last night. We told them that we had no dealings with the military authorities here, but the matter would be taken up with the Japanese Consul through the Chinese authorities.

Later the head of the Japanese Military Police, came up and was told the same thing. He however in course of conversation, told us that the Consulate had received a letter from me asking about the intrusion of armed Japanese soldiers (the Signal Corpsmen) on the British compound. He tried his best to get us to localize the present case and keep it out of your hands. Again this morning the Japanese Consul wished to discuss the matter, but we have informed him that the matter is now out of our hands.

Respectfully Submitted,
SHM

Margaret's last letter of the year 1921, revealed the fact that Stan had been ill for a long time. Fortunately, young Dr. Florence Murray was on her way and soon he would have help.

Dear Aunt Addie,

I am afraid I have been a long time this trip without writing. Poor Stan has been sick a long while (ten weeks) and is only this week well enough to go back to the hospital. I know you are very sympathetic with my troubles, but somehow I didn't like to worry you and make you anxious. There was such a long time when I couldn't say he was better or worse, just a low run of dysentery without any fever which kept him weak. But he is getting on pretty well now, and I hope the sea voyage will entirely cure him. We are expecting word any day now from

Cook's Travel Service in Shanghai about our boats, and I am gradually setting my house in order, for a long leave of absence. I have such a pile of sewing to do, I am fairly swamped. I have a good woman sewing on the machine, hard and fast nearly every day.

I wonder how Grandmother Barnes ever did it with seven children, and she didn't have as much help as I have either.

I still have some of the dinner and breakfast plates with the birds on them, the hen on the nest, and the precious sugar bowl that you gave me, after six years. There are other things too, the green glass finger bowls that I like so much for flowers. I try not to feel too badly over things when they get broken. I have had wonderful help in the home and they have worked for me a long time, I am proud to say.

If all goes well, we shall start our trip home the middle of February if we can get passage.

Babies well, and going to kindergarten.
Lovingly,
Margaret

Dr. Stanley H. Martin in his office.

XV

The First Furlough

When the New Year 1922 dawned on English Hill, there was excitement and great expectation in the Martin home. Young Dr. Florence Murray had arrived, and this was the year for the Martins' first furlough. "Furlough!" that long awaited time to get back to loved ones, to travel, to meet new friends and to report to the faithful supporting churches.

Margaret was writing to Papa. She barely got started, wishing him a Happy New Year when she wrote:

-Interruption- 8PM. Stan just sent up from the hospital for a cup of tea, as he has to do an emergency operation, and it is about a –10-degree night out.

He is getting along slowly, but his rheumatism in his knee is still so bad yet, that he is quite lame – a common sequel of dysentery, so the books say.

Dr. Florence Murray arrived a few days before Christmas, and is living with us. She is a very keen and clever young MD and we like her a lot. At her suggestion we were all prepared to put on a plaster cast on Stan's knee this evening, to give it absolute immobilization and rest for ten days, when this emergency operation came along and they are still at it.

Well to resume this letter, we have been checking the boat sailings. The *China Mail* sails April 27, from Yokohama.

Mr. Hylton is not able to leave his business, but his wife Edna, my dear friend and her three children may come with us. Remember our Edna is named for her. Our plans are to go to Pasadena where her sister lives, and then to Chicago. There, Stan will pick out his X-ray machine. After that, we'll go straight to Boston to make arrangements for fall study on the Rockefeller grant for Stan. Could you not meet us there? Stan thinks it best for us to spend the first two months in Newfoundland with his parents, then back to you for the remainder of the summer. We hope it will be at Mere Point in Maine.

We had a pleasant Christmas. I had fifteen at the table Christmas Eve, as we gave the Community dinner at our house this year. All the ladies helped, so it wasn't so hard. We prepared the ducks, and a few things, and Mrs. Fraser did the plum pudding. The girls (Ruthie 4 years 8 months, Margie almost 3 years old) helped me decorate the table with a small pine tree in the center. We decided not to give presents this year, but to send all our spare cash to the starving children in the terrible Russian famine. We received a lovely box from our dear Orillia congregation as usual, with dolls for the kiddies.

Christmas morning, we went to Korean church. We were asked to sing for them, so we made a double quartet and sang "Noel" in English. It was a big congregation. There are over six hundred people nearly every Sunday. Afterwards, Stan and I, and Dr. Murray were invited to the Chinese pastor's home for Christmas dinner. They live just behind the Chinese church, and we reached the church just in time to hear the close of their service. Little Chinese girls of the Christian Girls' school sang Christmas carols in their soft little voices.

At the end of the service, the pastor's wife took us to an upper room. It was cold and bare, with a tiny stove propped up on bricks, and the stovepipe disappearing through the window frame! They brought in a table and spread quilts on benches for us. After a long time of waiting – Chinese fashion, (they visit before a meal and leave immediately after) they gave us a fine Chinese dinner. There were about ten kinds of meat dishes, with rice and fancy cakes. In an adjoining room, the Sunday School children and some poor people were being fed. With us, were two of Stan's Chinese teachers, and a General of the Chinese soldiers in town who is a Christian. Also there was the wife of a wealthy Chinese man who had been the church leader, and was probably the donor of the feast. It was a novel experience for Dr. Murray, her first Christmas in the country, and very interesting for us as well.

It is fine to think of these Chinese Christians carrying on all alone here, with only an annual visit of a few days from their missionary, eight hundred li away.

I must stop as it is getting late. Stan has not returned. Dr. Murray went down to help him out.

Lovingly,
Margaret

Dr. Florence Murray wrote to the Mission Board of her arduous journey from Seoul to Yong Jung, and of the warm welcome she received there. She too enjoyed the Christmas festivities and the Chinese dinner described by Margaret. The plan was for her to take Stan's place at the hospital while the Martins were on furlough.

Dr. Murray's letter continues:

"The hospital here is very nice and pretty well equipped too. I was quite pleased when I saw it, as it is better than some I have seen in Korea. It certainly reflects great credit on Dr. Martin for when he came here six years ago, there was no medical work at all, and nothing to work with. Now there is a good hospital with accommodation for fifty in-patients and a fine operating room while the number of patients is past twenty thousand for the year. Nearly half of our patients here are Chinese, and Chinese women are not so ready to go to a man doctor for treatment as the Korean women are. Already several of them have come asking to see me, but I'm trying to give all my time to language study for the month of January. Next month I am to work at the hospital for part of the day."

On January 12th a telegram arrived, offering the Martins three cabins on the *SS China* sailing April 7th from Yokohama. Margaret wrote her father the good news, repeating the travel plans for crossing the United States.

She wrote to her father of preparations for the trip.

We are busy, sewing and packing. A Montgomery Ward order arrived – always a time of excitement – "our traveling clothes, two fine new raincoats for Stan and me, and handsome boots for all the children and Mother. My! It eats the money!"

In February she wrote again. I'm awfully sorry to disappoint you, but owing to a dock strike in Hong Kong which has become quite serious, we shall be delayed now a month in getting away. Many large boats, except one or two, which took on Filipino crews, have been held up. So it will be well into April before the "China" can make another trip. What worries me, is that we shall be having no mail from you for a period.

It may be just as well that we are delayed, for Stan could be a good deal stronger with benefit. We feel the Lord is overruling and that the delay will be for our good.

We have had our hot water heat with radiators, going for ten days now, and it is fine, so clean and comfortable, every room warm. All our old Russian stoves are gone and it makes so much more room. They were most unsightly, though they did keep us warm, and the dust and ashes, O my!

Dr. Murray is still living with us. She is a big healthy, jolly girl, like a fresh breeze from Canada. She saw active service in the Halifax disaster when that munitions ship exploded. She also was there during the great flu epidemic, as so many medical men were overseas, the students had to help. She is a Presbyterian minister's daughter and is certainly clever. Stan says she's a good surgeon.

Please write to me to Yokohama. I shall be anxious to hear.

Babies are well. Ruth looked at your picture and said "Whose is that grandpa? Is that my grandpa? I'm going to hug him." You will be tickled with our kiddies, I can hardly wait for you to see them!!

[On March 30th Margaret wrote again]. We are still here, and likely to be for another three weeks. A fine Chinese dinner was given to us and the other members of the mission about two weeks ago. Shortly afterwards, the Korean church people gave the Frasers and us a farewell feast. We have had some beautiful Korean costumes given to us for the whole family, even to baby Edna. So Doctor and I, and Ruth and Margaret went in Korean dress. I had a beautiful pale blue silk skirt and white jacket, *choguri* and white silk headdress, and the children were in gay colors. Little Mary and David Hylton were also in Korean dress.

After the feast, our children sang one of the little kindergarten songs for them, with the children in a circle. The dinner was nice, chicken and rice and *kimchi* [Korean pickle] and all sorts of fancy cakes.

One woman gave me a silk overdress, and a jacket of many colors, with striped flowing sleeves, and a bridal headdress of artificial flowers called a *gohkal*, which is worn by people of high station.

We are having a lull after the rush of getting ready. I have been spending a good deal of time with my dear Lydia who used to work for us, going twice a day to read the Bible to her. She is very weak and nearly dying, but quite conscious, and has such a beautiful faith. I went to see Chulsi yesterday too. She always asks about you. She was our amah when little Margaret was so sick.

The babies are well and they say and do such funny things! Margie woke up yesterday morning and said "Mama the doggie is barking," and baby Edna jumped up in her crib and said "Barkie, barkie" and wanted to be taken to the window to see him.

We are expecting to leave about April 20th from Yong Jung and sail about May 7th. I suppose your letters to me are piling up in Yokohama.

The Chinese are very fond of having farewell pictures taken with us, and we have now no less than three different groups who requested this, including the Chinese Christian Girl's School.

Hope you get your birthday letter.

Lovingly,
Margaret

P.S. Stan did a spinal splint yesterday. He took a piece of bone from a man's leg and inserted into the cervical and dorsal vertebrae for a tubercular spine, some surgery! Dr. Murray is a great help, and a very clever young woman.

The beautiful spring weather came, but Margaret's vegetable plots lay fallow. Just a few little volunteer flowers came up around the house. It seemed strange to her not to be busy with the gardening.

Gifts began pouring into the Martin's home from grateful patients. A silver vase, brass bowls and candle sticks, a beautiful white jade ornament, and many long silk banners of different colors. The banners had the Chinese characters for Stan's name, Min (his surname), San (mountain) and Hai (Sea) in gold letters on them, along with the donors' names and expressions of thanks. They were gorgeous. After they hung in the living room awhile, Stan rolled them up and packed them for the trip to the homeland.

At last the day for departure arrived, April 20th, 1922. They were fortunate that the delay meant warmer weather for the arduous twenty-three mile ride to Sam Bong. Margaret and baby Edna were in a sedan chair carried by two strong Korean men. Stan and the other two children, and Edna Hylton and her three little ones, rode in horse-carts. Interspersed with these carts were the horse drawn baggage carts. They made quite a procession as they went down to the hospital gate where a crowd had gathered to say good-bye. Miss Whitelaw and Florence Murray, Deacon Im and Lee Choon Chul (Alexander), and the faithful Korean hospital staff waved, as the carts came rumbling near. Stan jumped out and shook hands with all he could reach, and then they were off, as shouts of "Go in peace" in the Korean language, filled the air. A feeling of trepidation gripped the remaining people as the doctor's family moved away. A heavy weight of responsibility settled on all who gathered there.

After eight long hours on the road, they reached Sam Bong, and the group transferred to the railroad train, for the trip to Hoiryung. At Hoiryung they stayed with D. A. and Hazel Macdonald for the night – It was always a great pleasure for the lonely mission station to have visitors. The next day, another train trip took them to the seaport Chongjin, for the voyage to Japan by ship.

The hardest part of the journey was behind them, or so they thought. With six little children and all the baggage, it had been nerve racking to make all the transfers. At Chongjin, the little ones were especially frightened, as they were handed over the water from heaving sampans to the gang plank and ship's ladder. All were safe however, and soon they were on their way.

The arrival in Japan was exciting. This time the people and the shops were familiar to Stan and Margaret. Stan even spoke a little Japanese from what he had learned at the hospital. They had a time to shop, and they bought pretty parasols and trinkets for the children. A feeling of relief from missionary responsibilities seemed to slide from their shoulders.

After a few days in Yokohama they all boarded the *China* of the China Mail Steamship Line and set sail on May 3rd, Ruthie's fifth birthday. It was to be a twenty-day trip. The days passed pleasantly. With good food, and the fresh air out on deck every day, Stan gained strength after his long illness. Edna Hylton and the Martins were constantly on the alert to watch over the children. But one day they couldn't find three-year-old Margaret. The alarm was given to the whole ship. "A child is missing!" Cabin boys and passengers joined in the search from bow to stern. The call for lunch came, but the people refused to go to the dining salon and were swarming all over the ship looking for the child.

It was mother Margaret, searching frantically on the upper deck, who saw her daughter first, just a little bit of her blue dress showing on the other side of a life-boat. A life boat! These boats lie close to the edge of the ship ready to be swung out and lowered in case of need. There are no railings! There was barely enough room for two little girls to be there.

Margaret froze in terror. Gathering all her courage she calmed down and in her New England accent called softly, "Mahgret? Mahgret? You come here." And the little girl in the blue dress and the other child came crawling back. If the mother had screamed, they might have been startled and fallen overboard.

For years, the mother told the story to her children. "See how important it is to learn to obey? We might not have Margie now if she hadn't listened to me that day, and not come when I called."

The rest of the crossing was uneventful, but a few days before they reached San Francisco all six of the Martin and Hylton children seemed to have caught a cold.

The first whoop from one of the children told the story. They all had whooping cough.

Of course they were quarantined to the cabins for the last few days at sea. On arrival at San Francisco they disembarked, and the mothers and coughing children were hurried to the Ramona hotel, while Stan looked out for the baggage.

What should they do? They knew that Edna Hylton's sister was at Pasadena, and they had been invited there to stay for a week, in appreciation for helping Edna and her children make the long journey. They decided to accept the offer, and after a night in San Francisco they traveled to Pasadena. It was a hectic week with all the sick children. Edna's sister was a gracious hostess, but the Martins started looking for a place to rent. They found a little house to live in, for they were to be quarantined for a month. Edna Hylton's husband would join his family later, so she would be well cared for from then on.

The Martin children were fascinated by the new kinds of food in America – hot dogs and store-bought ice cream. As they became well enough to play outside, some neighbor children taught them the joys of chewing tar, which they promptly got all over themselves.

Stan sent a report of the trip to Mission headquarters with the travel accounts and the good news that he had been treated by a medical expert and his health had greatly improved. With his interest in astronomy he was fortunate to have a visit to the Mt. Wilson Observatory. There he had a long talk with an astronomer and a chance to have a look through the famous telescope. The forced month's rest was good for his health.

At last they were able to get on their way. But a new problem arose on the journey. Stan reported it to the Board:

> We left California about the 23ʳᵈ of June, having purchased our tickets in San Francisco which were OK'd by the Passenger Agent of the Main Office of the Southern Pacific Railway in Los Angeles. They were also passed as correct by the City Ticket office in Los Angeles where we were routed via Union Pacific to Chicago. We then went to Pasadena and showed the agent of the Union Pacific our tickets. He said they were all right, and gave us a compartment to Chicago. (Our children were recovering from whooping cough.) All was right until that afternoon at Las Vegas. The conductor said our tickets were timed wrongly. He held the train while I was forced to buy two new tickets! These were paid for without missionary reduction, because the agent had no clergy certificates for us to fill out at the station. They cost $160.28.

Missionary families were allowed $30 a month for rent on furlough so that gives an idea of the enormous sum he had to pay.

A report was made, a ticket refund was requested to the Union Pacific, but the little family arrived in Boston with hardly any money and had to wire the Mission Board for an advance.

Grandpa Rogers, Margaret's "Papa" who had waited through the long delays, met them at the station in Boston. He was seeing his grandchildren for the first time. He gathered his little granddaughters all at the same time in his big arms, and Ruthie got to hug her Grandpa. Margaret and her father stood smiling at each other, hardly believing they were together at last.

"Come, we'll have lunch in the station and transfer the baggage, for the Brunswick, Maine trip. Uncle Will is expecting all of us for the night here in Boston. You must be so tired."

The little group threaded their way through the crowds to the station restaurant. Stan carried little Edna, and Grandpa held Ruthie and little Margaret by the hand. The children were chattering with excitement.

While they had lunch, they had a time to catch up on the news. The month's delay with the whooping cough called for a change in plans. Margaret's father told them that his brother's cottage was available at Mere Point not far from Brunswick, and he could stay with them while Stan made a visit to St. John's, Newfoundland. It would be best for the children after their illness. Margaret especially needed to rest, because she was expecting their fourth child. The family talked it over and everything seemed to fall into place.

After the night in Boston, they took the train to Brunswick, and then on to the Roger's family home in the country at Cathance. It was the first time for Stan and the children to see the old homestead, with its attached barn with doors high enough for the hay wagons to enter loaded with hay. Margaret was home at last.

After a few days rest, Stan left for Newfoundland, and Margaret and the children went to Mere Point to spend the summer.

Stan soon wrote to Dr. Mackay at the Mission Board from his home at 171 Le Marchant in St. John's.

> Thanks for your kind welcome. I have been received both in Halifax and Newfoundland with open arms. The Women's Missionary Society here gave a reception for me, and yesterday morning the church was crowded. Everyone seems to be keenly interested in my story, so much so, that people came for many miles from summer resorts to hear of the work.
>
> I have been asked to go to Grand Falls and Bay of Islands. This I shall do on my way to Synod in Halifax September 12th.
>
> I am having some lanternslides made here, but am reserving some to be made at your lantern department in Toronto.
>
> Please advise how I meet my expenses from Boston to Toronto and Orillia, when I go to report on my work.

Later he wrote.

> I am getting in fine shape, and as I write, I am on an island, eating about three times what a healthy man should eat at one sitting. I'm making up lost weight.
>
> It's great to get home to tell the church about the work, but it will be better still to get back to work again.

On July 17, 1922, the St. John's, newspaper *The Daily Mail* reported of Stan's first visit to St. Andrew's Presbyterian Church.

> A larger and attentive congregation gathered at the morning service in the Kirk yesterday. The preliminary exercises were conducted by Rev. T. Darby MA. Around the pulpit were hung ten large handsome silk banners, inscribed in Chinese characters with expressions of appreciation, presented to Dr. Martin by communities and individuals who took this method of paying tribute to Dr. Martin's worth. Among the donors were, the Korean Presbyterian Church, the Chinese Presbyterian church, a village, the majority of whose inhabitants had been burned to death during a raid by Japanese troops, and an Academy which had suffered in like manner. One, especially valued by Dr. Martin was presented by the leading merchants of the district, all of who were non-Christians. Others were received from persons who had benefited by surgical attention; while one of splendid scarlet silk, richly overlaid with heavy gold leaf was the gift of a wealthy Chinese gentleman.

Dr. Martin's address, which lasted nearly an hour, commanded the close attention of the entire congregation. He prefaced his remarks with a testimony to the power of Almighty God, who alone had made possible the great results achieved by the workers of the station. He closed by an appeal for further help, not so much, in a financial way, but for prayer, which has a value beyond price.

The little family in Maine enjoyed the weeks of summer, the blueberries and strawberries, and the stories Grandpa told the children.

Margaret loved to take dips in the cold Atlantic waters, but her little daughters sat on the rocks and wailed wanting her to come back out of the water. Years later the girls were to do their "mile swims" off the coast of Wonsan in Korea.

All was well, until Grandpa fell and broke his leg. This changed the situation completely. With her father's leg in a cast up to his knee, he could no longer help her. So with her father an invalid, and the housekeeping and care of the children, it became too much for Margaret. She had to wire for Stan to cut short his time with his parents and the Newfoundland churches, and he returned to take care of the family in Mere Point.

By September it was time to move near Boston, so Stan could begin his medical studies. Stan wrote to Dr. Mackay at the Mission Board October 14, 1922:

> You will be glad to know that we are all well and living near the sea in a nice apartment.
>
> I have been fortunate in having met some of the best surgeons and physicians in Boston, so that each day I see operations at the Peter Bent Brigham hospital under Dr. Cushing, noted all over the world for brain surgery. I heard Richard Cabot yesterday lecturing to the graduate doctors and staff of the Harvard Medical school. I have worked also at the Massachusetts Eye Infirmary, and at the Mass. General Hospital. Seeing the way diagnosis and treatment is carried out in these fine schools of medicine, I think it is a great miracle that we are able to do the half of what we do in China. Seeing such beautiful operative work makes one keen to get back and put some of one's new knowledge into practice.
>
> Now to come down to the sordid earth again, we are finding it hard to get along. Having had to move twice, and in one case pay a month in advance before leaving, we find ourselves in cold weather without coal, and only able to get a limited amount of soft coal, and no hard coal at all.
>
> May we spread the payment of $125 we owe you over six months when we are paying coal bills. It will help us out, and this summer won't be so bad, as we hope to be in Newfoundland, where rent at least is cheap.

I haven't seen much real spiritual life since leaving Korea, I spoke at a church here and they seemed to be absolutely <u>dead</u>. I shall be glad to hear some Korean pastor preaching the <u>gospel</u> again.

Kind regards from all,
S. H. Martin

On November 29th Margaret went to her New England Baptist Hospital in Boston, where she had taken her nurses training, and gave birth to Gerald Arthur, a fine baby boy. His three older sisters were ecstatic. When the news reached Yong Jung, the Koreans rejoiced that at last Dr. Martin had a son!

The hospital, and Dr. De Normandie her obstetrician, who was an old friend of Margaret's, refused to take any money for their services. Miss Anderson the superintendent said it was "for the sake of the cause," a tremendous help financially.

December 8th, Stan reported the birth of his son to Mr. Armstrong and then continued the letter about his work.

I have been attending all the best clinics in Boston. Introductions from the Rockefeller Board gave me an "entrée" to these places. I have finished two courses in eye surgery, am now doing general eye work, and just starting a course in orthopedic surgery. I have had to use a great deal of my $300 study grant for travel to and fro from Boston.

I feel that the knowledge already obtained will be of great value in leading others to see the Kingdom, especially in eye surgery, which the doctors here think I do very well. They say, "Why waste your time out there, when you could make so much money at home?"

I told one man that "I should rather be a dog and bay at the moon," than stay home here and charge a poor schoolteacher $150 for cutting a simple eye muscle for squint, a case in point.

I am anxious to get busy again, and am going to look up some social service work here.

One rarely hears a real sermon but lots of lectures. We miss the spiritual life of the Koreans, and will be glad to get back home again.

I should be ready after February to lecture anywhere you wish. I want to finish my course in orthopedic surgery first.

He expressed his continuing concern that the Yong Jung hospital roof needed to be replaced. Later he reported that a doctor friend there in Boston, had promised two hundred dollars toward the project.

While the Martins were in Boston, Rev. William Scott wrote to the Board from Yong Jung, Manchuria, on October 24, 1922. He wrote of the rapid growth of the town.

Yong Jung has almost doubled in the last few years. The valley leading to Kukjaga, which used to be farmland, is now dotted with houses. The field that borders our compound is already well built upon, and we are now so closely surrounded that we can hear the Koreans talking in their houses. We are now the very center of the city, our very presence being a gospel message. Our hill is called "Yungkook Tok" or English Hill, and is one of the leading topographical landmarks of the city.

The railway from Sambong to Yong Jung opened a week ago. It is cheering to hear the sound of the engine whistle. There is now the feeling that you can always be sure of getting out of the place, without any reservations on account of wind or rain, or dearth of carts.

If you see Dr. Martin, tell him that he need have no worry about his hospital, his equipment or his staff. Miss Whitelaw has borne the burden of the superintendency of the hospital most efficiently. Her or rather "our" hospital is the best in the mission, and as far as my observation goes, second to none in Korea in point of service, organization, cleanliness and equipment. The hospital is worthy of the great church we represent.

I hope that both Dr. and Mrs. Martin will soon recover from their ailments and be able to come back to us again in the full strength our work here so much requires.

As Stan considered his return to his work, he often mentioned his recommendation that there be a two-man, or a man and woman station (missionary doctors) and a nurse at each mission hospital. He wrote to the Board December 8, 1922:

I believe the efficiency of our work went up 60% when Dr. Murray and I were working together for two months, although I was half-sick. Please let me know what medical policy the Board has for Korea. Also please let me know of the $5,000 given by the St. Andrews' church in Newfoundland for the X-ray. Is it still on hand for this, or part of it? I have picked out the machine. I should like to take it with me when I return, and I'm waiting to know if any money will be available by next fall.

In January of 1923 Stan was still writing to the Board about his X-ray machine.

The brother of the President of the Women's Missionary Society in St. John's is an agent of the Victor X-ray Co. and is arranging to get the best machine at reduced rates. This machine is used here in Boston in all the best hospitals, also in Peking in the Union Medical School. Ours will be smaller.

The lighting plant, which was installed by me, is quite powerful enough to light all our houses, the academy, as well as the hospital and run the X-ray as well. We got a 25% discount on this generator from a British firm in Shanghai. It was bought out of $500 from Miss Woodrow. The hospital is already lighted, and I hope to bring back some better fixtures for the operating room.

We hoped to have the Board allow us a small amount for wiring of the missionary houses, but this was cut out by our station when we were cutting everything we could last year.

The value of electric light in a crowded hospital at night cannot be overestimated. You should see the cheap type of lamp that we buy here in Yong Jung. My former training as an electrical engineer in the Marconi Co. has been of help in installing electricity and steam heat etc. in the hospital saving hundreds of dollars to the Mission. If I had not been in bed when the heating plants for the houses came, the money paid to Mr. Hylton might have been saved. It was at least $500.

You can't realize how much we long for another foreign doctor. It takes a lot of doing to look after your own wife during her confinement. I also care for other missionaries' wives, sometimes with only a nervous husband to give the chloroform, in difficult cases where both mother and child are threatened. I have faced this situation time and again, and often without a foreign nurse. We need the best nurses, as they often have to take great responsibility and need the best training. I mention this entirely for the good of the Lord's work.

A letter from Dr. Murray from Hoiryung where she is resting, shows me that she has been quite sick. She is finding her limitations and is trying to get the language too quickly. Is it fair to ask her to do all the planning and remodeling of the Hamheung hospital? No doubt she will be sent there when I return. The Japanese will not allow more than ten beds in the hospital until it is remodeled. This is a man's work. The men on the station are overworked with their large field, and the medical work will be sure to fall on one person. She will be left to do her worrying alone, and being more than energetic she needs someone to watch her. While doctors give their time and energies to protect others, they very often do not take care of themselves. I myself know, as I had three very serious illnesses in Manchuria.

One time I was operated on by a nurse, an assistant, and the man who gave chloroform, all natives trained in our hospital. There was no other foreigner on the station at the time. They were all in Wonsan.

Dr. Murray is an excellent surgeon and one of the best lady doctors in the East. We wish she could be allowed to work with us where she has been doing so much for Chinese women.

I am quite keen on native help. I have trained two men myself who are doing well as shining lights in villages. We also have two of our students attending Severance Union Medical College in Seoul and they will come back to us.

I should like to finish my course in orthopedic surgery at the Massachusetts General Hospital. I need $70 as I was forced to use up the last of my study money to keep the house going after Mrs. Martin came out of the hospital.

This orthopedic course will be of the greatest benefit to the many Chinese and Koreans who are suffering from diseased bones and joints.

With best wishes for 1923 from us both.

Sincerely yours,
S. H. Martin

On February 20th, 1923 Stan wrote to Armstrong from Winthrop, MA.

Re your letter concerning medical registration in Korea. When the Japanese took over Korea, men like Dr. Grierson were allowed to continue without a new license. Americans and Canadians such as Dr. Mansfield were required to write the exam in Tokyo. The exam in Tokyo is in two parts. They will not let you take them at the same time. I think six months must elapse between the oral and written exams. As you know, the Japanese copy the Germans in medicine and military tactics, so that Canadians and American men find it hard being examined according to the German school of medicine, by people who speak good German and poor English.

I would suggest, as I have already done, that British subjects should obtain the British license, and Americans should go to Tokyo and write the exam. This should entitle them to work in any part of the Japanese Empire.

If I were to work in Korea, I should write the Newfoundland exam. By adding five British pounds to this and sending it to London, I can receive the license to practice in the United Kingdom. I would take this to Japan and receive their license directly. Dr. Murray has done this with her Canadian exam, and all is fixed.

I am getting one of the best courses obtainable in orthopedic surgery. I'm speaking next week in the Boston YMCA. We are all well, but this has been a very hard winter.

I am more than anxious to get back to Yong Jung to help out the Russian refugees. We leave here for Newfoundland in June and expect to spend July, August and September there.

There is a lot of medical work I could do free of charge, but I must get to Orillia our supporting church as soon as possible. I wish also to see Mr. Kerr of Port Elgin, who gave us $4,000 for the hospital and also Miss Woodrow of Montreal.

Sincerely yours,
S. H. Martin

On March 6th Stan wrote Mr. Armstrong.

I have just received a letter from Dr. Murray. She says our hospital is filled, including a great number of Russian refugee cases – one a beautiful singer with pneumonia. She is the former wife to the Czar's Chancellor. It's the first time she has been in a bed for five years.

As you know, during the Bolshevik Revolution of 1917, thousands of the cream of Russian society, the nobility, have fled their country. They have made their way out through China and Korea, or to the West to Europe. Here in China, a large colony of them settled in Shanghai. It was hard enough for the peasants or *kulaks* to suffer these hardships, but this class of people have lived in ease and comfort all of their lives so it is more of a shock to them.

Stan continues:

Hamheung is pressing strongly for a doctor, and I expect that Dr. Murray will not be able or wish to go back to Yong Jung after Annual Meeting. As it would be a very bad thing indeed to have the hospital closed for even a month, I am anxious to get back early.

I am having a great time with orthopedic surgery. You should see how terribly deformed children are straightened out and made happy in this wonderful clinic.

I am especially following up tubercular cases and reading x-ray plates. I am determined to do better bone surgery when I return. If the St. John's grant for the x-ray is absorbed in the general fund I should wish to try and raise enough to get a small outfit.

I do most earnestly wish that we might have a second doctor at Yong Jung. What are the prospects for this?

Please arrange a travel or itinerating trip for me for April and May.

Sincerely,
S. H. Martin

Mr. Armstrong thanked him for the information regarding Canadian doctors securing British registration, and helped him to make plans for his speaking at churches. Margaret and the children were to stay in Massachusetts.

The Martin family then experienced the next trial on their furlough. All four of their children came down with measles. Margaret wondered what would be next!

After finishing his orthopedic surgery course, Stan made his trip to the Canadian churches to tell of his work.

The *Orillia Times* gave a lengthy report of his visit. Part of is as follows:

> The Presbyterians of Orillia have been renewing their acquaintance with their representative in the foreign mission field, Dr. S. H. Martin of Manchuria, during the present week. On Sunday evening Dr. Martin told the story of his own life and of the establishing of his hospital.
>
> He got the start for it, from a good Presbyterian farmer who sold his farm, and gave $4,000, practically all he had, to fund the hospital. This with another $4,000 from Montreal provided for the building, labor being cheap in the East.
>
> The Orillia Presbyterian Church had given $12,000 for the equipment of the hospital, which provided for the heating, plumbing and water system, and electric lighting plant, all of which he had installed himself. He had received other smaller gifts from the same generous source. He was now trying to get together enough money to install an X-ray machine. He already had a dispensary, and the mission buildings constitute quite a little settlement on what was a barren hillside.
>
> Dr. Martin tells his story in a simple direct, manly way, without embellishment of any kind, which was most effective, and he held the close attention of the large congregation. On Sunday he will take part in both services, and on Monday evening, he will be given a farewell under the auspices of the Ladies' Aid.

After his Canadian trip, Stan and Margaret were looking forward to spending some time in Newfoundland before returning to Manchuria. Stan wrote Armstrong quoting the fare for the family for a trip sailing on June 7th to St. John's.

> Would it not be possible for the Board to pay this for Mrs. Martin and the children, seeing that they are going for the first time to the home of my parents. If this can be done, please have Miss Cranston send us this money as early as she can with our salary.
>
> Ruth and Margaret are having their tonsils out tomorrow. It will cost $20 each. It is being done at the <u>Charitable</u> Eye, Nose and Throat Infirmary.

It seems strange that a person who has removed 20-gallon tumors for the equivalent of 25 cents in China, has to pay $40 for much smaller operations at home. As private cases however, we would have to pay $50 for each child.

With kind regards,
S. H. Martin

The response to the request for travel funds to Newfoundland was answered by the quoting of Board policy that traveling expenses will be met from the field, only to the point in the home country where the missionary and family expect to reside. The complication for their family was that two countries were involved. Margaret being an American and Stan a Newfoundlander.

It was true that Stan had made a short visit in July to his family and church, but the paternal grandparents, had not seen their grandchildren yet. Also, it was important that Margaret should greet their supporting church members, and renew her Newfoundland contacts with Stan's family and friends.

From the depths of her disappointment and fatigue from a trying year Margaret wrote to the Board on May 23, 1923.

> I can almost say there has not been one month since we landed in May 1922, in which there has not been illness in the family, and serious illness too. On top of that, we have had the constant anxiety of trying to make financial ends meet. Our two oldest children have had tonsil operations last week, and Ruth has developed a high fever today, another worry. My kitchen help is leaving today and I am forced to pay an outrageous price to get anyone for our remaining two weeks. I had hoped to have a little relief and a little time to spend with my father in the last days I may ever see him.

She reviewed the furlough year.

> From May to June 1922 the children had whooping cough, in July my father fell and was injured. In August we moved to Medford to be near Boston for Stan's studies, but we had difficulty in placing Ruth in school, resulting in a second move to Winthrop.

> In November, I gave birth to our son, and during my stay in the Baptist hospital little Margaret was seriously ill at home. On my return, I at once contracted influenza and was another month getting my strength back. In March, little Margaret had a violent attack of tonsillitis and croup, and Edna had a serious case of running ears, which brought on kidney trouble which is no light matter in a child of two and a half. This was followed by all of the children coming down with measles, all in Dr. Martin's absence in Canada. On his return there were

the tonsil operations as I have stated. During this time I had half-trained and incompetent help, or no help in the kitchen.

Please do not think I am hysterical, this is simply a statement of facts. We do not wish to be objects of charity. I should have been glad to go out and practice my profession this winter after the birth of our son, had I been able to leave the children. Nurses get $42 a week here, which would have been material help but this was impossible.

Please do not consider this a tirade or rebellion. We are just discouraged.

Very truly yours,
Margaret Martin

Both Mr. Armstrong and Dr. Mackay of the Board wrote sympathetic and encouraging letters to the harassed couple.

Armstrong wrote May 26, 1923:

I wish you would believe me to be a very real friend of every missionary since I was denied the privilege of being one myself. There is nothing I would not do were it possible to ease the difficulties of yourself or any of our missionaries. You have had an unfortunate experience in that I think you have been living under more expensive conditions, being in the United States and near a big city, than any others of our missionaries. Yours is therefore not a normal experience. Moreover you have been very unfortunate in the matter of illnesses. I was very much touched by your letter of May 23rd and I am heartily in sympathy with you in the struggles you have had during furlough.

Dr. Martin has given himself unstintedly to equipping himself further for the work in which he has rendered magnificent service, and which leads us to be very proud of him indeed. We look upon him as one of the ablest and most devoted of the medical missionaries of our Church. There is a great future ahead of him, and you must not be discouraged by your experience on furlough, for "the best is yet to be."

We have been passing through a financial crisis, but I think it is really "passing through" and that the future will not be as difficult.

Your condition is much the same as other missionaries who have lived in or near big cities, except that perhaps you have been living where it has been more expensive than even those who lived in Toronto have found it, and it is expensive enough here.

I am sure however, you are both eager to go back to the field, and I want again to assure you, that I want to be considered as a real friend in every sense and on all occasions. Please write me again if there is anything that you wish to say, and if there is anything special that I can do.

With kind regards, I am
Yours sincerely,
A. E. Armstrong

To add to the troubles of a difficult year, an added blow was word from Dr. Mackay of the Mission Board that Stan's x-ray machine funds were not available.

In God's good timing the refund from their transcontinental rail tickets came to Stan, and the Board gave permission to use that money for boat passage to Newfoundland, repayment to be made later.

Once again the family packed up and made the trip to Newfoundland. It came at a good time in their lives. Stan and his family were at home with his parents in their large house overlooking the harbor. There was plenty of room, lack of financial worry, and a royal welcome at the churches. At last the family found a much-needed time of peace and relaxation before their return to mission field.

XVI

Delayed Return

❧

After a few weeks with Stan's parents at St. John's, it seemed best to let the grandparents have some peace and quiet, so the young couple looked for a little place to rent.

They found a cottage at Topsail by the sea. Stan reveled in the time, observing the passing ships with his telescope, and watching his little ones play at the edge of the shore. He was often called away to speak at nearby churches. Margaret was cooking with a wood stove and trying to stay ahead of the laundry with a scrub board and a tin tub. With four children, age six and under, she was getting more and more exhausted.

On July 14, 1923, Stan wrote Armstrong:

> We are at the seaside. Mrs. Martin is not as well as she might be. She does not feel strong enough to start for China at the end of August, and we would prefer sailing in October. Even then, I may go alone if it can be arranged. It would be best for us all, and would save expenses.

In August the situation had not improved, and he wrote again to the Board.

Topsail, Newfoundland   August 22, 1923
Dear Mr. Armstrong,

As you are probably aware we have been corresponding with Mr. McGilvary, the Women's Missionary Society and several of the elders of the church at Orillia concerning the possibility of Mrs. Martin remaining there, while I returned alone to Yong Jung. This situation which is a very painful one for us both has been brought about by Mrs. Martin's overworking during furlough, without proper help, after the birth of our son. We had planned to go to Orillia, have Mrs. Martin operated on in Toronto, and then, either one of us, or both with the children return to China. The consensus of opinion of our friends in Orillia, the

Barkers and others, who know us well, is against any separation even for a short period. Now we find that after a summer in Newfoundland, she does not feel even able to take the journey to Toronto. This, with the difficulty of getting help in Orillia, and of renting a house there, leaves us the only alternative of remaining, and having the operation here. Mrs. Martin is less well than she was a month ago.

So we are obliged to request a further leave of absence of a year. We have left everything we own in our home in Yong Jung, including most of my medical books. Do not think we are not anxious to return to the work into which we have put the best of our lives. We hope in a year that Mrs. Martin will have regained strength, and that we may be able to pay off our debts, which we have been quite unable to do on our present salary.

We would like very much to hear any report of Annual Meeting, if it has come to hand. Meanwhile we hope some effort will be made to keep the Yong Jung hospital open, and that more doctors and nurses will be forthcoming.

We are wiring directly to Halifax to cancel the tickets, and are returning the two hundred dollars passage money with regret that Mrs. Martin's increasing illness has caused this changed of plan at the last moment.

With sincere regards,

S. H. Martin

During the summer of 1923 they heard of the disastrous earthquake in Japan. They wondered how it would affect all of Asia. They knew it would disrupt travel plans and especially affect the economy of the region.

At last the responses came from the Mission Board granting permission for an extension of their furlough. Soon afterwards, Stan was called to be a House Surgeon at Wellesley Hospital in Toronto. This was the opportunity they needed to pay their debts. The young couple was greatly encouraged.

Their supporting church at Orillia heard the new plans and offered to help in any way. Margaret and the children were to stay in Orillia, surrounded by church friends. One church family, the Coopers of Coldwater, offered to keep three year old Edna in their home for a few months.

Margaret needed surgery and they planned for it to be done in Toronto, as soon as she was able to travel.

In early September, they packed their few belongings and prepared to leave for Canada. Again it was hard to say good-bye to Stan's parents. The long years of separation loomed before them, and now the grandchildren had become close to their new grandma and grandpa.

In Canada there were some difficult weeks when the Martin children were "farmed out" to church friends' homes during their mother's surgery in Toronto. As soon as it was possible she and the children settled down to the new life in Orillia.

Ruth, Margaret, and Edna attended school, and baby Gerald grew to be a strong little toddler. Grandpa Rogers was able to visit for several months and was a great help to his daughter.

In October, they were glad to hear that E. J. O. Fraser had written to Armstrong from Yong Jung, that the hospital was in good shape, and it "needs only the doctor to make it better than it ever has been before." He also wrote that the town of Yong Jung had grown to about twice its size in the last year and a half.

Armstrong responded to Fraser's letter, with the news that "The Martins have been obliged to apply for an extension of their furlough, which has been granted. Mrs. Martin had an operation in Toronto General Hospital. She suffered considerably, but the Doctor speaks hopefully. This is very unfortunate for you all at Yong Jung but it is unavoidable. The Doctor himself would be only too delighted to return at once."

The Martins received Miss Jessie Whitelaw's report to the home churches written from Yong Jung. She had been a nurse there for four years and now had been the Superintendent during Stan's absence.

Dear Friends:

Here in Yong Jung we have a hospital that accommodates forty in-patients and have also a large out-patient department, having handled about 15,000 cases this past year before Dr. Martin left on furlough. We have only one foreigner (self) to supervise the hospital, nurses, nurses' home, answer out-calls, be hospital accountant, and exhort others to Christ. The hospital is well equipped with steam heat, electric light, and running water. There is also a comfortable nurses' home nearby.

Our staff members are all Christians and they try to teach and preach to the non-believers as they go about their work. There is also a Biblewoman who gives all her time to evangelistic work among the patients, and we are glad to report that many have decided to become Christians while they were under treatment in the hospital. Others who were served in their homes by out-calls have been greatly helped.

We are supporting a former hospital employee who is now studying at the Severance Union Medical College in Seoul, in order to better equip him for the work here. We also arranged for one of the staff to go to Severance last summer for special study in bacteriology. In our hospital we treat Koreans, Chinese, Russians, occasionally Japanese and English. Quite a babble of tongues, and at times, one's imagination is taxed to the utmost to know what a patient is trying to tell us. Our Korean doctor, who is a graduate of the Government hospital, speaks Japanese well, our secretary interprets Korean into Chinese, and we have a young Russian man who interprets Russian into English.

Much inconvenience has been experienced owing to the water supply system having broken down. Now we can boast of a water supply system equal to the best, Russians having reinstalled it.

Our greatest need now is the new roof we have been trying for some time to get, however our prospects for this are brighter than before. Probably the spring will see us with this long hoped for roof, as some kind friends in the homeland have provided money for this project.

The dispensary department needs to be repainted, we hope the where-with-all for this will also be forthcoming.

Our hospital is well on the way to self-support, so that in the future our help from the home-land should lessen yearly. On the whole our work has been very prosperous by the guiding hand of an All Wise Father.

The months passed quickly for the Martins, and the children enjoyed their time in Canada. They were dazzled by the Christmas decorations and celebrations. When Easter came, the Easter eggs and chocolate rabbits, and the smell of the candy shops were all new and exciting.

Before long their parents told them of their coming trip back to Yong Jung. Stan had made bookings on the "Empress of Australia sailing May 15, 1924 from Vancouver.

Margaret prepared for their return to the field, going over lists of food, clothing, and other supplies. She remembered the time eight years before, when she and Aunt Addie were checking her lists. This time she had a much better idea of what would be needed. Stan was busy with his surgery, but he took time to purchase medical supplies when possible. One Sunday at the Orillia church, the Martin children were told that they were not to come to Sunshine Mission Band that afternoon. They were puzzled and deeply hurt. They loved the songs and stories at those meetings.

Later they found out that the Mission Band children had been wrapping surprise farewell gifts for them – Ruthie, Margie, Edna and little Jerry.

At last the time of departure arrived. The Orillia, *Ontario Times* newspaper gave a detailed report of their last night in Orillia.

Dr. S. H. Martin and Mrs. Martin were tendered a farewell by the Presbyterian congregation at Orillia on the eve of their return to Manchuria, where Dr. Martin will again take up his work as superintendent of St. Andrew's hospital in Yong Jung. There was a large representation of the congregation present and a very fine spirit prevailed. The church showered them with gifts, both money and other useful articles.

Greetings were given from the Sunbeam Missions Band and they announced that a parcel of toys would be waiting at the "Empress of Australia" for the Martin children.

For some time Dr. Martin has been endeavoring to raise sufficient funds for the purchase of an X-ray outfit, so necessary in his work where there are a great many tubercular bone cases. Mr. Cunningham on behalf of the congregation presented Dr. Martin with a purse containing nearly $750, which, with what has already been received from outside sources, will be ample for the purchase of an excellent X-ray. The amount received from other sources include $500 from his home church in St. John's, Newfoundland, $100 from Queen's University, his alma mater, $50 from James Playfair, Midland, and over $100 received by Dr. Martin at various meetings which he addressed.

Dr. Martin was enthusiastically received when he rose to reply. He was overwhelmed with the kindness, which he and his family had received since coming to Orillia. The health of his wife had been restored, largely through the assistance of friends who had been most kind, and the months spent in Orillia would always remain one of the brightest spots in their memories.

Mr. Lincoln A. Rogers, father of Mrs. Martin, of Brunswick, Maine, who has been spending some time with his daughter, spoke a few words in appreciation of the kindness he and the family had received at the hands of the Orillia congregation.

Rev. McGilvary gave an inspiring closing message and told of the St. Andrew's Yong Jung Prayer Circle, whereby 250 members of the congregation had promised to remember Dr. Martin and his work in prayer at least once a week.

An autographed quilt, the gift of the Willing Workers Association, and a silk Union Jack from the Sunday School were also presented to them. It was reported that The Young Women's Missionary Society has undertaken the maintenance of a cot in St. Andrews Hospital at a cost of $100 a year. This Society had already given Dr. Martin $200 to buy new surgical instruments when he first arrived from the field. Word had come also that the W. M. S. in St. John's Nfld., had promised to support two Bible women at the cost of $100 a year each.

Dr. and Mrs. Martin leave tonight. Many friends in Orillia, besides those in the Presbyterian Church, wish them Godspeed and a safe journey to their far off field of missionary labor.

That night the Martins were taken to the Canadian Pacific Railroad station at Medonte as planned, and they began their long trip back to the mission field. It was uneventful to Vancouver. There, they boarded the beautiful *Empress of Australia* and set sail for Japan.

When the ship arrived in Yokohama, the passengers looked over the railings at a somber sight. Although much of the debris had been cleared away after the earthquake that occurred eight months before, there was still a lot of rubble, with only a few little houses near the shore.

The stewardess on board their ship, told them that the *Empress of Australia* was docked in Yokohama when the earthquake struck that summer. She was on the ship and on duty at the time.

She explained, "Most of the Japanese houses have "*hibachis*" (braziers) for stoves, small clay containers of charcoal. Their floors are covered with straw mats (*tatamis*). When the earth shook, so many of the hibachis overturned that the whole town burst into flame.

Frantic crowds fled toward the seaside, trying to escape the fire. They climbed onto every available little fishing boat, or on the ships that were tied to the docks. We took on everyone who could climb up onto our decks, until we couldn't hold another person. Then the flames reached the dock itself. The captain had no choice but to pull away, leaving the screaming, burning people to die. It was indescribable!"

The Martins were saddened by scenes of destruction everywhere, as they spent a few days in Japan. They then continued their trip, proceeding up the northeast coast of Korea to Chongjin and then overland to the Hoeryung mission station. It was so comfortable and familiar to hear the Korean language again. At Hoeryung, the Macdonalds welcomed them, and there was a chance to rest and tell of their furlough experiences, and to catch up on mission happenings. After a brief stay they continued their journey. When they climbed the steps to enter the train at Sam Bong, Stan and Margaret broke into broad smiles. This would be the first time to be riding on this new section of railroad. There they were safely on board with their four children and all their baggage on the last lap of their journey.

"Remember the long horse cart ride from here when we first came?" Stan asked Margaret.

"I certainly do, and it was bitterly cold on top of everything," said Margaret, as they settled into their seats. The train was already filling with passengers. The Martins noticed that the railroad car was very clean and had the smell of new paint. The children settled down as they looked out of the windows. The train started to move. Soon they were rushing by fields of soy beans and millet, with little thatched-roof farmhouse villages nearby. The crops seemed to be doing well.

Some Korean children in the train car noticed the foreign children and came by to stare at them. Ruthie remembered some Korean words. "How old are you? Where are you going?" The children answered, excited to hear her talk. Margie and Edna just listened intently. They had forgotten all of their Korean language. Little Jerry smiled and reached out his hands to them. One of the little Korean girls offered him some *yut*, barley candy.

Margaret said, "Thank you but he's too small." At the same time, she drew out some lemon drops and gave them to the little visitors. They were delighted and ran back to their seats to show their parents.

Some time later as the train approached Yong Jung, Stan and Margaret were amazed to see the changes in the landscape. Large buildings they had never seen before loomed up before them.

There seemed to be hundreds of new shops and houses. At the railroad crossing, the streets were filled with bullock carts and white-clad figures in the market nearby. They felt a rush of joy, as the train slowed and stopped at their Yong Jung station. In a few moments, they came down the steps, the little girls first, then Margaret, then Stan carrying little Jerry. Cries of welcome greeted them as they were surrounded by the large crowd gathered to meet them.

Members of the hospital staff welcomed them along with church friends, and the missionary families, the Scotts and Frasers.

"My, how the girls have grown."

"Welcome, welcome!"

"Mrs. Martin looks so well."

"Look! Dr. Martin's holding his son!"

The Martin family was home at last.

XVII

Last Days in China

As the Martins arrived in Yong Jung, horse-carts were waiting at the train station, and the precious x-ray machine and the hospital supplies were separated from the household baggage. The children were happily anticipating a ride in the horse-carts.

Crowds were waiting at the hospital door, as Stan rode up with the baggage. Word had gone out to the community that the "Min Dai Foo" had returned. It was explained to them that the doctor had to unpack and install the x-ray equipment and would be back on duty in a few days.

Margaret and the children continued to their House No. 4 on the Mission Compound, where Tabitha, Chulsi and Sahng Ha were waiting. What excitement as the Koreans examined the children from head to toe. Baby Jerry "a son at last," was clucked and cooed over the most. Margaret watched with mixed feelings, but after all, that was their culture.

A tremendous sense of happiness came over her as she walked to the living room, and saw the familiar furnishings and her beloved piano. The children ran from room to room squealing with delight as they explored everywhere. The house was spotless, and from the kitchen came the aroma of delicious Korean soup and rice that Tabitha had prepared for lunch.

That evening the families gathered at the Scotts' home for a welcome dinner for the Martins. The three Scott boys, Arnold, Lorne and Keith, and the Fraser children Jean, Clarence and John were glad for more children to play with on the compound.

The Martins heard the good news that a Miss Bradshaw was coming from Calgary, Alberta, to teach the missionary children. There would be six who were old enough to be in school and it was agreed that a Russian boy would join them. The room in the basement of the Eunjin Boy's School was already prepared with desks for the fall semester.

Stan and Margaret gave a report of their eventful furlough and they learned of the happenings while they were gone. Afterwards the adults played games with the children, for the children were always included in the activities as much as possible. Uncle Willie Scott did magic tricks, and they ended the evening with singing.

It took days to unpack and settle in, but soon the family was back to a busy routine. Margaret inspected her vegetable gardens covered with weeds. She then checked in the baggage for vegetable seeds that could still produce a little crop before winter. Stan was pleased with conditions in the hospital, and eagerly added to the supplies and equipment.

The summer went by, and the new teacher Miss Bradshaw arrived. She made her home with the gracious single ladies at House No. 3. The children started to school and the hospital became busier than ever.

Gradually the Martin children began to speak Korean again. Ruthie remembered some of the language from before furlough, and was soon off to the servants' homes to play with the children there. Margie and Edna followed her. They played "Hide and Seek" between rows of soy beans and Kafir corn. They learned to play Korean hopscotch, and heard Korean stories and songs. When spring came they took little baskets and went with their Korean friends to dig up the various herbs that the Koreans said were good for soup. Tabitha, the cook, was proud of them and prepared the soup. Their doctor father approved saying the herbs were full of good vitamins.

On April 24, 1925 they welcomed a baby sister named Phyllis. As the seasons passed, there was always something new and interesting. When the balsam flowers bloomed, they learned from the Korean girls how to dye their fingernails a lovely coral pink color. It was done by tying small poultices of the crushed balsam flowers to the fingernails overnight. In the morning there were pink fingernails. The color would last for weeks.

Vendors would come to the door with flowers or chickens. Sometimes a Chinese man would come to mend broken pottery. The children would hunker down beside him, breathing the cloud of garlic that surrounded him, watching him make two tiny holes in the china dish with an augur, and piecing it together with tiny metal clips.

One day a Chinese man came to the compound when the children were playing by the barns, beyond the servants' houses. He seemed especially interested in little Edna. This curly-headed one was the prettiest of all of the children. He talked to her in Chinese beckoning her to come to him. Suddenly he picked her up, put her on his back and started to run away with her. At this, all the children began to scream, so he dropped her and ran. This was a new situation and the children were warned always to stay together closer to the house.

Colorful funeral processions often went by on the road up the hill to the cemetery. The children would run out to watch. The banners and the sound of Korean flutes and drums were exciting, but the wail of the true mourners touched their hearts. The families of the deceased hired mourners to wail loudly. This vocal display was used to impress people with the importance of the person who had died. They plied these men with a good supply of rice wine, to add vigor to the noise. The children could see, however, those who were truly grieving, and they were touched by their pitiful sobbing. "They have no hope, they don't know about Jesus and heaven," thought little Margaret as she resolved to be a missionary when she grew up.

The summers at Wonsan, Korea, were the happiest times of all for the children, as they gathered in a community of missionary families from all over Korea.

At last Stan was able to write to his Orillia Church, and his report was printed in the *Orillia Times* in the fall of 1925:

> Dr. Stanley H. Martin, Superintendent of the St. Andrew's Hospital, Canadian
> Presbyterian Mission, has forwarded a report of his year's work. Dr. Martin is

the founder of the $30,000 hospital which was built in Manchuria in 1918. Dr. Martin relates many incidents of his work and says he is kept constantly busy. This year he is Chairman of the Annual Missionary Council which met at Wonsan in July.

He speaks of the excellent work being done by his X-ray machine, and instances a case of a wealthy Chinese man who might have lost his foot, had not the X-ray revealed his trouble. Attendance at the clinics average 50 to 70 patients a day, depending on the weather. Rain is needed very badly, as the season has been dry, and the crops are suffering. The new roofing has been put on and looks fine. It was purchased through the kindness of Mr. McNab of Orillia. The linoleum has also been laid on corridors and in the operating room and is a vast improvement. The money for this was sent by Mr. George Cunningham, treasurer in Orillia of the Dr. Martin Hospital Fund, and Secretary of the Prayer Circle. A large photo of the hospital staff is being sent to be put up in the Sunday school.

Dr. and Mrs. Martin send best wishes to their many friends in Orillia, and ask for continued prayers and support. The report continues:

Although this year has been exceptionally hard because of the crop failure, we have a great deal for which to be thankful, as we have managed to close our hospital books without a great debt. We are particularly pleased to again have a Canadian nurse, and are eagerly looking forward to the time when Miss Lenore Armstrong will be able to take up some work in the hospital where she is greatly needed.

Several trips have been made to the surrounding country where cases were seen, services held, and patients sent in for operations. The assistant doctor Dr. Choi (a Korean trained at Severance Medical School) is particularly fond of this work.

The number of tubercular cases of all kinds that come to us is tremendous, and we are considering a plan to alter one of our buildings so as to give these cases sun treatment.

Whenever circumstances permit, a Sunday afternoon service is held in the wards, and in every way the evangelistic work has been well cared for. A very efficient Bible woman was secured about six months ago, and since then, she has preached to 6,591 people, visited 440 homes, and distributed over 5000 tracts and gospels. The hospital secretary is also an elder in the church, and is a strength to the evangelistic work of the hospital. A recent patient, a Chinese Buddhist priest has been preached to daily by the husband of another patient, a Christian, his brother priests who visit him also coming in for a share of it.

A number of cases shot by bandits have been brought to us, one of whom, also badly tortured has just recovered after three months treatment.

Another man is one who was burned all over his body with red hot irons. He lived only six miles from here. The bandits burned his house too. He is out of danger now, though it will take some time to grow new skin. We have two Chinese soldiers with broken legs; the X-ray pictures are a sight to see!

Many Russian refugees here have had their miserable existence somewhat helped by the service rendered them by the hospital, many of their lives being spared by means of operation. Of the total number of patients 12,640, 7,190 were Korean, 5,050 Chinese and 400 Russian. The number of in-patients was 400, representing over 5,000 days in the hospital. A total of 356 operations were performed, the work being so arranged that the medical unit could carry on while operating was being done. All the pupils in two of our high schools were examined. Many diseased tonsils were removed, and those suffering from eye trouble were treated, and proper glasses fitted, 400 girls in all.

We hope that God's blessing will rest on this small piece of work, and will help with your support, to bring about the expansion of the Kingdom of God.

The months passed and again it was time to prepare for Christmas. The childhood joys of those days were described years later by daughter Margaret.

By the middle of December we were laboriously making colored paper chains and coloring fat Santa Clauses with red and black crayons. If we were lucky, we'd have snow, and we spent many happy hours sledding, snow-balling, or lying in the snow making "angel" patterns.

Then came the day the Christmas tree went up. Somehow in all that bleak land, where trees of any kind were scarce, there would always be Christmas trees, and joy filled every house on the compound. We decorated them with our paper chains and popcorn garlands and a few very precious "real" Christmas ornaments. Sometimes, if the circumstances are just right, I can still gaze into a shiny blue Christmas ball, and my heart will flip; with the remembered joy of the little girl of those early Christmases. There was the fragrance of pine and popcorn, and the piles of candy being wrapped for the Koreans. The candy packages were for our helpers' families, and for the hospital patients. We children watched wide-eyed, looking at the Korean *yut* (barley candy) covered with sesame seeds and the glittering, striped, hard candy balls. They were being wrapped in large white sheets of paper, the only kind of paper available.

There was always music, for mother had brought her *Ivers & Pond* piano all the way from Boston. We children sang carols and strung popcorn, eagerly waiting for Christmas. The early presents I remember were a box of seashells, a kewpie doll and a silk handkerchief. I was completely happy, and spent a long time by the window near the Christmas tree wrapping my tiny doll in the handkerchief and playing with the shells.

At noon the whole compound gathered at one of the homes for Christmas dinner and our community celebration. One Christmas, the other children told us there would be "crackers" with the dinner, and we Martin children couldn't understand what was so exciting about soda crackers! But they were much more than that. They were party-favor crackers, which banged satisfactorily, disclosing party hats and little trinkets. We were wild with joy.

There was no generation gap in those days. The grownups seemed to live for our happiness. There were magic tricks after dinner, charades and hours and hours of stories and games. We were the beloved center of attraction and looked to our compound "Aunts and Uncles" for our best entertainment. Often, long after we were put to bed, the laughter of our best friends, the grownups, would surround us and lull us to sleep.

Surrounded by love, and sharing with our parents the joy of the knowledge that we were in that land to bring the Christ of Christmas, our Christmases were complete. [7]

In April 1926 Stan wrote an article about his hospital work for the *Presbyterian Record*.

I have one man lying like "Toot and come in" in a plaster sarcophagus with a tubercular spine. He was a non-Christian and a difficult case to handle. Now he has become a Christian, and makes a joyful noise unto the Lord during hymn singing at the morning service.

Once we paused and leaned over the top of a five-foot crib to see an empyema patient of five years old that we had operated on that afternoon. To our surprise there was a woman of forty curled up, with her darling son under her wing. We left her there, as I was fearful for the crib and my own nerves, if she should attempt to climb over the rails.

---

[7]   *Christmases I Have Known*   Margaret Martin Moore
    Korea Calling Dec 1970 p. 3-4

When a patient comes to the hospital he is often accompanied by his immediate family, including "his sisters and his cousins and his aunts"! They camp around his bed with their fish and pickles, and the place soon smells like an Eskimo hut.

Daily we inspect the bedside tables and clean out the fearful food that is brought to comfort the sick!

Once, when calling at midnight to see a very sick patient, I passed through a ward and saw these cloaked and blanketed figures lying beneath and near the beds. These dear creatures think they are caring for the sick. Of course we have trained attendants.

I provided a wooden bed for one woman who insisted on caring for her husband, who had been blown up by his gun while trying to kill some wolves. I had heard her baby was sick and asked to see it. She stooped down and pulled out a quilt from underneath the bed, and here was the son and heir, reclining beneath the shades of his father!

Most of these ward conditions are due to the absence of our Canadian nurse at language school and to the leniency of the doctor in charge. It is difficult to be hyper-scientific, and yet love these people—for we really do learn to love them.

Let us look at some of our pathetic cases. Here is a young woman, forsaken by her husband who has taken another wife. She is one of three Korean women we have, who have taken lye (caustic soda) to commit suicide. The effect of the caustic is to close up the throat.

We operated on one woman twice and cured her; another has been treated and is improving; but after many unsuccessful attempts we must send this woman away, incurable, a starving woman without hope or home, and only twenty-five years old! I felt weak with sadness to let her go, but we have tried every method known to modern surgery.

The old lady in the last bed has been deprived of her closest friend, a tumor weighing twenty-five pounds that has been her constant companion for twenty-two years. Just after the operation, her friends arrived with a wash-basin of beef and pork to aid in restoring her strength—lots of love but no judgment.

One of our charity patients gave me a little black spaniel who has become my faithful companion, and is now curled up on a "Queens University" cushion in the most comfortable chair in my study.

As we go from bed to bed we see an unfortunate white woman, a Russian, who had gall stones removed. (These are thought by Koreans to be valuable in curing disease.) After cheering her up with the most useful of what we know of the Russian language, we pass on to the next case.

Next is a Buddhist priest who came in on a bed rigged on two poles drawn by a cow; from a village twenty miles away.

In a private ward you will find a Chinese officer who wished to send himself "west" by killing himself. Now that he is taking hold on life again, he is asking if he may eat more than one bowl of vermicelli.

And so on through the wards.

One of my cases returned yesterday. He was an old man whose life had been saved, after being shot by "careless" soldiers in 1921. He has great faith in this hospital, and is continually bringing in cases for treatment. Amongst these was his niece, who had a tubercular ankle. Permission was given immediately to amputate, which surprised us, as it often takes days to get permission. Her general condition was not very promising. Later this man came from two hundred li (seventy miles) away, and reported that his niece is going to market and coming home with large loads on her head and she doesn't even limp with her artificial leg of which she is very proud.

The wolfish dogs are very bad here and people are often bitten. Let us hope they choose the right foot when they attack this woman, as Eskimo dogs once did, when they attacked a friend of mine in Labrador who had his game leg splintered.

I will not take more of your valuable space to describe the rest of the patients. I would like to close by suggesting that whether we are at home or abroad, under God's heaven, let us do what we can to further His kingdom.

The missionaries in Yong Jung were acutely aware of the surrounding dangers. The hospital staff heard the latest news from patients brought there who had been shot or tortured by bandits. People stayed indoors after dark, but on certain nights there were church meetings and the parishioners walked in groups for safety. The long grey hospital and the missionary homes glowed at night with precious electricity, but the Korean houses were dark except for the small oil paper windows that gave a soft yellow light, lit by kerosene lamps. When there was no moon, the streets and alleys were pitch-black dark.

One night when Stan was returning alone from their church in this kind of darkness, he was aware of furtive footsteps behind him. He walked for awhile, and then made up his mind. For a moment he froze in terror, and then he swung around to strike the follower. His fist struck the man's chest on his padded coat. The giant stalker blurted out in Chinese, "Oh Min Dai Foo! It's all right! I'm, Wang Ho Chin, I'm just following you home to protect you!" He was the unusually tall member of the Chinese church. Stan then remembered that he had recently delivered the man's baby son. Both men laughed, and Stan impulsively hugged his friend as he thanked him. They walked together the rest of the way.

"Yea though I walk through the valley of the shadow of death. ..."

Another troubling piece of news was that young Korean Bolsheviks were out to destroy the Christian leadership of the churches. Several of these men had been trained in Moscow and sent back to the towns and villages of Manchuria to do their dastardly work. In town after town, a gang of them would raid a church service, pluck the minister from his congregation, and the man would never be seen again. It was well known that the Communists were saying, "The only thing that can stand against us is the Christian church. It is our enemy number one!"

One night in Yong Jung, Stan and Margaret were attending their church near the hospital gate. Margaret was playing the organ as the congregation sang. Suddenly the doors at the back of church were flung open, and with a shout, a group of armed men stormed into their midst. Stan jumped up and held a hymn book over the little electric light bulb hanging over the organ. The church congregation knew immediately what was happening. A woman whipped off her outer skirt that tied at her waist, and threw it over the preacher's head. Women at that time often wore a skirt head dress, so he was unnoticeable. The other women joined hands in a circle singing the hymn "'Tis so sweet to trust in Jesus." Margaret kept playing the organ. In the confusion the minister slipped out a side door and was safe.

How it all ended is uncertain but no one was hurt. It was a mystery. The armed men knew they had failed in their objective and vanished as suddenly as they had appeared. The protecting hand of God was over His church that night.

As Stan and Margaret went home on the dark path that night, they were thoroughly shaken. It brought memories of the nights when they had seen distant villages burning. This time these armed men were a few hundred feet from where their children were sleeping. The thought gripped them. "How long can we stay in this work, with these people we love?"

KOREAN ECHOES

THE KOREA MISSION

OF THE UNITED CHURCH OF CANADA

VOL. XII.   OCTOBER 1935.   No. 2.

A CABLE FROM THE FOREIGN MISSION BOARD.

A cable from Toronto, received on Sept. 14th., decoded reads as follows :—

"It is necessary to reduce budget of the Board $100,000. Korea appropriation for 1936 $42,625. Possibly

The Canadian missionaries are the only Protestant missionaries north of Wonsan, in North East Korea and East Manchuria.

additional amount of $5000, conditional early action Women's Board."

This means a cut of $25,000. A cut of $40,000, or sixty percent of this year's budget, had been suggested. That would have meant an irreparable disaster to the Mission work in Korea, as it would have meant the withdrawal of eight out of fifteen families, and the serious curtailment of our evangelistic, educational and

medical work. We are thankful that we are spared such a wrecking of the work so well begun in Korea. But even the present cut of $25,000, which is 37.2% of our present reduced budget, means a very severe blow to the work. It will probably mean the withdrawal of five men from the already small staff, with further reductions in salaries of the remaining families, and severe cuts in grants to our evangelistic, educational, and medical work and the Union Institutions.

We have already had the hard task of closing the hospital in Sungjin, founded and conducted up to this time by Dr. Robert Grierson, one of our pioneers. This leaves only one F.M.B. hospital and one W.M.S. hospital for our five stations.

We would remind the Home Church that we are the only Protestant missionaries in a population of over two and a half millions, of whom only one in a hundred are yet Christian. Can we believe it is God's will that men should be withdrawn from this field where they are so sorely needed, and return to Canada, where there is already a sufficiency of ministers?

A. F. Robb.

KOREA'S FOREIGN MISSION CONTINUES.

E. J. O. Fraser.

Non-Christians jump at the opportunity to point to weakening in the Church wherever found. At the recent meeting of the General Assembly of the Presbyterian Church in Korea there were many indications of the rapid development of a spirit of self-centredness and narrow denominationalism that shows the church in this land has yet to go a long way to reach the spiritual heights it should have. Local newspapers made much of it, and especially of the suggestion that was made by a party to withdraw one of the three missionaries the Church maintains in Shantung Province in China.

The question of withdrawal of one man, so as to make it possible to send a man to Manchuria, which is really home mission work among Koreans there, had been laid on the table last year. It was taken up this year, and a spirited and lengthy discussion took place. Among the various arguments used in favor of withdrawal was the statement that now that Western countries, especially Canada, are cutting down so much on foreign mission work the Korean Church must look after its own people, and so should cut down the foreign work in Shantung, by withdrawing one man now, another in five years, and the last one in ten years.

After several strong speeches had been made on both sides, the aged blind minister, Mr. Kil Syen Joo, made an impassioned plea which won applause. It was then decided by a large majority to continue the work in Shantung, among the Chinese there, at full strength, and an endeavor will be made also to send a man to Manchuria.

Can our Canadian church afford to accept a policy of serious retrenchment in the face of this challenging situation in Korea?

Map of Mission Stations in Korea, 1935.

197

XVIII

The Winds of Change

For many years, some of the Canadian churches were considering a new chapter of church history. There was talk of Methodist, Presbyterian, and Congregational churches joining to form a United Church of Canada. However, there were churches that preferred to remain as before, refusing to unite. This struck the mission fields in a painful way, as some of the home churches dropped the support of valuable, hard-working missionaries, because they differed from the home church's stance.

The problems were compounded as mission properties would have to be divided on the mission fields between the Presbyterians and the new United Church.

The Martins wrote Mr. Armstrong that they wanted to stay in Manchuria regardless of the Board under which they would serve. They felt loyal to their Orillia church that had done so much for them. This church was remaining Presbyterian. As the months went by, however, the situation changed. The Korea and Manchuria missionaries were predominantly in favor of union.

In 1925-6 discussion between the United Church and the non-concurring Presbyterian Church led to the suggestion that the Korea Mission be divided between the two. The mission replied. "We reiterate our decided opinion that the work should be carried on the basis of cooperation under one mission, and urge the Board to press for that decision." [8]

The fear was that "two Canadian missions working in close proximity would lead to confusion and friction among both missionaries and Korean brethren." [9]

The Board finally agreed, and three of the Canadian Presbyterian missionaries were assigned to work among Koreans in Japan. The name of the mission became the Korea Mission of the United Church of Canada.

Stan wrote again to his Mission Board.

---

[8] *Canadians in Korea* – Rev. William Scott p. 98
[9] Ibid.

We do not know our future, but wish sooner or later to go to Severance Hospital in Seoul where we might do one thing well, -- help a great number. Ten years as a "jack-of-all-trades" medical man is sufficient for any doctor and I should like to have a share in the great work of Severance which touches all of Korea before I die.

While Stan and Margaret agonized over the future and waited, the work went steadily on in Yong Jung. In the spring of 1926, Stan wrote to his home town of St. John's, Newfoundland, to the editor of *The Daily Mail*.

Dear Mr. Editor:

I don't forget the warm "welcome home" your paper and other city papers gave me when reaching dear old St. John's after my first seven years in medical missionary work here. As Easter day brings many reminiscences, I thought I may send greetings to you, and many friends of the Kirk and others who ask for us.

Last month was our busiest month for some time. Patients total 1468, 940 paid fees, 248 will pay later, 380 free or charity. Outside calls 136.

We had an epidemic of whooping cough here, and all of our children are sick. Our one year old baby Phyllis developed influenza on top of it, which is dangerous for children. But we enjoyed our Easter Sunday, as our stone of anxiety was rolled away. The churches in Canada are now discussing the division of property and territory in this Korean Mission and we are not sure what will happen. I have received an offer to be a doctor on the staff of eleven missionary doctors in the large Severance Hospital and Medical School at Seoul, this chief city of Korea. It has a population of six hundred thousand. The Executive of our Mission Council has asked our Board in Canada to have me transferred to Seoul. We pray that God will guide us in the way He wishes us to go. There will be better opportunities for education for the children, and things lately are very much disturbed around here through Bolshevik propaganda. There is strong agitation that China and Russia shall fight Japan, if Japan shows any further attempt to annex Manchuria. We should be glad of the transfer to Seoul for better protection.

Our medical student Choi whose course at Severance Medical College has been made possible by Canadian friends of the hospital, is giving excellent service as an assistant doctor this year, and will complete his college work next year.

The hospital's appearance was greatly enhanced by the new green asphalt shingle roof, making it one of the best looking buildings in town.

The X-ray machine a gift from St. John's, Newfoundland, and Orillia, Ontario has been invaluable in bone surgery and other work.

Sincerely,
Stanley H. Martin MD

After many negotiations, Stan and his family were to be transferred to Seoul. The plan was for an interim doctor, a T. H. Williams to come from China to take over the work at St. Andrews Hospital until a new doctor, Dr. Donald Black, could come from Formosa (known now as Taiwan). As Dr. Williams was fluent in the Chinese language he would be able to handle the work well.

In April of 1927 after sad farewells, and many feasts and gifts given in appreciation for Stan and Margaret's years of service, the Martins boarded the train to start the journey to Seoul. There had been tears at parting, and the Martin family had mixed feelings as the train moved away.

Each phase of the trip was so familiar, the rest stop visit at Hoeryung, and the journey by Japanese ship down the east coast of Korea to Wonsan. There they took the train to Seoul.

When they reached Seoul, the little Martin children stared in amazement at the Seoul railroad station, the immense stone and brick structure designed by a German architect. Announcements blared from the station's loudspeakers in Japanese, and there were many Japanese families among the crowds of people milling around. Across the street, and up a hill, stood the large Severance Hospital buildings. Stan pointed them out to the children. The streets were bustling with ox-carts, pedestrians, trolley cars and a few automobiles.

Missionary friends met them, and soon they were at the Canadian Mission house outside the West Gate area of Seoul. This house had been built for Dr. and Mrs. T. D. Mansfield, and their six children, but by this time he had given up his mission work and had returned to the homeland. There were four large bedrooms, a bathroom, a smaller bedroom, and a sleeping porch upstairs. Wash basins with running water were in every bedroom, because Dr. Mansfield was fastidious about cleanliness. They found a fireplace downstairs, and one upstairs in the master bedroom. The large living room, dining room, a half-bath, kitchen and fine big study for Stan made up the downstairs. This was to be the Martins' home for many years to come. It was ideal for a large family.

The next day Stan walked to where he could take a trolley car to Severance hospital. There were no taxis. He reported in to his Canadian friend, Dr. O. R. Avison, the founder and superintendent and was introduced to the hospital staff and the medical students at morning chapel. They were all pleased to welcome him. He was shown to his office rooms where he would develop his Chest Clinic Department specializing in tuberculosis. Later he was to start giving lectures at the Medical School building next door.

Since it was April, the Martin children had to pick up their schooling at an unusual time of year, continuing at the grade level where they had left off in Yong Jung. Because they had come from a seven-pupil schoolroom, they were extremely shy at the Seoul Foreign School. About one hundred students were enrolled. Ruthie was in fifth grade, Margaret in third and Edna was in second grade. They were especially bewildered at recess time, with so many foreign children running around. The students were mostly American and Canadian missionary children, with a scattering of other nationalities from the business and diplomatic community.

The school curriculum was based on the New York system and was taught by teachers who came on three year terms, from some of the top schools in America.

The interdenominational Seoul Union Church was an important part of their lives, with Sunday school and church services held in the large auditorium upstairs in the school building.

Eight-year-old Margaret started violin lessons with a German professor, Mr. Joseph Huss, and Ruthie and Edna had piano lessons at home with their mother.

It was a twenty-minute walk to the Seoul Foreign School, and as the Martin children came home for lunch each day, they had an hour and twenty minutes of built-in exercise. The streets were not paved, so it was dusty. When it rained, the mud was like chocolate pudding. On rainy days the few cars were required to have mud guards on their wheels to prevent the splashing of mud on the pedestrians.

As the children walked among the Koreans on the way to and from school, they heard comments on their clothes, or the color of their eyes or hair. Once in awhile a missionary child would turn and ask in perfect Korean "Is that so?" startling the one who was making comments. The Koreans were always friendly though, and the city became more used to the foreigners. The children were aware of the Japanese presence in the country, so different from their days in China. Japanese policemen stood at every street corner, and Japanese families lived across from their mission home. Downtown, there was an area called Honmachi, where all the shops were owned by Japanese merchants. It was easy for the children to pick up Japanese words and soon they could shop in the Japanese language. The girls especially enjoyed the colorful doll displays.

During the year there were Japanese festivals, such as on the Emperor's birthday or for the New Year. It was especially interesting when at a certain time of year the Japanese homes displayed large colorful banners in the shape of fish, the numbers of fish according to the number of sons in that home. At Japanese restaurants the family enjoyed the famous dish *sukiyaki*.

The Martins however were closer to the Koreans in their everyday life. A wonderful woman, Kim Chong Hi, became their cook, and Chulsi became the *amah*, nurse-maid to help with the youngest children. An outside man tended the furnace, did the heavy cleaning, and took care of the Holstein cow on the hill behind the house. With five children they needed the milk. Commercial dairies were nonexistent then.

The servants' houses were near the mission compound gate. This made all the difference to the Martin children as they spent many happy hours playing with the children there. At first the Korean children teased the Martins for their North Korean accents and words. Imperceptibly the Martins began to sound more like their friends with their "Kyung sung" or "Seoul talk." Their cook, Kim Chong Hi, had two boys, Yong Koo and Yong Suri and a pretty little girl, Hee Sooni. [Kim Yong Koo was to grow up and attend the Seoul Methodist Seminary. Later he went to the United States on a scholarship. He became an editorial writer for the *Hankuk Ilbo* newspaper. In his travels he had the opportunity to interview outstanding scholars such as Reinhold Niebuhr at Union Seminary in New York. He later became the editor of a popular literary magazine called *The Flintstone.*]

Although the Martin children talked Korean as they played with the Korean children, Kim Yong Koo later became very proficient in the English language. This was a great help for his future studies.

In the Martin home the squeaky violin music turned to a more melodious melody, Beethoven's *Minuet in G*. There were also more difficult pieces heard on the piano. The family often gathered to sing with their mother, Margaret, at the piano. It was a peaceful haven for Stan as he returned from the pressures of his work.

Transportation to his work was an immediate problem. To walk daily to the trolley line and to squeeze onto the crowded streetcars became unbearable, especially on his way home at the end of the day. The Mission and the home churches realized this, and he was able to purchase an Overland from J. H. Morris, a businessman in Seoul. He taught himself to drive by making a practice area on their large lawn. He pounded wooden stakes into the ground at intervals. Then he drove back and forth between the passage ways. The children loved to sit in the back seat as he drove, sniffing the smell of the new car. They thought it smelled like bananas.

The first summer was coming after their move to Seoul, and it was time to think of the children's vacation. Stan was aware of the summer epidemics of cholera, typhoid and other diseases in the city, so he planned to get the children away to Wonsan as soon as school was out. This summer would be different for the family, as a new baby was expected in August. Margaret, Stan and little Phyllis were to stay in Seoul for the summer, to wait for the birth of the new member of the family. Stan took the older four children, their cook, and a fine young Korean medical student, by train to Wonsan to their summer cottage. He then returned to Seoul.

The children remember a happy summer in the Wonsan community with Canadian missionary "Aunties" and "Uncles" to keep an eye on them. They especially remember the fun on the beach when the young Korean student took wet sand and molded wonderful sand castles and "automobiles" big enough to sit in. All was well.

At the end of the vacation they returned to Seoul with great excitement to see the new baby sister, Mary Elizabeth, born August 1, 1927. Now there were six children in the family, five girls and a boy.

The people of Yong Jung (*Lungchingtsun* was the Chinese name) were greatly relieved when Dr. T. H. Williams arrived from China to take Stan's place at the hospital. Soon after his arrival Dr. Williams wrote this report for the Korean Mission Council.

Lungchingtsun Medical Report
St. Andrews Hospital
June 1927

"It is an ill wind that blows nobody good." The Aryan phobia obtaining in the Chinese mind against the white race, which caused so many of our West China Mission to withdraw to the coast, made it possible for one of the doctors to come to Lungchingtsun to tide over between the leaving of Dr. Martin for Severance Medical College and the arrival of Dr. Black of Formosa. It also afforded me a much appreciated opportunity of seeing the Korean Mission and the medical work here and getting a broadening of missionary experience.

One is deeply impressed by the evidence of the loving esteem in which Dr. Martin is held here by Koreans, Chinese and Japanese, and I have great admiration for the most excellent hospital plant he has slowly and laboriously assembled and outfitted. Many of the fixtures and fittings are the work of his own hand and brain, and the unit, and its usefulness to the community stand as a memorial of the years of unremitting labor he has lavished upon it, and the ability of a fertile brain to find a way or make it.

I find the hospital here has established a reputation, and trained a staff which of its own momentum carries on, and it has been my privilege to assist to some small extent in that carrying on. The Korean graduate Doctor Choi of our Severance College is a very fine man and a capable one, and I long for the day when our West China University shall be able to provide graduates for our Szechuan hospitals. Here we find also Christian Korean graduate doctors practicing in many towns and wielding a great influence for Christ. Nearly all of them are the product of Dr. Avison's untiring labors.

With figures of the years work I will not bother you. Sufficient that they are obtainable else where in the Field report to satisfy that inordinate appetite for figures with which some suffer. But I do want you to know that the hospital here is serving a very real need and making a very real contribution to the impact of Christianity on the minds and hearts of the people. We have had many serious cases even since my arrival here recently and some pitiful ones. My usefulness has been greater than I expected because my Chinese Mandarin language is understood here and we have many Chinese patients.

The high incidence rate of tubercular disease is appalling and when we get back to the reason we find it largely economic. Poverty everywhere fosters unsanitary, ill-nourished living conditions. Many of our surgical cases are tuberculous bones or gland infections. We have also had a very wide range of operative cases, some of whom have come to us as a last resort and most of whom we have been able under God's guidance to restore to health again.

What a privilege it is to be His helper in His great work.

Dr. T. H. Williams MDCM

Martin home in Seoul, Korea

XIX

"Lest They Die"

As Stan became involved in his work at Severance Hospital in Seoul, Korea, he learned more of its scope and history. The name 'Severance' was given to the hospital in honor of Mr. Louis H. Severance of Cleveland, Ohio, whose first gift of $10,000 was given in 1900. He and his family gave much more later.

It's an amazing story. Mr. Severance was listening to the Korea Presbyterian missionary, Dr. O. R. Avison, speaking in New York at a conference on foreign missions at Carnegie Hall. The doctor was making an appeal for a United Hospital saying that there were seven small denominational hospitals in Seoul, Korea but none were properly equipped and each one was handled by one doctor and no nurses. "If three or four of these doctors could work together in one properly equipped hospital they could do more work than the seven, under the present circumstances." [10]

Years later the president of Wooster College, told Dr. Avison another part of the story. "When you were making your appeal that day, I was sitting with Mr. Severance, way up in the back of the gallery. You had not been reading long, when he turned to me and said, 'What would you think if I gave that man a hospital?' And with that he got up, went down to the main floor, made his way through the crowd until he reached the platform, and waited till noon to meet you." [11]

Dr. Avison had said to himself before he spoke that day, "If I speak clearly and loudly to the man in the farthest back row of the second balcony, if I can make him hear, all will be able to hear." [12]

Other people have said, that Mr. Severance told people later that he felt the whole message was spoken directly to him.

That was the beginning. By the time Stan joined the staff in 1927, the institution of Severance included Severance Union Medical College, Severance Hospital, the Severance Hospital School for Nurses and Midwives, the Severance Pharmacy, and the Severance Optical Shop.

---

[10] *Avison of Korea* – Allen DeGray Clark p.113
[11] Ibid.
[12] *Avison of Korea* – Allen DeGray Clark p.112

As Stan examined the many patients who came to him in the Chest Clinic, he became more and more convinced that disease prevention was to be an important part of his work. So many tuberculosis patients who came to him were beyond recovery, when earlier treatment could have saved their lives. He was especially concerned for students who lived in crowded conditions, often malnourished, and under great pressure in their studies. One of his oft-repeated expressions was "Lest they die with all their music in them." It was time to sound an alarm, to warn and teach.

He used audio-visual methods – lantern slides and a "moving picture" from the American National Tuberculosis Society to educate the medical students at Severance and the East Gate Hospital. These films were also shown at schools and churches.

The Seoul Press and other city papers printed several of his articles on tuberculosis in Korea, and his articles in The Korea Mission Field kept the missionaries aware of this tremendous problem.

He wrote a little booklet on the diagnosis and treatment of tuberculosis. These booklets were bought by the hundreds and distributed throughout Korea. Some have said that this booklet helped to bring down the rate of tuberculosis in Korea at that time, the country being fairly stable then.

Because symptoms of the disease are so similar to the common cold and influenza, many were unaware of how dangerous and contagious this disease was among them.

A tuberculosis survey of Korea was started, with forms sent out to the Korean Medical Missionary Association and the alumni of the Severance Union Medical College, gathering statistics. The work was done by a Korean, Dr. Paul Choi, and missionary Dr. Norman Found.

Stan was also concerned about the leprosy problem (Hansen's disease) in Korea. He traveled to Soonchun to his friend Dr. R. M. Wilson, to the largest leper colony in Korea to examine the hearts and lungs of the patients there.

He wrote however, "In Korea there are about 20,000 lepers while there must be several hundred thousand suffering from pulmonary tuberculosis in different stages, exclusive of bone and intestinal tuberculosis."

Lepers, minus a nose or hands, are automatically shunned and avoided and are not allowed in crowded eating places and inns. Typhoid, typhus, and smallpox are ordered by the police officials to be reported immediately. On the other hand, tubercular patients in the third stage of the disease, and just as dangerous to the public, are not reported by any doctors and are to be found daily spreading disease in the eating houses and inns throughout the country in every direction.

"What can we do here in Korea towards tackling this important problem?" [13]

After serving for a year at Severance Hospital Stan took time to write of his work.

A Day with a Mission Doctor in Korea

Come with me through the crowded clinic of Severance Hospital and pick your way among the hundreds of patients on any afternoon and you will see Chinese, Koreans and Japanese, all mixed up, in all conditions of health and wealth. Many

---

[13]   *The Tubercular Problem in Korea and Japan,* S. H. Martin, MD, CM

are lying on the floor, and here and there a leper may be seen trying to hide his loathsome disease beneath a few dirty rags. Many are so sick that often we have to be called from important duties to administer first aid, or to be just in time to see a neglected creature die while he is waiting to see a doctor.

One of these patients walked three hundred miles and reached Seoul. I found an apparent bundle of rags lying on a box behind the hospital. Leaning over this collection of skin and bones, I heard it say through blackened lips, "Jesu Poolachoo," meaning, "Oh, please call Jesus." He had no pulse and was almost a skeleton, having begged his way those many miles from the southern part of Korea.

There was no bed in the hospital, so a mattress was taken from my office table and he was put on the concrete floor of the basement, near other charity patients who had been more fortunate in finding beds, pathetically few in that ward.

We filled him up with hot intravenous medicine, fed him like a newborn baby, and after a few hours he could speak. After weeks of nursing, the X-ray showed us that his stomach outlet was occluded by an old healed ulcer. He was then specially fed to give him enough strength for an operation, which we performed a month later. The food now finds its way through a new passage. He actually grew fat, and one day without warning, he stood up and thanked God before the ward, and was bubbling over with praise for the kindness he had received.

At Christmas, we found that this man, instead of receiving a Korean Bible as a present, he preferred a new book called Studies in the Acts of the Apostles. He already had his own Bible, and was on the way to becoming a clever and sincere Christian. A gift of money from a missionary in our station at Lunchingtsun bought him a complete outfit of clothes – at a cost of $3.45, and the balance paid his way back to his home in the South, to which the present writer took him, and where he is now employed. The age of miracle is not past. Here we have a fine Christian gentleman who was once nothing but a bag of filth and bones.

Yet there are some people who still do not believe in miracles. I do, and they happen in institutions like Severance and other mission hospitals.

After admitting two beggar boys that day, (one with dysentery) I comforted a young woman who had lost her baby. I started out on rounds with a Salvation Army officer, a French lady. We visited a new section of "dugouts," where we found whole families on the verge of starvation. ["Dugouts" were simply small caves dug into the side of a hill.] The mother in one cave was dying, but we rescued her three children. The two girls, one a baby, were taken to the Salvation Army Home for Girls, and the boy to the Salvation Army Boy's Home.

It was about eight pm when I wandered home, tired but happy. The moon rose over East Gate and shone through the mist that covered the homes of thousands of people, most of them poor, yea, doubly poor because they knew not the love of Christ.

It gave Stan great satisfaction to work with Salvation Army officers of many nationalities. He gave the orphan children of the Salvation Army Boys' Home and Girls' Home medical exams, and helped to eradicate hookworm and other diseases from the homes. There were about sixty-five children at the time.

After a few months in Seoul, Stan had patients coming to his clinic who had strange wrinkled hands. They were the silk-mill girls. For long unbearable hours these girls sat in the Japanese-owned silk-mill factories, with their hands in very hot water unraveling the silk from the cocoons. Their wages were low. They hardly had time to eat their meals, and like many of the students they were in poor health and susceptible to tuberculosis.

Stan had a special concern for these girls and invited some of them to his home. The Martin children were fascinated to meet them and to learn about the process of making silk.

One of the girls brought the children a square piece of paper on which there was a circle filled with silkworm eggs. She told them to place the paper on mulberry leaves. Fortunately there were mulberry trees in the Martin's garden. Soon, there was a large tray of chopped mulberry leaves with little silkworms crawling around in them. The leaves had to be fresh, so more had to be added constantly. Once Margaret found her daughter Ruthie chopping leaves for the silkworms in the middle of the night.

The worms grew large and it was amazing to hear the sound as they crunched and devoured the leaves. Eventually they started to spin their cocoons. By then it was time to go to Wonsan, so the cocoons went with the family to the summer cottage. There, the children watched the silk moths emerge from their cocoons, and soon some of the moths were flying around and laying eggs in the mosquito nets. The family had learned a lot, as the silkworm eggs had come full cycle.

Stan continued his special interest in the silk-mill girls, many recovering from tuberculosis in his care.

Another time he wrote of one cold night in this article, "Our Doctor makes Midnight Rounds."

Our Doctor makes Midnight Rounds
S. H. Martin, MD, CM

How would you like to make rounds with me in an eastern city at midnight with a full moon to help you in your work? After getting some hot cocoa into our systems, and some good gas into my little "Ford," Ensign Widdowson, a Salvation Army officer from South Africa and I started out.

The thermometer was playing around zero when we first started to search the sewer-like stream that drains this ancient city from west to east. Under one of the bridges, on the ice covered by straw, was our first patient. But unfortunately for the doctor and his medical kit, he was dead. A young man about twenty-five frozen to death! We found over thirty urchins sleeping under bridges on straw or on the ice and covered with sacks. We distributed food tickets to them.

Then we went through the back streets and side alleys, some of these streets being only a few feet wide, leaving the car where we could reach it easily. Outside some government property, we found boys sleeping in some huge unused drain-pipes, behind a rock wall. We heard heavy snoring. On investigating, and pulling up a corner of some straw matting, we flashed an electric torch upon a wriggling mass of arms and legs and many pale, frightened faces. "How many are here?" "Seventeen, sir." "How many have eaten today?" "Four, sir." "Here, take these tickets and come to the Salvation Army soup kitchen between one and four o'clock tomorrow. Good night, remain in peace and sleep well."

Our itinerary led us behind the famous big Korean curfew bell at Chong No. Here, many years ago, when its notes boomed over the city, all the men disappeared from the streets and the women took their turn at coming out. Behind this bell, we found a moaning figure trying to keep warm on the frozen ground. His feet were bare, and his face and hands were swollen with the cold. I found that he had pneumonia and only a warm bed could save him. We gave him a stimulating injection and went to get the car, to return as soon as possible, only to find that he had passed on to join the thousands in the great beyond.

We passed through a great market place, now empty, and there on the frozen ground saw scores of boys and young men sleeping behind shelters of various kinds. Many of them were without food. One poor little fellow about ten-years-old was crying with pain and having examined him I found him in frail condition. I then turned to his sleeping companion who had short, matted hair. This poor creature turned out to be a young woman. The boy was put in my canvas automobile cover, and picked up like apples in a handkerchief and deposited in the back of the car. Later I got the young woman, who we found had formerly been a dancing girl. They are both on the way to recovery.

We had seen and given tickets and medicine to over sixty destitute homeless people in a small section of the city and coming back to the car, kicking open ash boxes as we went along, we found a boy of six, sleeping in an ash box.

He was afraid that we were police at first. I think that I had the best bit of fun in my fifteen years out here when I saw these boys the next morning. But I didn't sleep at all that night, thinking of that patch of straw on the frozen ground under which lay the shrunken shivering form of the young woman. Thank God she is not there now, but supposing the missionary doctor and the Salvation Army officer hadn't decided to take a walk every Saturday night in the dead of winter!

"Inasmuch as ye have done it unto the least of these," and these were "least" but just as precious.

He wrote of the need for more sanatoriums for tubercular patients. "There is no reason why all hospitals should not be asked to set aside beds or isolate wards for the exclusive use of these patients until more sanatoriums can be provided. Several mission hospitals have tubercular units such as ours at Severance.

Dr. Sherwood Hall of the Methodist Mission is doing an outstanding work fighting tuberculosis at his fine hospital in Haiju, Korea. Also he has started the campaign of Christmas anti-tuberculosis seals that are sold for publicity and funds for the work.

In the meantime all general hospitals and private physicians when treating tuberculosis should use the latest methods of lung collapses, such as pneumothorax, phrenicotomy and throcoplasty, by which 25% of those coming to clinics could be definitely saved. In our own chest clinic of 300 cases treated by lung collapse, 48% are clinically well, and 32% completely cured. Most of these are from the educated classes of Korea.

We are most fortunate that by the generosity of a good friend of the Korean people, a fine new brick building has been erected on the Severance compound. It's capable of taking care of twenty patients. This building is up-to-date in every particular; it is fitted with special ultra-violet glass windows and has a large roof garden for sun-treatment. Here, one hundred and sixty medical students get full instruction in the diagnosis of this disease." [14]

In his 1928-1929 report he wrote.

> Fourteen hundred students have been examined by me in an effort to find incipient cases of lung tuberculosis – students of Paiwha, Ewha, and Kyungsin Schools and three Bible Schools. Seventy-four cases were found. Forty-four cases of tuberculosis were found moderately active. Seventeen of these were removed from dormitories, and seventeen have died. Forty-eight students in the Salvation Army institutions and forty-five students in the Pierson Memorial Bible School were examined and four cases of tuberculosis were found and isolated. About thirty percent of our medical cases at Severance Hospital have tuberculosis of the lung. I have seen as many as eight new cases in one class and all of them incurable.

As care and treatment for tuberculosis patients often took years, Stan became very close to his patients. Many stories could be told but he wrote of one very special patient.

---

[14]   *The Korean Mission Field*, S. H. Martin, MD, CM p. 100

A Story of Ada Lim
"This heart was woven of human joys and cares,
Washed marvelously with sorrow and swift to mirth,
The years have given her kindness and dawn is here."

I was called to see a pastor's daughter who was supposed to be suffering from influenza. I very soon found that the upper third of her left lung was in a state of rapid destruction by tubercular disease. I carefully explained the situation to her, and from the beginning she had absolute faith in God's power to cure her, and in her physician's ability to assist in that cure. After one year's treatment on the veranda of the East Gate Hospital, she was persuaded by parents and friends to return home before the next winter. Conditions in her home were anything but ideal for her recovery, but she left the hospital against our wishes. Soon a large hemorrhage took her down and outwards and almost through the portals of Death. When she was very low, she asked God to spare her life so that she might become a Bible Woman.

During this time a Korean doctor of the old school was administering various herbs and decoctions containing tiger's teeth, beetles' wings, etc. I continued to see her daily and was often present at the same time as the Korean doctor, still waiting my time until the parents would let me transfer her to Severance Hospital. This permission was finally granted and the frail form of this much loved young college graduate was taken in Miss X's closed car, and then the recovery began. It was an uphill fight, but the love of several ladies, particularly of one, Miss X, together with Ada's great faith soon changed her weight from fifty-five pounds to one hundred and ten pounds. She spent almost all the summer on the hospital roof, where she had only the stars for company at night. Fresh air was an important part of the treatment.

Today Ada is without exception the brightest, jolliest and finest girl spiritually in a hospital of one hundred and fifty beds. In fact she was moved in before the building was finished. Every other day she goes home to see her family, and Christmas day was spent with her physician as one of the family.

Any day at noon if you were to come into the Women's tubercular ward you would find three college girls all praying for the work of the Severance Anti-Tubercular Society and especially for the writer. Ada prayed long that her friend Miss Ahn, who was seriously ill with tuberculosis in a country village, might be given the treatment she has had. Another Miss X stepped into the breach and so Miss Ahn is in the next room to Ada and is on the way to recovery. I cannot take time to tell of Miss Chiu, another pastor's daughter, and ten others. Remember these three college girls patiently fighting for life, as they pray each day at noon for a sanatorium where we can take care of the tubercular youth of Korea whom we love so much.

Our new tuberculosis wing is complete and we now have eleven patients. The hardest problem is that of refusing incurable cases. To date, four patients have been discharged well, and those at present are responding to treatment. We are planning to ask the Korean Government for permission to hold an "Anti-tuberculosis Day" in Seoul, when the double cross badge of the Anti-Tuberculosis Society will be sold. These badges act as very effective propaganda, for people are always asking what they represent. The Society asks the support of every missionary and teacher throughout the country in its effort to remove this most dreaded of diseases. [15]

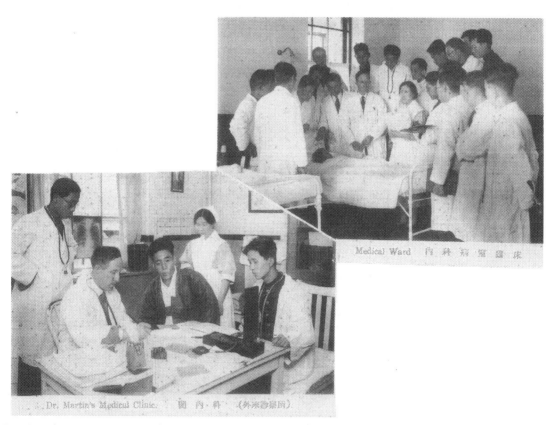

Dr. Stanley H. Martin with patients and medical students. Severance Hospital, Seoul, Korea

---

[15]   *Ref. Article, Anti-Tubercular Work At the Severance Union Medical College, Seoul, Korea, S. H. Martin, MD*

Martin family in Seoul. Seated: Betty, Mother Margaret, Edna, father
Stan. Phyllis on floor. Standing: daughter Margaret, and Jerry

XX

Stan's Furlough

It was time for the Martins' furlough again. Missionaries served seven years between furloughs in those days. Stan and Margaret decided that taking six children on the long trip home, with the deputation visits and the disruption of their schooling was not a good idea. They decided Stan would take a study furlough for a year, and Margaret would take some furlough time later.

For some time Margaret had been urging her seventy-nine-year-old father Lincoln Rogers to come for a visit and this would be the ideal time. He could help to care for the children and be good company for the family during the father's absence. They made plans for his coming.

Stan's eventful furlough year began in June 1930 and was recorded in the beautiful pictures he brought from Europe, and the newspaper accounts of an unexpected adventure to come.

Travel around the world is so common these days. With air travel, people flit around in no time, but in those days travel was slow and time consuming.

He planned to go by the ports, through Southeast Asia, the Suez Canal and Europe. His first ship after Japan was a German freighter. He told his children later, that every morning he heard a gruff voice outside his cabin door saying "You're bad!" meaning "Your bath." It was the ship steward saying he had drawn water for Stan's bath and it was ready.

Stan was always sensitive to color and beauty and as he traveled from place to place he expressed himself in poetry.

Sunset from the Peak in Hong Kong

Come! Leave the sun baked narrow streets and mount once more into the paths
of space;
To gaze like Cortez o'er a molten sea
From Hong Kong's Peak of Cathay's ancient race.

Here, lost in reverent contemplation gaze,
Into the western gate of golden glow;

And watch the silhouette of laden junks
To far off islands, wrapped in silence softly go.

Then all too soon the day has gone,
And stars rush out and fill the vault o'erhead;
With Milky Way and planetary dust.
The Southern Cross glows brightly near the Virgin's bed.

And far below, the man-made galaxy
Breaks forth in stars of golden glow;
The stately ships now silent, rest like swans
While o'er them southern zephyrs softly blow.

Sumatra Jungle at Midnight

Enwrapped in silence, I before the
Mighty jungle bow in awe and wonder.
Yet with bolder feet push on into the great unknown.

The path is lighted by the fireflies glow,
As I move along the lonely moonlit path alone.

The moon sails on into the silent tropic night,
The Malay Kampong push their roofs of nipa through jungle screen;
But over all there broods so near I even feel
The presence of the Great Unseen.

Sunrise on a Mosque in Singapore

The ship's bell sounds the hour of five,
A radiance is seen to eastward o'er a palm-groved shore.
The Southern Cross now low, pales out of sight.
Behind the jungled slopes of Singapore.

But lo! Behind me in the morning mist.
A silver mosque with minaret;
A firefly glistening in a golden glow
Entangled in a web of silver net.

Stan journeyed on through the Suez Canal, and on to Florence and Rome. There he reveled in the beauty of art and architecture. He especially bought paintings of the Renaissance artists to take to his children. He later told how disgusted he was to see tourists playing cards in their hotel rooms, instead of appreciating all there was to see and learn.

In Rome Stan made the tour of the catacombs. While there, he paused to examine some object more closely, but the tourist group moved on and turned around a corner. Just then his little candle went out and he was in total darkness.

"Now children if this ever happens to you," [he told his family later.] "Stay where you are. Don't move. If you wander around it'll be harder to find you." Stan stayed in his place and after what seemed like hours, a crowd of flickering candles appeared and he was safe again.

In Vienna Stan took a short course on heart diseases, and then moved on to London, where he took a study course at the London Heart Hospital. On a visit to the London headquarters of "The Mission to Deep Sea Fishermen," he was warmly welcomed, because of his work with Dr. Wilfred Grenfell in Newfoundland and the Labrador.

Then he crossed the Atlantic to St. John's, Newfoundland, to have some rest with his family and church.

The quiet days were suddenly shattered on March 16, 1931. The story was told in a letter sent to Korea from Arthur Martin, Stan's father.

171 Lemarchant Rd.
St. John's, Newfoundland
March 21, 1931

My dear Margaret, Mr. Rogers and the children,

Although the envelope has the address written by Stanley you will be surprised to find the letter and news is from me.

We had a happy Sunday the 15th, when Stan listened to the radio to Rev. Hugh Lyon the new Presbyterian minister. Fine man. Good preacher. We had a nice dinner, veal, peas etc. Stan then went to George St. Church (their family church) and taught Rev. Ira Curtis' Bible Class. (Rev. Curtis was married to Stan's sister Gertrude.)

On Monday morning Stan was writing letters until 11:30, he then started out visiting patients until 1:00PM returned to dinner 2 to 2:30. Two patients here for examination and prescriptions – Left for hospital to join Dr. F. to perform an operation. About 3:00PM phone message from Dept. Marine and Fisheries, the Hon. Mr. Lake. "Is your son Dr. Martin there?"—"No sir, gone to General Hospital." Little later. Phone from Mrs. Lake, "Can you find out where your son Dr. Martin is? The *Viking* has had an explosion and is sinking. 128 on ice, many injured, feared many lives lost." I phoned the hospital myself, got in touch with Stanley. Reply – "just heard of it myself. Will be home in 20 minutes. Tell Mother to get all warmest old clothes out of trunk, heavy underclothes, brown sweater, with shaving gear packed in valise. Warm tea as I have to be on a boat sailing from dock at 5 o'clock. A little later he came in and we helped to see that he forgot nothing. Got a loan of a warm fur cap and gloves from his friend next door.

Ira Curtis [Stan's brother-in-law] and Gertrude heard he was going, and rushed up. My sister, over 70, came in and also our niece Marjorie a trained nurse going to be married next summer. So we had a nice party of relatives to join in wishing him "Godspeed and Goodbye." I was glad for his mother's sake, it comforted her a lot to have Gertrude to stay with her as her husband and I went off in the car with Stan, staying until the rescue steamer the *Sagona* left dock. Lots of gentlemen, all our best people, on pier shouting out "Good luck Doctor."

Thank God there was great joy that at 5 o'clock just 24 hours later they sighted some wreckage. They took off Captain Kennedy Navigator, Clayton King, Marconi operator, and Mr. Sargent a New York moving picture man. They are doing as well as can be expected on the *Sagona*. It is very unfortunate we find wind forecast still northeast and north tomorrow. It makes it colder for all. I enclose you several cuttings, which I have numbered. The weather is wretched here, fog dense. Northeast wind keeping ice on shore packed tight.

Yours faithfully,
Arthur W. Martin and Minnie C. Martin
Love to you and children from everybody!

The next letter Margaret received in Korea about the event, was from Stan himself, written on the rescue ship the *Sagona*. Part of it is as follows:

I heard of the accident at 3PM on March 16th and volunteered to help and was accepted at once by the Minister of Marine and Fisheries. Erin drove me home quickly and I got fitted out with old clothes, sweaters etc. and here I am. I'm so sorry I will miss getting a letter off to you in the next mail – but my dear I couldn't resist the temptation to come out here and help, and I'm tickled to pieces to be here. We are lurching all over the place as we butt the ice. Will write more later. I expect to walk ashore to Horse Island tomorrow AM. Au revoir for now.

He added at the bottom of the page.

I walked (jumped) by myself over this loose ice to the island carrying drugs. (Further words are missing.)

The whole of the story eventually became more clear, with pictures and many newspaper articles in the Newfoundland papers and *The New York Times* and *Herald Tribune*.

A film crew from Paramount Pictures of New York had been on the *Viking*, a sealing ship near Horse Island, north of Newfoundland. They had been filming a movie called "White Thunder," based on the life and work of men in the sealing industry.

On March 15th this ship with one hundred and fifty-five men on board, was wrecked by an explosion. About twenty-nine men were never seen again. A wireless was sent. Healthy ones helped the injured into flat-bottomed boats called dories, and got them away from the ship that was on fire and sinking. A party of seventy men dragged and pushed the dories ten miles to Horse Island. It was sixteen hours of hard struggling during which time the dories were split asunder by rough ice. The ice was loose with a heavy swell but the sky was clear. The people of Horse Island came out a distance to greet them with food. Tired and hungry and suffering intense cold, the survivors were more than elated once more to set foot on dry land. In a short while, the wearied crew were located in the homes of the people and everything was done to comfort them. Later, a second contingent, and smaller groups made it to the island.

Meanwhile the rescue ship *Sagona* was moving toward the disaster area. On board were Stan and two other doctors, Patterson and Moore, and two nurses Miss Berrigan and Miss Payton. They were subject to a heavy storm for twenty-four hours. Miss Payton reported later on "the awful rolling of the ship." All of the medical people took to their bunks except Stan, who had experienced many storms at sea as a teenager.

The Evening Telegram, St. John's Newfoundland, March 24, 1931, reported, "Dr. S. H. Martin one of the medical men on the *S.S. Sagona*" describing what he saw from the ship says "We were providentially directed." "We were sweeping the sea with powerful binoculars when into our vision came a dark object that at first looked like a pack of seals. Traveling toward it we could see a flag waving and soon discerned two figures, and another moving as a blinded man might. We bore down as carefully as we could on the ice-pan which was about six feet across and in a bad condition and in danger of breaking up. A dory was slung out and Clayton King was gently lifted into it and swung aboard the ship. Many hands helped the other two men from their hazardous position and at once everything possible was done to relieve their suffering and restore their strength. The ship at the time the rescue was made had drifted 21 miles from the disaster area. At once a search was made on the surface of the sea but not a single trace of living or dead was found before darkness set in." [16]

The three survivors were Wireless Operator Clayton King, Henry Sargent of the film crew and Master Mariner William Kennedy. They told their story. King had been blown out of the side of the ship. His face and eyes were badly burned, and one leg was fractured. . Sargent with a head injury had been flung out with the stern of the *Viking* that had landed on the ice-pan. He had pulled King up to safety with him. They then were joined by Kennedy. Sargent and Kennedy had managed to gather from the ice near them, some of the debris including tins of milk, baked beans, some clothing, two flags, and a piece of burlap which they wrapped around the helpless Clayton King. They had drifted off into the night and all the next day, suffering untold hardship from exposure to the cold. The pan in which the wreckage was embedded broke with the swell

---

16   *The Evening Telegram*, St. John's, NFLD March 24, 1931.

and was gradually becoming smaller. The drifting men watched it dissolving as they approached open water. Then to their eyes came the welcome sight of the *S.S. Sagona*.

After picking up the survivors the *Sagona* proceeded towards Horse Island, but because of tightly packed ice she could get no closer to it than six miles. The next morning the sealer *Imogene*, the most powerful steamer in the vicinity was able to reach two miles closer to the island.

Otis Bartlett the twenty-one-year-old wireless operator on Horse Island stuck to his job night and day for four days, appealing for help and giving news of the survivors. He was highly praised for his work. Soon more sealers were steaming toward them. The Governor of Newfoundland was advised of events, and Mr. Lake the Minister of Marine and Fisheries supervised the rescue efforts from a distance.

As the news of the tragedy spread, the family of Varick Frissell heard of it, and they were frantic with anxiety. Varick was the movie producer. Dr. Lewis Frissell, his father, sent a large Sikorsky amphibian from Boston to aid in the search for survivors. It also carried food and medical supplies. It was piloted by a man name Belcher who had extensive Arctic flying experience.

A St. John's newspaper reported a letter from Doctor Martin dated March 18th.

> Here I am on a relief ship out in the ice, with five seriously sick men on board, with broken legs and gangrenous feet from frost-bite, one man with pneumonia. There are three M.D.s Patterson, Moore and myself, and two nurses, Miss Berrigan and Miss Payton. We picked up three men on a pan floating loose, waving flags from some wreckage, which consisted of the stern of the Viking which blew up and caught fire. 118 men have landed on Horse Island to which we are now endeavoring to force our way butting ice. Among the 118 men who are short of food there are more injured men. Moore and I may walk ashore tomorrow about five miles on the loose ice. We want to get all the injured men off as soon as possible, get out of this ice before we are jammed, and up to St. John's where we will have several amputations, unless we are stuck, then we will do them on board. We are lurching all over the place as we butt the ice. [17]

Soon, however, the *Sagona* was jammed in a solid pack of ice stretching for miles around. The decision was made to send assistance to the island from the ship. A party made up of twenty-five men and Doctors Patterson and Moore prepared to haul medical supplies and food over the ice. Dr. Martin was to stay with the seriously ill on board.

The trip was difficult, and the dory was completely demolished but the group arrived safely. The sick and injured were given attention, and the doctors, the cooks and the crew of the rescue ship, served food to the survivors and islanders whose food supply was practically exhausted.

The same day, one hundred eight of the uninjured men arrived at the *Sagona* from Horse Island, having walked the span of ice from the island.

Stan and the nurses were now the only medical help on the ship as the rescue party was still on the island.

---

[17]   *The Evening Telegram*, St. John's, NFLD. March 18, 1931.

Miss Payton, one of the nurses wrote of those days, "Diligently we worked and eagerly we waited for the return of the relief party. After what seemed a year to us the whole of the relief party arrived." The islanders had assisted in dragging the dories with the injured. High praise was given to them, saying the work could not have been done without them.

Troubles were not over. A wire was sent from Captain Kean of the *Sagona* to the Minister of Marine and Fisheries.

> *S.S. Sagona* via Fogo, March 20, '31 Wind east northeast blowing strong thick snow; can't possibly move, as the ice is packed tight. No prospects of getting clear without a change of wind. If weather conditions don't improve our position will be serious as there is shortage of food and the ship is over-crowded, while sick men occupy the saloon. Doctor agrees with this arrangement. *Beothic* and *Imogene* jammed about a mile and a half inside us. Impossible for us to move either way.

> Signed Kean

Adding to the tragedy of the *Viking* disaster at that time, another sealer the *Sir William* foundered in the open water, and twenty-eight men had been rescued by the *Eagle*.

Stan, with his years as wireless operator, checked in when he could with the wireless operator on board the *Sagona*. They had many stories to share. Imagine his delight and relief when the message came in that the *Prospero* was on the way to bring help.

"Why, that's the ship that took my Margaret up to the St. Anthony hospital to be a nurse for Dr. Grenfell nineteen years ago! She later became my wife. I know the ship well."

The *Prospero* had been ordered by Mr. Lake, Minister of Marine Fisheries to take all men possible from the *Sagona*, to transfer full food supplies to that ship, and also to take from the *Eagle* the twenty-eight men rescued from the *Sir William*.

Help was coming but that was available only in open water. Five days passed and the crowded *Sagona* remained fast in the ice. Captain Kennedy's pneumonia became more serious and unfortunately he died on the way to safety.

The nurse, Miss Payton, wrote a report of those days.

> Once again the human was helpless. Unless the wind should change we were powerless even to turn. The condition of two of our patients was so serious that every day meant a lessened chance for them to live.

> It was Sunday March 22nd, and we were reminded that in hundreds of churches prayers would be going up on our behalf. We could do nothing but wait. Suddenly at 11PM the wind veered and the ice began to break up. It appeared miraculous! So rapidly did the ice break, that in half an hour the ship had turned, and was following in the wake of the two sealing vessels which had been jammed. Two hours only did it take to plough through those miles of ice. We reached the open sea. The *Prospero* was waiting and transfers were made. Then the wind changed

and was blowing east again sending the ice back to practically the same position as before we started!!

The headlines of the *Evening Telegram* St. John's Newfoundland March 24, 1931 were:

'SAGONA' BRINGS

'Viking' Survivors

Heroism of Masterwatch is Outstanding Episode of 'Viking' Disaster

----

William G. Johnston Stood by Injured
for 52 Hours

Devoted Services of Doctors and Nurses
Praised by Injured—Work of Dis-
embarkation Efficiently Carried Out

At two o'clock this morning the rescue ship *Sagona*, Capt. Jacob Kean entered port, bringing back from the scene of the disaster which overtook the sealer *Viking* on the night of Sunday, of 15th of March, many survivors and the sick and injured, numbering twelve, and the body of Capt. William Kennedy the Navigator.

To the gathering of the spectators on the pier, her dark bulk as she came through the Narrows, and slowly and silently approached was impressively significant of the tragedy that had occurred. Men moved about her deck softly as in the presence of death. There was an absence of the usual shouting and bustle as the ship was berthed, and those present at the early hour stood in silence that spoke their sympathy far more eloquently than words. Before the arrival of the ship, the Prime Minister of Newfoundland, also Mr. Lake, Minister of Marine and Fisheries, with several other members of the government had assembled on Harvey & Co.'s wharf.

The Evacuation

As soon as the ship was made fast, the work of removing the victims commenced, Doctors Moore, Martin and Patterson directing the removal of the injured on stretchers, Dr. Macpherson looking after the transfer to the ambulances and Nurses Berrigan and Paton seeing to the comfort of the patients. Those who were uninjured were taken to boarding houses or to their homes in motor cars, and as soon as there would be no impeding of the work, the press correspondents boarded the ship to learn the particulars of the disaster. From Captain Jacob Kean on down they were met with courtesy, but the piecing of the story required many interviews before the tragic occurrence and the work of rescue could be learned. Stan was interviewed later, as he and the medical staff went immediately to General Hospital with the patients.

The *Evening Telegram* made the event clearer.

One question was uppermost. "How did it happen? Why the explosion?" There were many theories. The reporters learned that on the fatal night, Sargent, Penrod and Varick Frissell all members of the film crew, were located in the cabin at the stern of the Viking. To understand the situation, a brief description of the ship's structure is necessary.

The powder magazine was on the starboard side in the very stern of the ship. Next to this was the boatswain's cabin in which it was said was an oil lamp. The captain's cabin was next forward. On the opposite side of the ship were rooms occupied by assistant Best, Navigator Kennedy and wireless operator King. Between was the cabin in which were sitting at a table, Penrod on port side, Sargent in the middle, and Frissell on the left.

The latter who was the director of the film crew, had been speaking of the danger of having the powder magazine in which a ton of explosives was stored. He had just said "I'm no artist but I'm going to make a danger notice." Penrod was engaged with some films, and Sargent was discussing the next day's operations. Just behind him was the sternpost. Frissell had scarcely spoken when the ship lurched, and almost immediately came the explosion that tore the whole stern off the ship taking it is estimated 29 lives, and hurling men and wreckage in all directions. One blast pushed forward along the starboard and the other along the port side sweeping everything before the terrific force, and combining forward of the cabin, cleaning out the whole of the engineer's quarters in which there were three engineers. Sargent was flung out with a piece of wreckage which pitched on a pan of ice.

These details of the last moments were given by Sargent of the film company.

Following the explosion men scattered in all directions. William Kennedy said he saw Varick Frissell, the New York movie producer, and A. G. Penrod cameraman, caught in falling rigging and unable to get away. It was the presence of mind of Captain Abram Kean Jr. the Viking's master that saved the situation. Injured as he was by being flung from the bridge to the ice twelve feet below, he ordered them to keep together. This undoubtedly saved many from wandering away blindly or of finding death between the ice pans.

Many of the crew were on the ice without boots, others had no mitts or caps, and practically no food. Captain Kean badly injured, though able to stand, shouted to the crew to cut the dories loose. It was a very dangerous task owing to the flames which spread so quickly, and the fear that at any moment the boilers might explode. Several men got on board and secured eight dories. On the other side of the ship men were also cutting dories clear.

As soon as they could, the men moved away from the burning ship and started toward Horse Island. The first group arrived after sixteen hours dragging the dories holding the injured—another large contingent arrived later. Some smaller groups also reached the island.

There were many stories of the courage and bravery of the survivors. Two stories remain to be told.

A survivor who came in on the *Sagona* that night was William G. Johnston, the masterwatch. The pluck and perseverance of this man is one of the outstanding achievements in the grim story of the disaster.

He was forward attending a prayer meeting, when the explosion occurred. When he reached the companionway, he saw that the ship was all on fire aft, and the bridge was swinging with the roll of the ship. He took his oil clothes, chart and compass and collected some fifteen men. They secured a dory into which they put the mate Alf Kean who had been blown from the bridge and was found 20 feet from the ship with a broken leg, and Fred Best of the film crew who was found near the stern of the Viking, and was being assisted by some men. He had burns on both feet.

With ropes attached to the dory the 15 men started towards land. The ice was running and very rough. After proceeding about 7 miles the men began to show signs of exhaustion; the dory was badly battered by the ice. Under these conditions Johnston told the men to go on towards the island and get help, and he would remain with the injured men.

All went except Mike Roch, Richard Walker and a third man. Johnston could not remember the man's name. The three remained until Tuesday morning (the explosion was Sunday night) and no sign of assistance coming. Then Johnston sent the three to the land and he was left alone with the injured men.

About 3PM on Tuesday seven men from Horse Island came to the rescue with food. It was impossible for them to move the dory with the injured men over the ice and they returned to the shore. The little group spent another night huddled in the dory. The morning of the third day broke. There was no sign of assistance until about 10AM Wednesday when the sealing ship the *Beothic*, with Captain Carter, was sighted.

Shortly after, the plucky Johnston saw the two injured men safe aboard ship. Mr. Johnston is about 48 years of age. He has been going to the ice for 25 years and this was his fourth spring as master watch.

The other story was that of Harry Brown. The newspaper headline was, "Salvationist's Devotion Which Saved His Life."

Among the crew of the *Viking* the Newfoundland sealing vessel which met with disaster in the Arctic Circle a few weeks ago, was a Salvationist a soldier of the St. John's III Corps Newfoundland who had a marvelous deliverance.

The *Viking* met heavy weather soon after leaving St. John's. None but the crew were permitted on deck during hours when seas were sweeping the gallant little wooden-sheathed sealer.

As Sunday night approached, the ship was steaming in loose running ice which was piling high on the swelling sea. Brother Brown who worked in the aft galley, a cook to the captain and his officers, became possessed by the idea that if no one else conducted a Sunday service with the one hundred men in the forequarter of the ship, he would do so himself.

Telling his helper to carry on until his return, when he would finish the work to be done, Brown left the cabin, and never saw his friend again.

He had his hand on the door to descend to the forecastle, when he was accosted by a man, whom he knew slightly who said, "I notice that you do not swear or smoke."

"Oh, no" replied Brown. "I don't nowadays get any pleasure out of these things, for I am saved."

Suddenly a tremendous explosion shook the vessel, and our comrade knew nothing more until he found himself on the ice, yards away from the ship, standing by an injured man, whom he discovered to be the mate. Near about him were twenty men dazedly and aimlessly wandering about.

Aroused by the sound of detonations aboard the wrecked vessel, the mate asked Brown if he could go aboard again and get some clothes. The whine and whistle of exploding ammunition, and the boom of bursting tins of blasting powder gave a warning but our comrade said, "Ay, ay sir!" and started toward the part of the *Viking* that had not blown away. Aft of the engine room was now an inferno.

Within a few minutes he had secured from the mens' quarters, a large quantity of coats, caps, oil clothes, and heavy blankets for the injured men. At any moment the ship might slide from the gripping ice back into the hole that the explosion had made at the stern, or the balance of the blasting powder might blow the ship high in the air with everything on board.

The mate had in the meantime, thought of food, and Brown was again requested to secure supplies. This task led him to a room almost immediately above the region of the ship's magazine.

Securing a few loaves, he threw them over the ship's side, and with two other loaves under his arm, rejoined his party.

Placing the wounded men on the two blankets well covered with coats and clothing, in a dory to which was connected just one rope for hauling the pelts of seals, the twenty-five men started for the shore.

After twenty-two hours of Herculean effort a halt was made, and it was decided that it was impossible to get the wounded men farther in the dory, without food and drink to restore lost strength. The island was some two miles away and it was decided that having made the wounded men comfortable, and leaving with them with three men who had volunteered to stay, the remaining twenty should make for the shore, seeking aid and provisions.

Some idea of the conditions prevailing can be understood when it is realized that six hours were expended in making the short distance to shore, where the men staggered to the nearby houses, and in most cases, collapsed for long hours. Brown was picked up unconscious about fifteen yards from the nearest of the fifteen houses in the little hamlet.

Those who heard the story praised God that Brown had gone forward in the ship to hold a service, that saved his life.

These stories are similar, but over a hundred men made it to the island—most of them being able to walk unencumbered by the dragging of the dories with their injured companions.

After the *Sagona* returned to St. John's and the patients were turned over to the capable medical people at General Hospital, Stan returned to the arms of his family. For days he could hardly move he was so tired, but calls kept coming for him to come and tell his version of the story. So after he recovered, he fulfilled many requests. The churches especially wanted to hear all the details because they had been praying for the whole situation.

The rest of his furlough was peaceful, and he set his mind towards returning to his family and work in Korea. Margaret was an excellent letter writer so he had been kept in touch. En route back to Korea he attended a six week course at the Trudeau Sanatorium at Saranac Lake, NY.

Stan wrote a report of his visit there.

> Trudeau Sanatorium was named for Dr. Edward Trudeau the first physician to use the treatment of tuberculosis by complete rest in the open fresh air. His work brought hope and life to thousands. This center became a place of scientific research and the best place for post-graduate work in this disease in the world. There were lectures by specialists in occupational therapy, diagnosis, and seriological and bacteriological aspects of the disease.

> There are thirty-three doctors attending this course. They are from sanatoriums all over the world.

> Before the closing of our course, I was asked to speak on my TB work at Severance and my eleven years missionary work at Lungchingtsun. They were greatly interested and called out "Go on! Go on!" until after eleven o'clock.

> I'm on the way to Korea. Through the great kindness of Sir Wilfred Grenfell a very reliable electrocardiograph has been donated to me to be used in the Chest Clinic of the Severance Union Medical College and Hospital, Seoul, Korea. This machine which is over $2,000 is used in detecting the slightest derangement of the action of the heart. With the special study of the many forms of heart disease under experts in Vienna last fall and with the machine I feel as though I could handle any problem.

Group of Korean doctors and medical students at Martin home. Lincoln A. Rogers (Margaret's father) with Stan and Margaret. Surgeon Dr. Koh behind Mr. Rogers.

XXI

Grandpa "Halabooji"

When Grandpa Rogers came down the steps of the train in Seoul, he was no stranger to his happy squealing grandchildren. Margaret looked on and beamed as he hugged each one – all six of them. He then embraced his only daughter, their mother. It was like a happy dream. He had kept in touch by writing to each child at different times, and mother Margaret had carefully checked the Trans-Pacific sailings to be sure that letters were crossing steadily to his home in Maine. He had followed the events of their lives, so it was easy to pick up from there.

Stan was still away on his furlough, so when her father settled in the spacious guest room, and blended into the family routine it seemed so right. Margaret was comforted and strengthened to have a man in the house again. Grandpa was seventy-nine years old at the time.

When Lincoln Albion Rogers reached the family he brought the wisdom and experiences of a completely different generation. He was born in 1852. He told that as a little boy he was watching his mother make an apple pie, when news came in that Abraham Lincoln had been assassinated. He was a Latin and Greek scholar so he was able to help his high school grandchildren with their Latin. He was a graduate of Bowdoin College in Brunswick, Maine, class of 1875, and a friend of Henry Wadsworth Longfellow. The family had some treasured Longfellow letters from those days. Lincoln Rogers had a long career as an educator. He was principal of Topsham High School in 1876, he then taught for the next two years at Castine Normal School before leaving for Chicago to take a position in the Dearborn Seminary there. Two years later he became the principal of the New Britain Seminary in Connecticut, remaining for four years, while for the five following years he taught in the New Britain High School. At that time he established the Paterson Military School in New Jersey, continuing as its head for 14 years. His graduates were well received in the Ivy League schools.

Returning to Maine, he was superintendent of schools for Mexico and Dixfield for 1908-1909. A year later he engaged in the real estate business from which he retired in 1923.

All this was in the past and now he was "Grandpa" in a busy household. He was *halabooji* in the Korean language. The Koreans were amazed at him for several reasons. They watched as he strode down the street so vigorously, even though his hair was grey. He was not bent over nor did he need a cane. He took over the shopping for the family. He learned to ride the street-cars and took off to distant markets bringing home treasures. He found Mocha coffee beans and pineapples in Honmachi, the Japanese market. The coffee beans he found piled up in woven grass baskets. He brought them home and ground them in a meat grinder. He bargained with the vendors at the kitchen door, picking up some of the Korean and Japanese languages enough to know prices and the currency.

He was an experienced gardener. Soon, white grape and concord grape arbors grew by the house. He knew how to prune the vines and care for them through the seasons. Wild grapes were at the back of the house. These were left to climb through some chestnut trees. Wild grapes though small, made excellent jelly and juice. He planted a strawberry bed, and with the family cow up on the hill, he had good manure for fertilizer. He produced some splendid crops. He made six garden plots in the vegetable garden – one for each grandchild, telling them they could plant anything they wanted there. This led to an interest in gardening and appreciation for flowers the rest of their lives.

Grandpa Rogers took a great interest in the culture of Korea, and the mission work on the various mission stations. He made several trips around the country and wrote articles on what he saw for the *Seoul Press*, for his Brunswick hometown newspaper, and for the missionary news magazine *The Korea Mission Field*.

In June, Stan returned from his furlough. The three years Grandpa Rogers spent with the family went by quickly. One of the most exciting times was the summer of the typhoon.

The family had gone north to Wonsan for the summer. Grandpa was with them but Stan was at work in Seoul at the time.

When the family woke up that August morning, the sky and sea were yellow, and the waves were churning angrily at the shore. It was the day of the Friday night entertainment, and twelve-year-old Margie was to play a violin solo that night. In the afternoon she and her mother went down to the big auditorium to practice. Her mother was her accompanist as usual. As they were playing, suddenly the large shutters of the huge place began to slam down one after another. The wind was lifting them and the shutter poles clattered to the ground. Margie was playing the lullaby "Sweet and Low," of all things. Startled, the two Margarets stopped rehearsing, packed up the violin and started for home. A short distance from there, at the shore, they saw many of the teenagers standing, holding out their arms facing the wind as it blew from the angry stormy sea. The sand stung their arms and legs. Then they saw a sight that terrified them. The sea was leaving its bed and creeping up over the shore, filling in the flat areas. The cottages at that end of the beach were closest to the shore. The Martin's house was a little farther inland.

They hurried home to find Grandpa already busy going around the house nailing down all of the shutters. Luckily some strong, long nails were available. The children were all safely home and the family settled in to an early supper wondering what would happen. There were no radios and no weather warnings. The wind grew stronger and stronger and the rain came down in torrents. This was only a little two-story wooden cottage that shuddered from time to time. The oil lamps were swinging. The children finally went to bed but Grandpa and Margaret stayed dressed and awake all night.

In the morning the rain and wind still blasted against the house, but the roof held. Margaret said to the children, "If this keeps up, we may have to evacuate and go inland."

"Where? When? May I take my dolls?" the little ones asked. The question was not only where, but <u>how</u> could they even go outside of the house?

Margaret urged the children to eat a breakfast of hot oatmeal and they waited. As the morning passed, the wind began to die down and they looked out of their kitchen door. The large acacia tree that stood there was stripped of every leaf, just as in winter. At last Grandpa said he was going to walk to the Beach House, the guest house for those who did not own cottages. It was farther back from the ocean. There he could hear the news of the rest of the community. Nine-year-old Jerry went with him.

When Grandpa came back he said, "At the southern end of the beach all the cottages were flooded, because the creek had backed up. The waves had been pounding on the cottages at the shoreline but no one was hurt or missing. A fishing boat had been smashing up over and over against the Boots' cottage. Many had waded hip deep to the Beach House. A Salvation Army mother woke up in the night to see her baby's crib floating beside her, but all was well.

The rumor was that if the typhoon had continued at peak ferocity much longer they may all have been swept into Wonsan Harbor beyond them.

Although the missionary community was safe, the storm's destruction became apparent when mountains of debris began to pile up on the shore. It was made up of mostly willow trees torn from the river banks. Bodies of oxen and other animals and some human bodies were found among them. The Martin children were not allowed to go near the shore. There was a strange smell in the air from the decaying willow trees. It took several days for the seashore debris to be carted away by Korean villagers, so the children were content to play in the many rain pools in the meadows.

A few weeks went by, then came a surprise! The acacia tree burst into full bloom with its fragrant white flowers, just as if it were spring!

By now it was almost time for school to start again. Wash-outs had developed on the railroad lines, but now the trains were running again, and the family packed up to return to Seoul. With so few communications, Stan had been frantic for news of the family so he welcomed his family home with heartfelt gratitude. Margaret told him what a tower of strength Grandpa had been. In Seoul they learned from the newspapers of the terrible loss of life and property due to the typhoon. It was a summer to be remembered.

Martin family. Seated left to right: Edna, Jerry, Phyllis, Betty, mother
Margaret. Standing: Ruth, father Stan, daughter Margaret.

XXII

Guglielmo Marconi

❦

As Stan returned to Korea after his eventful furlough, his workload increased. Word spread that many were recovering from various illnesses after visiting Dr. Martin at Severance Hospital. Often grateful patients came to his home with strings of eggs, or a few apples in a kerchief. Eggs were carried in a long container woven of barley straw, ten at a time, not twelve as in the west.

As Stan faced each day, he never knew what strange event would take place. He wrote of his experiences for newspapers and the churches back home.

A Doctor's Daily Dilemma

The day broke through smoke and cloud over the South Mountain, and into empty corridors with their clean smell of Lysol disinfectant. The clinic workers were singing "What a Friend We Have in Jesus" "making a joyful noise unto the Lord." The doctor and his assistants were starting the long round of treating the sick, and of giving bedside instruction to his medical students, in the main wards of Severance Hospital. Many acute cases were rapidly becoming normal and others were patiently holding their own. Beside the bed of an unconscious young man – an attempted suicide – was the photo of a smiling modern girl. The smile was part of the cause of the poisoning. In the ward above, a young woman with the face of a sphinx, lay staring at the ceiling. She was not sick, her pulse and temperature were normal. She was heartbroken (*sok sang hesso* in the Korean language). Her young husband had died the night before.

But it is after 10:00 a.m., and the doctor must hurry to the clinic, where the waiting room is filled with suffering humanity, waiting in turn beneath a huge painting of "Christ Healing the Sick" when He too was a practicing physician. The first patient, a youth of twenty, accompanied by many uncles and aunts, sat

232

with the shoulder blades of his emaciated chest flaring, a replica of the *Winged Victory* at the Louvre! But this picture represented defeat. What answer could be given to the anxious father's "How many days will it take to cure him?" when it was a matter of years, and even then no complete cure!

Many other cases such as these were seen. One young Japanese woman of university standing was told quietly and honestly, that she had not a weak lung, but the truth, which she already knew, was that she must be treated for tuberculosis immediately. She received the shock with tears in her eyes, and the trace of a "Mona Lisa" smile playing around her lips as she said, "*Shi kata ga nai.*" (It can't be helped) She departed with faith in her heart and six Kagawa books in one of her sleeves. One of the books was entitled, *The Thorn in the Flesh*, and another *Meditations on Christ*. [Toyohiko Kagawa was an amazing Christian who went into the slums of a large Japanese city to live with the people there. He wrote many fine Christian books.]

An old man with visible stomach cancer, tried to get the doctor to tell him that it was due to indigestion, although he really knew that the demon that had seized his vitals was cancer, and there was little hope.

A Chinese "dancing girl" with a Shantung accent told her many woes and was advised to go to the Christian Home for women with her type of problems. He gave her the address.

It was time to pick up some homeless he had found in the night. He had told them to wait at the Salvation Army headquarters that noon and he would drive them to a home of rest, warmth, and good food, outside West Gate, to the Salvation Army Boys Home

Leaving them there, the doctor, having opened all the windows of his car for ventilation, rushed off to the other end of the city, to a very clean Japanese home. There, all was silent save the sound of Japanese slippers on the polished floors within, and the sound of rain without. The patient, a dignified matron was waiting there with her son. The doctor spoke in Japanese and gently told her about the results of her tests that had been made at the hospital. They showed the onset of insidious cancer. He drew diagrams to illustrate the operation to be done the next day.

Elaborate bows were made and No. 51 after being driven, drenched and cleaned, was housed again for the night, or so the doctor hoped. He climbed the hill to his home, and opened the library door to find a poor woman who had been waiting two hours. She apologized as he tried to dig up from the depths a Christian smile of welcome. She had come to thank him for saving her son's life, and with many words of gratitude, she placed on the table many "sticks" of eggs. She departed into the mud and rain (Koreans hate mud), and the doctor felt a lump in his throat as he saw her going off alone into the darkness, and again he questioned, "Should I have sent her home in a taxi?"

And so to bed, until the roar of the city again steals to his window, and a lurid red breaks over the South Mountain, and the corridors of the city hospitals fill again with the sick and suffering. As the doctor starts anew, he wonders, "How many shall I turn away today, and how many times shall I fall short of what Christ would have me be and do?"

Three of the Martin children, Ruth, Edna and Jerry were given the experience of having some high school years at the missionary boarding school in Pyeng Yang up north. There they were in school with missionary children from Korea, Japan, China, and even Tibet. Rosa Bell and her sister, Ruth, who later married Billy Graham, were some of their classmates. The Bell sisters came from China to attend school. Stan checked on the health of many of the Pyeng Yang students including Rosa Bell. The Martin daughters Margaret, Phyllis and Betty stayed in Seoul.

Once in awhile patients came to Stan who had served time in the Japanese-run prisons. He was angry and grieved to hear of their treatment including torture. He became aware that many healthy young people came out of their experiences in prison, "as white as a sheet," in the second – or third stages of tuberculosis. He protested vehemently to the prison authorities.

In the midst of the days of gloom and problems for Stan came a bright experience that had roots in the past. He wrote of it in his own words in 1933.

Seoul, Korea

On this great highway of the world, in Seoul the capital of Korea, the foreign community was greatly disappointed when they heard that the famous Marquis Guglielmo Marconi, who was now in Seoul, was indisposed because of so many engagements in Japan. He could only accept an informal tea-party with the Governor General of Korea. The writer was therefore surprised when in the midst of a busy clinic, a telephone message came from Marconi's secretary asking me to call and see him (Marconi) if he could spare the time. The work of the department was arranged, and the writer took with him Dr. Ludlow, a surgeon on our staff, well known for his research in cancer and other diseases. They were soon ushered into the Marquis' private suite. Marquis Guglielmo Marconi and his secretary Mr. Umberto Marconi gave us a very warm welcome. (Umberto Marconi was a personal friend of the writer, with whom he had been associated in Manchuria for ten years.) In a few minutes they were asking us searching questions about our research work at Severance Medical College. Signor Marconi said, "I am extremely interested in medical research and am in a small way connected with it in Italy."

Dr. Bastonelli, the renowned Italian surgeon who is well known to both of us, is a close friend of Marconi's and had recently operated on the Marquesa for appendicitis.

The Marquis then told us of experiments on mice, using only ten centimeter electro-magnetic waves (micro-waves). He told us how by protecting a mouse in a metal case and leaving the tail out – the tail sloughed off after an hour's exposure, but that the mouse was unaffected in any way. However, the mouse would be killed almost immediately by exposure to these short waves without protection. The relation to cancer of lesions produced by X-ray burns was discussed, also the theory of cancer being due to the omnipresence of electro-magnetic energy in highly civilized centers of the world.

The Marquis was greatly pleased with the type of research that Dr. Ludlow was carrying on, and took with him a package of reprints on cancer and other diseases which have been especially studied at Severance. Later I was glad to give professional service to the Marquesa who was not feeling well.

They were interested that I had been there on Signal Hill, St. John's Newfoundland when Marconi received his first Atlantic signals on December 12th, 1901. I was eleven years old. Later in the day I was again invited to a private interview. At this time our family gave the Marconis a Korean brass bowl, our sixteen-year-old daughter Ruth making the presentation. It was a gift I had received from the second wife of the late Korean king in gratitude for healing from an illness.

Signor Marconi has not lost his famous boyish smile, and when not in deep thought his keen sense of humor flowed through his conversation. On being congratulated again for his great work, he said, "If you set your heart and soul upon doing a thing, you can do it."

The charming Marquesa with her patrician dignity, yet motherly eagerness was looking forward to speaking to their three-year-old daughter Elletra by wireless telephone from Shanghai to Rome.

It was a never to be forgotten hour to see again the face, and talk with the man who had made possible for humanity the famous SOS call, and to hear him discuss how we might use the same electro-magnetic waves in the future.

Soon afterwards some troubling news reached Korea. The Board of Foreign Missions wrote that, "Owing to continuous decline in receipts from the Missionary Maintenance Fund and depletion of its own reserves, there will be a reduction of approximately $100,000 in field expenditure in 1936. This meant that several missionaries who were on furlough were held back from returning to their work. The appeals for help from the countries affected, showed in a vivid way how much the United Church of Canada was doing around the world. The Martins were secure in their work but Margaret sold some of her family silver heirlooms, and a piece of her timberland in Maine to make ends meet.

Dr. William Scott a missionary educator added to the appeal from Korea saying, "There stands the pressing need for a nation-wide campaign against tuberculosis. At present this work heads up in two men, one whom is our Canadian representative on Severance staff."

Korea's cut was to be $40,000 but was later reduced to $10,000.

Stan was further cheered to hear that 28,000 of his booklets on *The Care and Prevention of Tuberculosis* had been sold, and that missionaries at several stations had sent in enthusiastic reports, asking for more copies.

He was also in the midst of a study of the relation between sprue and pernicious anemia. He had many cases among the missionaries who were completely cured through his plan of treatment.

XXIII

"Silhouetta"

The Martin family had many friends in the missionary community. However no family was closer or more loved than the Newlands of the Southern Presbyterian Mission in Kwangju, in the southern part of Korea. Rev. Roy Newland and his wife Sarah had five children. All of the family was welcome to the Martin home whenever they visited Seoul. Stan Martin and Roy were especially good friends.

From the Newland house at Kwangju, one could see a great mountain to the south. The Koreans called it *Mudung San* meaning the "Incomparable One" or the "Unsurpassable Mountain." It was special to their family because Roy had built a little cottage there for their summer vacations. They had spent several summers there. Other missionaries had chosen the community beaches of Sorai Beach on the west coast, or Wonsan Beach on the east coast, or the mountain community of Chiri San in the southern mountains of Korea.

When the time came each summer, the Newland family had to climb up a steep mountain path to reach their destination, the little house in a clearing. It took about two hours.

In the summer of 1935, Stan was invited to spend some time with the Newlands at their cottage on *Mudung San*, so he joined the caravan that started out that early July morning. Sarah Newland was carried in a sedan chair by two strong Korean men. Other Korean men carried boxes of food and other supplies. Each Newland child carried a suitcase. Their woman cook was with them, and this year the procession was followed by the family cow and a young Korean dairy farmer to care for it. With all those children they would need the milk.

Upon reaching the top, what a relief it was for them to feel the cool mountain air, after the steamy, unbearable summer weather below. It was absolutely thrilling to be there. The children raced around the cottage exploring their favorite places. It was a wonderful safe place for the summer, or was it?

As the family unpacked the supplies, the farmer took the cow to a little shed that was to be it's shelter for the summer.

That night they slept soundly in the cool air after the hot sleepless nights in Kwangju. Life took on a happy routine. The children gathered wild tiger lilies and bluebells, and played in the area near the cottage.

"Don't go too far – stay in calling distance." said the parents. The cook baked wonderful bread, and with milk and simple canned foods everyone was satisfied. Water came from a mountain brook nearby. The evenings were spent listening to Stan's stories of his Labrador and Chinese adventures, or playing games.

Stan had brought his precious four-inch telescope in its large rosewood case. So they had lessons in astronomy on clear nights.

One late afternoon, they were all out on the little lawn enjoying the sunset. In the distance was a long low-lying cliff. As they watched, to their amazement the figure of a tiger was silhouetted against the sky, slowly slinking along the top of the cliff. It then disappeared into the bushes beyond.

Stan was amazed at the lack of fear. The children laughed and said, "Let's call him Silhouetta because he is silhouetted against the sunset!" The parents were relieved that the children took it so well, but red flags were up, in the minds of the grownups.

The next evening, the night was beautifully clear, and Stan had promised to show the rings of Saturn through the telescope. They would stay near the lighted house. Roy, Sarah and all the children were there with him.

As they clustered around waiting for their turn to look through the telescope, suddenly in the bushes beyond them was the unmistakable snarl and cough of the tiger!

With one startled motion, the group flew through the door of the house all at one time, and landed in the middle of the living room floor, sprawled in every direction! This time there were shrieks of fear with the laughter.

Later Stan said "No one remembered whether they let Mrs. Newland in the front door first or not," and he laughed.

That was the second encounter. The children were kept very close to the house for many days. Eventually they became restless and begged to go on a hike. The parents realized the need for a change, so they consented.

Tom, the oldest, the high school son, said, "I'll keep us all together, and we'll make a lot of noise. We'll be all right."

The children took off in the direction of the cliff, and stayed close together as promised. It was quite a climb. When they reached the top of the cliff they looked down onto a large flat area dotted with bushes.

"I wonder where "Silhouetta" is today," one of the children said. They started throwing rocks down on to the flat area. Suddenly below them, the great beast came slinking from right to left. He slowly crossed the area and disappeared down the mountain. This time the children were terrified, as they hurriedly found the path and started home. They shouted and sang songs to keep up their spirits. Tom remembered that he had seen the tiger pass over a large flat rock below them as he had crossed the area. When they reached the rock, six-foot Tom lay down on it, with upstretched arms, measuring the size of the tiger. He could estimate that it was huge!

There were no more hikes. The children stayed right by the house. Indoors, Rook, Dominos and the few books they had to read were getting dull. What should they do?

One night, when they were having supper, the kitchen door flew open and the milkman came flying in, his eyes wide with terror, not a drop of milk in his bucket.

He gasped, "I was milking the cow, and the cow was very restless. I didn't know what was the matter! Then I saw between the cow's legs just a few feet from me, the <u>tiger</u> crouched like a big cat, just watching me do the milking! That's when I left!"

That was the final straw. They decided that the cow was part of the attraction for the tiger. So they sent the cow with the dairy farmer down to the lowlands, with the urgent request that the men who helped them before, should come up to help them as soon as possible. They packed their belongings, and in a few days when the Korean workers arrived they headed down the mountain. The children were wistful as they looked back. "Now we have a new name for the mountain, 'Silhouetta!'"

As the years passed it was time for Ruthie, the Martins' oldest daughter to return to America for further education. She had graduated from Pyeng Yang Foreign School in 1935. She planned to travel with other college-bound students, going by the trans-Siberian railroad to Europe. Her schooling was to be for a year at Ricker College in Houlton, Maine, then on to the New England Baptist Nursing School in Boston. She had a beautiful soprano voice, and sang in recitals and an operetta in high school, but she always wanted to be a nurse from the time she was a little girl bandaging her dolls.

That same year, mother Margaret took her six-month furlough as planned. She was eager to see her father who had returned to Cathance, Maine. She was also able to be with her daughter Ruth who was in college at Houlton. This was the town where Margaret had grown up in her Uncle Francis Barnes' home. Friends and relatives still lived there.

Stan, with the good help of Chong Hi, the cook, and Aoni, the amah for the little ones, managed to care for the family while she was gone, but was greatly relieved when she returned.

When Margaret, the second daughter, graduated from Seoul Foreign School the next year, 1936, an interesting request came from the Southern Presbyterian missionaries in Kwanju.

"Five of our children here are too young to go up to the Pyeng Yang Foreign School. Come and be our school teacher for the school year '36-37.' One child will be in the fourth grade and four in the fifth. They are Jeanie Avison, Martha Brand, the Paisley twins Martha and Florence, and Keith Newland. Since your parents are due for furlough in '37, you could spend one year in teaching, and return to the States with the family when they go."

After thinking it over, it seemed the right thing to do. However, Margaret would have to commute by train back to Seoul for bi-weekly violin lessons. So seventeen-year-old Margaret was a "school marm" for the year, rotating around to the parents' homes for room and board. They had their own little school room and the year passed well. For the parents they even put on some scenes from Shakespeare's "Merchant of Venice." Also, not many kids get to have their teacher play "Prisoner's Base" with them at recess time, as they did!

Meanwhile, the churches in the country of Korea were facing a growing problem. As Japan was spreading its empire across Asia, there was a heightening of nationalism. A large Shinto Shrine had been built on Nam San (South Mountain) in Seoul. The Japanese believed that their emperor had descended from the Sun-Goddess and national ceremonies were to be held at this Shinto Shrine. The Koreans were told that the ceremonies were not religious but civil rites. But when the first ceremony was held, the Koreans saw Shinto priests dressed in their full regalia, clapping their hands, calling down spirits from heaven. The assembled people were then to bow down to the shrine. Again the priests clapped their hands and the spirits were supposedly sent back to heaven.

Christians were shocked, and many refused to go. As a consequence there was often a knock at the door in the night, a person would be seized, have a sack thrown over his head and he would be spirited off to prison, many to face torture or even death.

Imagine the people sitting side by side in the Korean churches, some having family members in prison, others having obeyed the Japanese and gone to bow down at the shrines.

There were long discussions around the missionary dinner tables. It was easy for a missionary to the Koreans to say "Don't go, don't bow down at the heathen shrine," but it was the Korean who would have to bear the consequences. All they could do was pray.

All Christian churches were required to fly the Japanese flag, to sing the national anthem and to recite the creed of national loyalty on special occasions. Considerable pressure was brought to bear on the Christians to bring about attendance at the shrines. Some preferred to have their schools closed rather than go to the shrines. Others accepted the government's assurance that the rites were civil rites.

Much more could be written about this problem. It was evident that increasing pressure was coming upon the churches with the threat that they would be closed. In loyalty to the church, Christians made agonized decisions, but greater changes were to come.

In Pyeng Yang, one of the largest mission stations in the world at that time, many Christians refused to bow at the shrine in their town and were thrown into the Japanese-run prisons. One day, word came to the relatives of these prisoners that their loved ones were to be transferred from one prison to another prison outside of town. Crowds gathered and lined the city street. Then came the long line of prisoners dressed in their burnt-orange colored prison garb. Each prisoner had a unique basket covering his head like a helmet that had a narrow slit at eye level so he could see. The family members strained to figure out who each one was, as they came stumbling by. Some were on crutches as the result of frostbite.

"Is that Yong Suri?" "Is that Uncle?" "Oh I know that's Kee Ho – he's so tall!"

There was a growing murmur from the crowds by the side of the road, as the prisoners passed. The words were <u>not</u> "Give up! Come back to us!" but they became clearer and clearer in unison.

"Goot gajee! Goot gajee!" ("To the end! Stay true to the end!")

On this wave of encouragement the ragged group moved on to their new prison, some to their death.

XXIV

Gathering Clouds

❧

The Martin household in Seoul seemed strangely quiet in the fall of 1936. With Ruth in America at nursing school, young Margaret teaching in Kwangju, and Edna and Gerald up north at the Pyeng Yang Foreign School, only Phyllis and Betty were at home to brighten the days.

Young Margaret, called Margie, continued her trips back to Seoul every two weeks for her violin lessons. She was preparing to give a violin concert for the Seoul Music Club in the spring. The glowing dahlias, and spectacular chrysanthemum displays came and went. Then the sad news reached the family that Grandpa Rogers had died. He was eighty-four years old. His daughter Margaret said wistfully between sobs, "He was waiting and waiting for us to come home." She was more grateful than ever that he had made the visit to Korea, and for the time he had spent with the children.

At the hospital Stan was caring for his many patients. He wrote of an experience that moved him deeply. He entitled it "A Bereaved Mother."

> In the midst of a busy clinic I was interrupted by a sad-faced woman who begged me to please come and see if I could resurrect her nineteen-year-old student son who had drowned, and whose body had lain at the bottom of the great Han River all night. Because she was a "mother" I left my important cases and went with her to the Police Station at Yong San, an area near the river. Here we found the body of another student aged twenty-two who was not her son. After helping them to arrange to drag again for the son's body, I went back to the hospital, only to be called the next morning again, this time to find a lonely group by the riverside. There was a howling rainstorm and some men were standing near a hastily constructed straw shed in which lay a pale figure watched over by an anguished mother. Although dead and stiff for two days, she insisted on my seeing if there was yet life in the body that remained. When finally convinced that there was not, she said, "Oh, tell me where his spirit has gone! Is it still in the river?" I said

"I know one thing I am absolutely sure of. His spirit is not in the river, but is at this moment in the presence of the Heavenly Father."

She said nothing, and as I left the shelter, I noticed boats patrolling the river scattering various kinds of food to appease the spirit of the river, and along the shore rose the wail of beating tom-toms, the beaters hoping with the noise to frighten away the unwelcome spirits of the underworld. As I was returning to the hospital, the distance being great, the father of the boy asked if the mother could ride back with me. There was silence, with only the roar of the little Ford car as it went up the ravine in low gear. As we crossed the lone mountainside, the mother put her hand in mine and said, "How do you know that my son's spirit has gone to the Heavenly Father?" I said, "I only know that when I die I most certainly will again see my mother and that she has gone to rest with the Heavenly Father." There was silence, all but the roar of the little Ford car as it went up the ravine in low gear. Then as we passed under the stately pine trees she said, "I am so glad that he has gone to be with the Heavenly Father," and the anguish went out of her face and a light appeared in her eyes as she thought of the future when she would see her son again.

"Tis moonlight—the rain has ceased—and all is fresh and rare." But in a Buddhist temple by the East Gate, sounds the cry of a frenzied devil dancer or *Mudang* who is trying to appease the evil spirit of the river. But a mother at the foot of the hill does not hear the sounds that come to her as she sits by the newly-made coffin. She sighs for the time when she may go and meet her son in the presence of the Heavenly Father.

How I wished I had my own mother there to comfort this poor woman as only she could—and how I felt and feel for all mothers who do not know of the Christian Hope of the Hereafter.

A happier time came with an invitation to the Martins to come to Shanghai for a visit that Christmas. The Kilbourne family, an Oriental Missionary Society family that they knew from Wonsan Beach summers, gave the invitation. Of course the whole family couldn't go but it was decided that mother Margaret would accompany the teens Margie and Edna, *especially* Edna, for this special trip. So near Christmas the three of them crossed by ferry to Japan, took a train to Nagasaki and then took another ship across the Yellow Sea to Shanghai. It was a rough trip and they were all sea-sick. They were met at the Shanghai wharf by a crowd of shouting Chinese coolies who *all* wanted to carry their suitcases! They were so glad at last to see the whole Kilbourne family, Uncle Bud, Aunt Hazel, Ed and the twins Elmer and Ernie. What a relief it was to hear someone talking English!

They were taken to the beautiful Kilbourne home on the O.M.S. compound. It was decorated for Christmas. There followed days of reminiscing, good Chinese food, sight- seeing and music.

Margie had brought her violin. It was Ed who was happiest of all, because Edna was his girl friend from summer days at Wonsan. They were sweethearts, and were married a few years later. Edna was still in high school then, and Ed was attending St. John's University in Shanghai in his first year of college. As the days passed the families enjoyed beautiful Christmas services in the Chinese churches.

One of the places they visited was the Willow Pattern Tea-House. This charming place was set in a garden, with ponds and bridges and pavilions, in the area called "Old Shanghai." This tea-house was the inspiration for the Blue Willow chinaware that is still popular today. A short trip was made to Soochow, the Venice of the East, where they saw walls that were standing in the time of David. Back in Shanghai, what truly dazzled the visitors from Korea was Bubbling Well Road with its many fluorescent lights. They had never seen anything so beautiful!

Too soon, the Martins were home again and their busy life resumed. One evening Stan sat and listened to his children singing as their mother played the piano. He was enjoying the moments, but now there was a sense of foreboding. Doctors know too much, and this doctor, a heart specialist, knew the symptoms of an illness he could diagnose all too well. As the days went by, Stan cut down his office and teaching hours to conserve his strength. He was forty-seven.

On February 3, 1937, W. Burbidge, the Mission Secretary, wrote to Dr. Armstrong.

I am sending you today the following cable.

"Dr. Martin ill with heart trouble; ordered to return home by Mission on account of health; coming at once alone; leaving via *Empress of Russia*; telegraph approval." I am quoting from the circular letter which has received the approval of the Mission and was issued from the Hamheung Station.

"We are issuing this letter in consultation with Mr. Fraser who has just returned from Seoul where he had a conversation with Dr. and Mrs. Martin, and with Drs. McLaren and Avison of Severance Hospital. Furlough for Dr. Martin and family in the summer of 1937 has been voted on by the Mission and approved by the Board. Recently Dr. Martin's heart has been causing him unusual trouble. Since he would have to be extremely careful of himself and be able to do very little work, if any, from now until June, and since an early departure is considered advisable by the doctors of the Mission, do you agree?"

Permission was granted and plans were made that he would go to his sister Mabel's home in Toronto. The rest of the family would come on furlough later when school was out.

On February 16th Stan boarded the *Empress of Russia* in Yokohama, and was on his way to an uncertain future. The Pacific Ocean is often stormy in winter and this year was no exception. Fortunately he was accustomed to rough seas. As he watched the grey heaving waves, and counted the days until landing, he felt very alone. All he could do was to trust God, and pray for his family, and his Korean friends he had left behind.

The ship arrived in Vancouver, B.C., and Stan continued across Canada by train to Toronto. It was refreshing to see the beauty of the Canadian Rockies, and to watch the snow-covered scenes across the country, but he was very tired when the train pulled into the Toronto station. There he was met by his sister Mabel and Dr. Armstrong himself. The plans were for him to be examined by a doctor that very day, but he asked that the appointment would be postponed a day or two. He would later be in the hands of Dr. J. Gilbert Falconer, a heart specialist recommended by the Mission Board.

Dr. Armstrong drove them to Mabel's home in North Toronto. There his sister showed him to a quiet front room, with a southern exposure, very sunny as there was a vacant field apposite. Dr. Armstrong said to Mabel as he left them, "The very best will be done for Stanley." Stan was pleased and began to relax. Now it was up to him to just rest and wait.

Back in Korea, Margaret received reassuring letters from Stan, Mabel and their Board Secretary. She now had to turn her mind to travel plans for the rest of the family.

Rev. and Mrs. John Thomas of the O.M.S. Mission who were stationed in Seoul, had told her about Asbury College (has since been renamed Asbury University), a Christian college in Wilmore, Kentucky. They said they gave fifty percent reduction on fees for missionary children, and that there was a good possibility of students earning their school expenses there. Dr. Marion Stokes, a Methodist missionary in Seoul, also highly recommended Asbury College. Margaret was persuaded, and made plans to spend their furlough in Wilmore. She also realized that if Stan couldn't carry on his work, this would be the best place for the children.

Steamer passage was booked on the *President Lincoln* sailing from Kobe May 24th. The next problem was that of immigration documents for entrance into the United States. Margaret was an American, and Stan from the Commonwealth of Newfoundland traveled on a British passport. The American Consul in Seoul told her that with four children born in China, one in the U.S. and one in Korea, she would have the people all tied up in knots, trying to figure out where they should be placed. He advised her to try to get Canadian passports for four of the children. Jerry was an American because he was born in the United States. She contacted the Canadian Legation in Tokyo. After some anxious waiting she received word that by special concession, Canadian passports were granted for the four children. Young Margaret also needed a China quota number because she was born in China, and was entering the States after she was eighteen!

In April, good news came from Dr. Falconer in Toronto, with a report on Stan's health. He wrote "Dr. Martin made surprising and gratifying progress while here." He gave details from the medical tests such as fluoroscope and electrocardiogram findings. He closed the report saying, "With rest, increased food intake, and change of surroundings, he has improved very greatly. His heart has not been causing the present illness. He will eventually be able to do his work again." With this new lease on life Stan left Canada and proceeded to Lynbrook, Long Island, to visit with his brother William and to wait for his family to come home. His brother was an electrical engineer, and had been a pilot in the Newfoundland Air Force in World War I. The two of them shared fond memories including the time they had climbed Signal Hill as children to watch Marconi's historic event, the receiving of the first transatlantic signal by wireless.

In Korea, the news that Stan was recovering, buoyed up Margaret's strength and courage as she prepared for the trip home. Young Margaret finished her teaching, and gave her violin concert. She would plan to go to the New England Conservatory in Boston in the fall. Edna, Jerry, Phyllis and Betty also finished school, and on May 24th the Martin family was safely on board the *President Lincoln* on their way to Los Angeles. Four of the children hadn't been in the States for thirteen years, and little Betty had never been in America.

When the family arrived in Los Angeles, Margaret reported later, "The Immigration Officer let us all into the country 'in good faith' since Dr. Martin was already in the United States on a non-quota visit for residence. He showed me every courtesy." Stan meanwhile had traveled to Kentucky to wait for the family. It was a great relief to them when they all reached Kentucky and were together again.

Stan described the new situation in a letter from Wilmore to Dr. Armstrong, June 19, 1937.

> Yours received with thanks. We are now all settled in a nice home on the hill quite close to Asbury College, and the primary and high school. Already many of the Korea missionary children attending high school and college have been up to see us. There is quite a crowd of Korea folks here and Dr. and Mrs. Stokes are arriving in a few days. The church pastor met the train and brought us all in (17 miles) from Lexington. The Presbyterian pastor made us a long call yesterday. Mrs. Martin and I will send our expense account in a few days.
>
> Asbury is strongly missionary minded. They broadcast a devotional program every morning.

That same month Dr. Armstrong received a letter from Korea from one of Stan's former patients.

> Pai Chun, Korea
> June 16, 1937

> Dr. A. E. Armstrong
> Toronto 2, Canada

> My Dear Sir:

> Are you in peace? I hope you will excuse me, but my heart is so full of thanksgiving to God for what he has done for me through your servant in Christ, Dr. Martin, while he was at Severance in Seoul. I have T.B. but am fast on the road to recovery they say. I tried to end it all but was found just in time—to dress the wound and keep me from bleeding to death from the place I had cut in my throat.

> I was just telling Dr. McLaren of Severance of how Dr. Martin had saved my life and soul, and wanted to know if it were possible for my people to have him back now. We do not want to be selfish and take him too soon from his rest, but oh how we Koreans that have T.B. need him.

He cures our bodies and loves us so much we find Jesus through him. He is so gentle with the Koreans. I think his voice must be like that of Jesus. It has been said a Korean never heard him raise his voice, or say an unkind word to anyone. Dr. McLaren said "He truly has a compassion for humanity."

I just met a Japanese teacher in Seoul who had tuberculosis. Dr. Martin treated her two years ago and helped her financially until she was well. Now she is spreading the love of Jesus to her people.

The by-ways in Seoul have lost a friend while Dr. Martin is away. He befriended the homeless, fed the hungry, cured the sick, and found a job for those that wanted to work. Our people love him so much that there is nothing in his office except what the Koreans have given him.

Please send our friend back to us as soon as he is rested. God doesn't give us a friend like Dr. Martin but once in a life-time.

Our hearts are full of appreciation to you for giving us such a friend.

I wanted to write sooner but just today got your address.

Please tell Dr. Martin that my people are thinking and praying for his return to us.

Sincerely,
Kim In Ho

In the fall, young Margaret went to Boston as planned. Having her sister Ruth nearby at the New England Baptist Nursing School made a big difference, as she settled in the big city. Dr. Goodrich, the Director of the New England Conservatory of Music accompanied Margaret on the piano, as she played a concerto for him for a placement test. He decided that Harrison Keller was to be her violin teacher, and she was to be in the Conservatory orchestra. Usually the students had to take a year of preparation before they joined the orchestra.

In Kentucky, Edna, Jerry, Phyllis, and Betty started school and the Martins adjusted to life in Wilmore. Stan was regaining his strength and began to take speaking engagements at the college and the nearby churches. Margaret was very pleased with Wilmore and wrote enthusiastically to Dr. Armstrong.

We are fortunate to have a large cool house on a hill at the edge of this town, with acres around it for the children, and plenty of milk and fresh air, yet only ten minutes walk from the college. From a health point of view this place is even finer than I had hoped.

She was the family financier and sent in the report of their travel expenses down to the last penny.

> We saved eighteen dollars because Gerald came in as an American citizen. Also, through the kindness of the Seoul travel agency our daughter Margaret was given clergy rates on the American R.R. as a teacher in a missionary school. This saved nearly half on the transcontinental fare.

In November Stan wrote to his Board.

> I think that as I am doing well down here in this mild climate, that I had better stay here until spring. However I would like to take three more medical magazines for study purposes. If that could be a legitimate expenditure on post-graduate study. (3 medical magazines for 6 mos. $15-$20) If I went north now to Toronto I should have to board at the YMCA as my mother is sick and at my sister's. (No spare room)

As the months passed he was asked to speak in Louisville at the American Medical Association Meeting. He spoke on "Crisis in China" with the president of the Association in attendance. At that time he heard of many opportunities for him to work or study.

On February 4th, 1938 he wrote again to Dr. Armstrong.

> Just a line to report – We are all well. This town has been one of great spiritual activity. I spoke before 150 new Student Volunteers for Overseas, after Dr. M. Stokes and I had spoken for a week in special meetings here. This last week, and now continuing there is a revival on in the college and churches. Hundreds have been "converted" or "changed." I have been having small groups of students in my home. All these boys have come out for Christ.

> I am going next week to speak three days at a Student Volunteer Conference for Southern Colleges at Columbia, S.C. A China missionary, the Rev. Percy Culver from Foochow and I are traveling in his car, raising money for Chinese orphans and refugees. Wish I were in China.

> Kindest regards,

> Sincerely,
> Martin

> P.S. Spoke in Lexington at two large Presbyterian churches last Sunday. In one there were hundreds of University of Kentucky students.

In the spring, Margaret wrote the Board concerning the booking of Trans Pacific passage for their return to Korea. They were expecting to take Gerald (16), Phyllis (13), and Betty (11) back with them. She also told more of Stan's travel experiences with Mr. Culver of Foochow, China. They were holding services in New York City when Mr. Culver's son Maurice or 'Frex' was returning from Europe on the *Queen Mary*. He and three other Asbury students had spent a year in Europe and the Holy Land. They were called the Crusader Quartet. As the young men were asked to tell of their experiences in the church of Rev. Walter Moore, a Christian Missionary Alliance pastor, Stan didn't know as he listened, that Rev. Moore's son James, one of the quartet members, was to be his future son-in-law.

Later, Stan and Mr. Culver traveled to Florida where they were asked to speak in so many churches they stayed two weeks longer than expected. Dr. O.R. Avison of Severance Hospital, who was now retired at St. Petersburg, gave them some fine contacts. There was a good response as they raised money for the Chinese people. Japan at that time was continuing a reign of terror on the Chinese mainland. They had heard that out of 10,000 dead in Shanghai, 7,000 were children in January 1938.

Margaret gave news of the family. Ruth was half way through her nurses training and young Margaret might get a scholarship for another year in violin, or she will come to attend Asbury College with Edna and teach violin.

In April of 1938 Stan traveled north to Toronto to attend the Board meeting and to do medical study there for the month of May. On the way, in Cincinnati, he visited Dr. Reid the one for whom he had installed an x-ray machine in the Songdo (now Kaesung) Ivey Hospital. They were the closest of friends. He also visited again with his brother on Long Island cherishing the time spent there.

While in New York he met some of the Northern Presbyterian and Northern Methodist heads of mission boards and was concerned about news from Korea. He felt things were really upset out there. Later in the summer Dr. Armstrong wrote Stan that he had had a talk with Dr. O.R. Avison, and Stan need not fear that Severance Hospital would close. "Our Mission Hospitals are in great need of you. You can eagerly look forward to your return. These are the times when the Korean Christians need all their friends."

Referring to the growing pressure of the Japanese on missionaries and Christian institutions he quoted Stan's fellow missionary E JO Fraser in Wonsan who wrote, "We have found for years that we in our Mission are much less troubled with visits and questionings from the police than are those of the Missions where there is a constant feeling of opposition. I have heard men from Pyeng Yang and other places say that detectives were always around them and never a day passed without some detective being in their office trying to find out something of what is going on. We have had none of that. In fact I have had a visit only on an average of about once a month and then for some perfectly proper purpose."

After spending the month of May in medical study, Stan returned to Kentucky in time for Edna's graduation from high school and special meetings at Asbury College. Ruth and Margaret came from Boston and the family had a few last weeks together before Stan and Margaret and the three youngest ones left for Korea in the fall.

XXV

Sunset Years

When Margaret and Stan returned to the field in the fall of 1938 it was with new vigor, and new surroundings. A missionary home had become available on the Severance Hospital Compound. "It is very convenient for me," Stan wrote, "and for the hospital too. – Can't get taxis for 'love' or 'money' – gasoline restriction – no permits allowed for new cars – glad we didn't bring one – street cars jammed."

The children walked to school as they did before. Time revolved for them around the Seoul Foreign School, the Seoul Union Church, and the Seoul Union – a tennis club with a small swimming pool. It was a happy, challenging time. Jerry did well in tennis, and of course all of the children swam like fish from their Wonsan summer days. Jerry took up violin and Betty began violin too, with Mr. Huss.

It was a time when ladies still wore hats and gloves to church, and if you were invited to dinner the ladies wore evening dresses. Many of the dinners were with Korean friends.

Stan's letters were upbeat as he kept in touch with Dr. Armstrong.

> Everything going well here, lots of work and opportunity. We are very happy – Enclosing a story to help our work and the schools. Dr. Scott's school in Hamheung and Severance Hospital are doing very well. Best 'spiritual glow' I've seen in 24 years. Finances also good.
>
> Please have this article put in the "Outlook."
>
> Cheerio.
>
> SHM

In April 1939, Dr. and Mrs. Black were leaving the field, giving up their mission work. He was the doctor who continued the St. Andrew's Hospital work in Manchuria. He didn't like the political situation there with their small children in danger. His father was urging him to come home. Changes were also coming to Korea.

Stan wrote to Dr. Armstrong at this time:

> Dr. Black is kindly taking this letter. Please let church papers and people know that it is <u>difficult</u> to let them know about our work, because of censorship etc. Please tell Wallace "Observer" old friend of mine, Queens – <u>we do not receive</u> the church papers. We had two "embargo" notices from police <u>censors</u>. I have received <u>3</u> copies in one year. Manchukuo, strange to say is different, they allow anything in there. All of our Reader's Digests – Time–Life, all magazines have three and four pages removed at a time. Many books are banned. Fine spiritual glow through the missionary group – revivals breaking out all over the country.

> Severance is going strong. I am teaching Clinical Medicine to the 3rd and 4th year students (seniors). We've had special speakers at chapel services. Very little pressure on colleges. I am studying and using Japanese but I doubt whether evangelists need much of it. The new missionaries, the Roger Cole Nunn couple are a <u>great</u> addition to the work. They are <u>fine</u> <u>Christians</u>.

> We have discovered and are using a new method of finding activity in TB cases. It is being published in "American Review of Tuberculosis." 28,000 of our TB booklets were sold in two months.

> If you see Dr. Falconer or any of our Medical Board members tell them I'm doing full time Medical Clinic – teaching etc. including night calls. It's especially convenient that we live on the hospital compound.

> There is much poverty. In the winter, six beggars were dead and left on the street in front of Severance for four days, only covered by heaven sent snow.

> I was down south in Soonchun with my friend Dr. R. M. Wilson, examining TB cases at his leper colony. Twenty people were trying to get inside the "leper heaven," although they had not a trace of leprosy. They preferred being inside with leprosy, than outside with nothing to eat and nowhere to live and nothing to do.

> All the best rice has been commandeered and sent to Japan and to the Japanese soldiers and an inferior quality is imported from Rangoon. Our cook, Chung Hi, stands in a queue, twice a week for six hours with 500 people, and gets ten handfuls of barley. First it was rice, maize and barley – then rice and barley – now only barley. Foreigners with the others must have a ration ticket to get a pound of rice. All real gold articles must be given up by us. The ladies have been ordered by the British Consul to ask ahead of time for permission to keep their wedding rings.

In our hospital we cannot get quinine, aspirin, iodine – no foreign drugs of any kind. We use paper dressings and paper bandages. There is no opium or codeine and very little morphine (with special permit), yet the Japanese are debauching the China coastal cities with tons of opium derivatives.

Medical work is very difficult here, as we must substitute, substitute. In surgery, we can't get ether or chloroform, and are using mostly spinal anesthesia.

The loving Father is taking care of us all, and we are having the privilege of suffering a little with the Korean people. We are going to miss Dr. Black, but he and his family have surely made a grand contribution to the spread of His Kingdom 'overseas'.

In June 1939 he wrote again sending the letter by Rev. Burbridge.

We greatly enjoyed Board Member Dr. Arnup's visit, but had three police visits after he left. He spoke at our chapel and saw a lot of our work, and met some of our best people. I have never been so busy or so happy. So far, the Japanese are treating us well. But there is liable to be a 'flare up' in international affairs in the Orient at any time. The British and French are now convoying their liners and shipping, with warships along the China coast. We are only allowed long wave radios. All of our magazines have whole articles and pages removed. Montgomery Ward catalogues are badly mutilated. Pressure is being severely applied to close the Australian Presbyterian schools which refused to go to the shrine. Our mission is quiet. Severance also is quiet. The spiritual tone never better. Dr. Choi (studied at Toronto) and Dr. E. W. Anderson of the Methodist Mission have been elected President and Vice President respectively. Dr. McLaren, Australian Presbyterian, is on the Executive Committee. The Japanese people on the street are not anti-foreign. The Christians are friendly. The military and ex-soldiers are anti-foreign. They are now guided by a Divine Mission to establish the Peace of the Orient. They congratulated Berlin and Rome on their military pact.

We are busy about our own interesting work. I continue with 200 students now in Clinical Medicine class, the 3rd and 4th year students. I get fine attention and interest. I'm having many good results with TB cases. I'm writing a book in Korean and *han moon* (Chinese characters) on TB treatment. We are all well, Jerry is 6' 2." Plays good tennis. Betty, Phyllis, and Mrs. Martin are well.

We often think of you and Mrs. Armstrong and your little daughter.
With best regards to one and all,
Stan and Margaret Martin

As the summer of '39 approached, their thoughts turned to vacation, and the new summer resort called Whachinpo a few miles south of Wonsan on the East Coast. The Japanese had commandeered the missionary summer resort at Wonsan to make an airfield, but had compensated the missionaries for their houses. Whachinpo was not disappointing however. It had a combination of a lake, nearby mountains and the sea, all in the same area. The first ones who visited it, raved about it to the missionary community. Some had built their cottages in the spring, and were able to enjoy their summer there. The Martins were able to rent that first summer, but Stan enjoyed supervising the building of their new cottage while there.

According to their letters to their daughters back in the States it was a very hot summer part of the time. Margaret wrote in July from Whachinpo.

> Having a hot spell – awful! Daddy got pretty tired in all that heat, and one night he was short of breath. After the heat broke we all felt better. Next summer I'll send him to the Diamond Mountains if it's hot like this. I didn't eat much, kept going on coffee and watched the kids to make sure they wore their hats! Phyllis and Betty are well, getting tall and tanned. They swim well. Jerry is ice-man and worked hard during all the heat. Missionary teen-agers can earn money delivering large blocks of ice for the families' ice-boxes. No electricity. Daddy is doing well. We came here June 18th. Daddy plans to stay until August 20th. I shall stay with the kids until September 3rd. I have a nice light boat to row.

When they returned to Seoul the children started school and Jerry began his senior year of high school. The family dreaded the time he would be leaving them the next year. Margaret wrote to the girls in the States, Christmas night 1939.

> We had a lovely Christmas day. Jerry took our pictures. Hi Sooni snapped one of us all by the tree after we opened presents. We had prepared five long stockings for the servants' children. They came in, wearing their pretty Korean clothes and sat around the tree. Then they opened the stockings finding nuts, candy, fruit and little presents. Their eyes just popped. It was their first experience of our foreign custom. It was fun to see them.

> We had just the family for lunch, then I played Diamonds with Betty and rested. In the evening we had Korean friends in for dinner, and we played music afterwards and sang carols.

On December 30th Jerry and Phyllis went to Peking for a week with Carol Appenzeller, Paul Haines, and Miss Conrow the Ewha College teacher. The exchange rate was such that many of the foreign community took advantage of it, and made the trip.

The New Year 1940 dawned on an unsettled fearful world. Stan and the family kept up with the political situation, following the war in Europe and Japan's ravaging of the Far East.

In Korea itself, drastic changes were taking place under the slogan of "Japan and Korea One Nation." The Government General began to enforce measures aimed at complete integration of the two countries. Exclusive use of the Japanese language was required of all. Korean language and literature were dropped from the school curriculum and the use of the Korean language by students was severely punished. Public buildings, schools churches and even homes were required to fly the Japanese flag. The school day began with obeisance to the flag, and in the direction of the Emperor's palace, followed by the loyalty oath. Individuals were pressured in to abandoning their Korean names and adopting the Japanese equivalent.

Christian organizations were required to renounce their international affiliations. The Korean churches were compelled to make radical changes in their constitutions, dropping all references to freedom of faith, conscience, worship and government, and deleting all articles dealing with the status of work of foreign missionaries. [18]

In the Martin home there was concern for fifteen-year-old Phyllis who continued to run a low grade fever after scarlet fever in March. In May her mother wrote to the girls in college.

Phyllis is much better, wants to play the victrola until she drives me crazy. Dr. Rogers saw her and advised sulphanilimide which brought the improvement. It takes all my time to look after her. We've had our walls painted. They look lovely. We'll have station meeting here next week. There's a Japanese house nearby with five gay fish flying. I would like to send the lady something for her five little boys.

I miss you more than words can say. All I have now is your letters. I wouldn't change our missionary calling but it doesn't grow easier as the years go by!

As the school year drew to a close, thoughts were on Jerry's high school graduation activities. He played a difficult Seitz violin concerto, and sang two solos at the Senior recital. His father was so proud of him. He made good grades and was on the honor role. For the Junior-Senior banquet Mrs. Dexter Lutz rehearsed Jerry, Paul Haines and Bob and Charles Sauer in a quartet number, "Sleep Kentucky Babe" and the parents were invited for the rehearsal. Margaret wrote: "That song had me in tears several times, both for Kentucky, and for Jerry's leaving. He will sail on the *President Pierce* August 15th. I plan to go as far as Japan to see him off. I must be brave at the ship."

Jerry's class graduated and it was time to prepare for Whachinpo. It was decided that Jerry, age seventeen, and <u>twelve-year-old</u> Betty would go there first. A letter from Betty tells of an adventure on the way.

---

[18]   *Canadians in Korea*, Rev. William Scott, pg 138

July 4th, 1940
Whachinpo
Dear Margie and Edna,

I'm sorry I haven't written you, it's been ages, but its hard work to try to sit down to write a letter at the beach when we're getting settled in a brand new house, but just the same that's no excuse. Whew! What a long sentence. Take a deep breath when you read that!! Our *chim* (baggage) is at the station now and my violin is in the big trunk. I'm so excited I can hardly wait to play it. It's been such a long time since I played it. Jerry and I came up here before the rest of the family to open the house and we brought the kittens with us. Boy did I have a time on the train!! Susie the mother of Ginger, Cream Puff and Snowball had the time of her life. I was at my wits end!! The cats were terrible. First one would let out a squawk, then the next, then the next etc. until I thought they were having singing lessons. The car door opened and the conductor came around to punch tickets. The cats were all quiet until the man came to our section. What do you think happened? Susie somehow slipped out of the basket, walked to the edge of the bunk and stuck her head out between the curtains and let out a "meeeow." That was about the last straw. The ticket man turned around in amazement and said in Japanese, "*Nikko?*" which means cat in Japanese, then "Rrat? No, cat?" I nodded my head. It was too late to yank the cat in behind the curtains, anyway the trio in the basket started up. The man said, "More cat? How many?" I meekly put up three fingers and he said in Japanese to put them at the end of the car, so I got Susie in with the trio and marched them into the rest-room. That was all the trouble we had with them, enough too!!

Today is pouring rain. Even though it's the 4th of July I guess nothing much exciting will happen tonight.

Loads of love to all,
Your sister Betty

Despite the uncertain political times the missionary community gathered and followed the summer schedule. Rev. Roger Nunn, so admired by Stan, wrote an article for "Korean Echoes," the United Church of Canada paper describing the activities. He introduced all of the Canadian missionaries there and came to the conclusion that "our United Church people out there are the salt of the earth." He was writing of all the Mission groups when he wrote –

"I would like to say that nowhere could a more wholesome, lively bunch of kiddies and teenage young people be found than at Whachinpo this summer. On many expeditions, at tournaments of tennis, croquet, swimming or whatever was "On the Boards" they cooperated with each other and shared each other's fun in a way that was an example to us all. They were a fine advertisement of the missionary cause."

The Martins from Seoul (including four kittens) made up the complement. It was a good summer for the Martins, for they had Jerry with them before he left for America. All Whachinpo was sorry to say goodbye to Jerry when he left in the middle of August for Yokohama, and the ship which took him, and a number of other missionaries' children to America for their University education. One of the last things Jerry did was to fulfill a long cherished ambition and come in first in his precarious sailboat *Sweetie Pie* at the weekly regatta. The boat had a spill in the morning and apparently considered it had better be on its best behavior in the afternoon when the race was held. His father Dr. Martin spent a good bit of time this summer in the boat, or with his pastel art work.

We all appreciated the religious services at the Beach and the one that stands out in my memory most vividly is the Thursday prayer meeting held during the critical days of July. Dr. Martin gave his witness to God's power in answering prayer and told us three stories out of his own experience which illustrated his message in a telling manner. The hymns, and fervent prayers given by many missionaries present added to the impressiveness. [19]

On the day that Jerry, accompanied by his mother Margaret, left Whachinpo, there were many to see them off. It was a sunny day but there were many tears. Stan stood grieving as the train pulled away. Then flanked by his daughters Betty and Phyllis he slowly walked back to the lonely cottage. A few days later at Yokohama, Japan, Margaret stood on the dock as the *President Pierce* moved out. Jerry was at the stern of the ship. Jerry waved and his mother waved to him — waving until they could no longer discern each other. After Margaret's return to Whachinpo the family finished their vacation and returned to hot, noisy Seoul. They all resumed their busy schedules.

Fall is beautiful in many places but nowhere is it more beautiful and satisfying than in Korea. As the days grew cooler, the golden gingko trees and the red maples made a blaze of glory in the palace grounds. The sky was very, very blue, and the chestnuts, grapes, apples, and Korean pears were in abundance. It was an invigorating time after the heat of summer. When Jerry's first letter came they all felt better.

---

[19]   *Korean Echoes*, Rev. Roger Nunn, Vol. XVII, October 1940.

XXVI

The *Mariposa* Evacuation

Aafter the good summer of 1941 at Whachinpo, two crises began to converge on the Martin family, and all the missionary community. As Stan returned to his work of teaching and his clinic, at Severance Hospital, he realized his strength was failing. At the same time the American State Department warned that the political situation was becoming more serious. Then word came that Americans were to leave Korea, and that the Matson Line ship the *S.S. Mariposa* would come to Inchon to evacuate them on November 16th. The orders were given by Consul General Gaylord Marshal.

Dr. Florence Murray reported to Dr. Armstrong about Stan's condition and that the Mission Council advised sick leave. This was granted and Margaret booked passage for the family on the *Kamakura Maru* sailing from Kobe, Japan November 18th. Margaret was American, but Stan and the three children were not, so they did not qualify for passage on the *Mariposa*.

As the political situation became more tense, the Canadian missionaries also planned the return of their missionaries to their homeland. They chose Japanese or the Canadian *Empress* ships for their travel. They were divided into groups. The first group, were those with children, and some who could best be spared. The second group, were those whose work could go on, so they could stay longer in Korea. The third group was to be made up of a minimum of four missionaries who would stay to the last and do their best to hold things together.

Stan wrote to Dr. Armstrong during those last days in Korea on November 3, 1940:

Dear Dr. Armstrong,

You have heard by cable that we are 'bound back' on sick leave. We hate to be leaving now, as I ordinarily would enjoy being in a 'crisis,' but the body doesn't match the spirit, and I could barely walk to the close-by hospital for my last lecture. (2½ hours) I gave them my best, finishing with "May God keep you always in His grace." The (boys) (100) students rose in a body and bowed, clapped and shook hands with me, with tears in their eyes. I found it hard to navigate the stairs. I have been in bed since, (two days) and sorry I could not go to church because of chest pain and discomfort.

Our ship the *Kamakura* will take us by the southern route as the northern route is very rough this time of the year. Our daughter Phyllis is still not well and may need sinus surgery when we get home. Margaret will take her to Boston for treatment, but Betty and I will keep to the south in Kentucky where young Margaret and Edna are at Asbury College. They will graduate in the spring.

I wish to avoid the cold as much as possible. Dr. Murray has sent medical reports and x-ray pictures of my heart. Dr. Falconer and the Medical Board know of my condition.

We feel that the only thing that can be done is to <u>rest</u> completely until spring and see if there is any improvement. I haven't the strength to consider crossing the Canadian border. Because of the war situation it is more complicated now. I will be fortunate to get as far as Kentucky. – But I have completed my full <u>25 years</u>.

So we are going slowly and quietly knowing that His Presence is with us even unto the end of the world.

Best regards from both of us.
Sincerely,
S. H. Martin

This sudden call for evacuation struck the missionaries with pain and surprise. The term 'minimum baggage' was repeated over and over by the Consular authorities. Within about two weeks time they would have to get rid of treasures of a lifetime.

Margaret sat in her living room trying to evaluate the situation. She said later, "I was glad I put money into music lessons, and not into some of the beautiful Korean brass-decorated furniture. It would all have had to be left behind. It was the boxes of family letters that I grieved over the most. I sat before the fireplace, read some of them, took them by the handful, kissed them, and threw them into the fire."

As the Martins prepared to leave for Japan, a visit to the American Consulate made a sudden change in their plans.

E. J. O. Fraser wrote to Dr. Armstrong November 15, 1940. "Dr. Martin and family are leaving Seoul tomorrow, on the American *Mariposa* after all, as the American Consul refused him a visa to land in the States unless he went on an American vessel. Mrs. Martin has an American passport."

Arrangements were made and the British Dr. Martin and all his family were granted passage on the *Mariposa* sailing November 16th. It was best in every way, because the trip to Japan would have been complicated for Stan. The harbor of Inchon where the *Mariposa* due was just a twenty-two mile train trip from Seoul.

On Evacuation Day when the Martins left Seoul, Chong Hi and her family and many of the Severance doctors, nurses, and church friends were able to go on the train with them to Inchon. There the missionaries were to be placed in small boats to be ferried out to the large waiting ship. But first they had to go through Japanese customs.

Mrs. Arthur Emmons, wife of the American vice-consul, reported when they reached the pier. "Although the Consulate-General at Keijo (Seoul) had been assured there would be only a perfunctory examination, the passengers were delayed while only one customs official at first (later an assistant joined him) proceeded to go through their baggage with utmost care, looking in pockets and taking out each article and examining it – the customs offices tore up photographs – including their family and other personal photographs." [20]

The Korean friends were herded over to an area that was roped off by the Japanese authorities. A cold wind was blowing on them as they waited for hours. There were tears, and calls of farewell from these loved ones as they stretched out their hands to wave good-bye. Chong Hi and her family were watching for a last glimpse of the Martin family.

Years later, a Severance medical student told of this incident. He said, "Just before we were pushed away from our missionary friends at Inchon, Dr. Martin stepped forward and taking his Severance Medical School badge from his lapel, he leaned forward and pinned it on to me."

This young man later became a doctor at the Seoul Reformatory for Juvenile Delinquents. He related the story to Stan's daughter Margaret as she visited that institution.

Finally, all passengers were on board and the *Mariposa* blew the signal of departure. The railings were crowded as the ship slowly moved away. One can only imagine the thoughts of the people there, as they saw the Korean shore-line fade into the distance. Some family members were separated. Friends and co-workers of a lifetime were now left behind. Anxiety for the future of Korea and of God's work there weighed on their minds as the distance grew between them and those they loved.

As time passed, the passengers fell into a steady routine. Grieved, but relieved they tried to comprehend all that had happened so suddenly.

There were many children on board, and plans were made for their entertainment. The *Mariposa* was a luxury ship with all day food service, movies and a band. The youngest Martin, thirteen-year-old Betty and her best friend Boo Langdon, daughter of the American Consul Bill Langdon explored the ship. They even had dinner with the Captain one evening. Religious services were held and a room was set aside for meditation. In the lounges there was serious talk among the missionaries. Had they done the right thing in leaving Korea, as their government had ordered?

After rest, and the good meals on board ship Stan felt well enough to write the Mission Board.

---

[20]   *Living Dangerously in Korea*, Donald N. Clark, p. 255

On board the SS Mariposa
November 28, 1940

Dear Dr. Armstrong,

We were offered a chance to leave directly from Inchon near Seoul on this large evacuee ship. We found ourselves on board with some 530 missionaries traveling Tourist Class. We heard that Miss Lawrence, one of our Severance head nurses was removed from a Japanese boat at Yokohama by the police, and sent under guard without being allowed to speak to anyone – to Seoul where she is now in prison. (The charge is Communism!!)

On this ship we have had many inspiring meetings and conferences, in which we have heard statements of the problems of the missionaries, and also of their many trials and persecutions. Also we heard of the faithfulness of the Koreans amidst persecution, and the overall pervading miraculous protection of Almighty God.

Because of the difficulty of passing between the USA and Canada and vice versa – during this war period, also because of the need of immediate rest in a warm climate as ordered by the doctors in Korea. I am having a complete medical examination by Dr. Brush at Nashville, TN en route to Kentucky. Dr. Brush is the medical advisor of the Southern Presbyterian Mission Board. Dr. Murray who examined me last advised me to get a report for our Board Medical Committee and I have been advised to see Dr. Brush.

I will have him give me a complete line of treatment to follow out in Kentucky until spring when Edna and Margaret graduate from Asbury College. Dr. Smith of Korea is also sending an electrocardiograph which he kindly came to Seoul to do. Dr. Falconer has all the details of my medical report in Canada.

Just before leaving Korea I was unable to dress myself. Since resting on this boat I feel much better especially since taking digitalin and nitroglycerin tablets.

Please keep us informed of our Korean friends and Mission.

With many thanks and kindest regards,
S. H. Martin

As the Mariposa approached San Francisco on December 4, 1940, Stan and Margaret realized it was exactly twenty-five years to the day, since they had sailed from Canada to go to the mission field. All the rush of culture shock came over them as they prepared to disembark, however, they were buoyed up watching the excitement of their daughters Phyllis and Betty.

The plan was to travel on to Wilmore, Kentucky, where friends and family were waiting, but first there would be a detour to Nashville, Tennessee for Stan's medical checkup.

From Nashville, Stan wrote to Dr. Armstrong

> I have just completed a two-day very thorough examination. Dr Brush the examiner for the Southern Presbyterian Board of Missions was exceedingly courteous and would not accept any fee and would not send a bill. He will gladly send a full report to our Medical Board through you. Dr. Falconer will be able to compare the old and new records.
>
> Dr. Brush wishes to keep in touch with me and offers to check me up again in the spring. I have been ordered complete rest for four months now and then gradually increased regulated exercise.
>
> I also had a long and friendly talk about Korea with Dr. Fulton their Board Secretary. He thanked me for what I have done for their missionaries through the years. He had a draft cashed and arranged a good hotel for us. Please thank D. Brush when you write.
>
> Just leaving for Wilmore, KY
> Best Regards,
> S. H. Martin

When they arrived in Wilmore, Edna, a senior at Asbury College, was waiting for them with many friends they had met before. Jerry was to come from school at Wooster in January, and young Margaret was to come from Nyack, NY in February to finish her college years in June with Edna.

Stan lost no time in reporting to Dr. Armstrong on December 9th, 1940.

> After the long trip I am tired – but coming along. Your letter addressed to Yokohama worried me quite a bit. You seem to have the idea that I was not planning to go back to Korea. That is not so. We are all hoping that with the rest I get here – as I did before, near my family and in a warm climate and under Dr. Brush's outline of treatment that I may be able to return to my work in our mission which I dearly love. I shall be glad to have advice from our Medical Board in Toronto, after they see Dr. Brush's report. As Brush advised there is nothing I can do or plan now, until I have four months rest and another checkup.
>
> In case our work cannot be carried on in Korea—I would be glad to do work in Canada, so please keep any contact you can with the TB sanatorium you mentioned. I have a British license, and with it, and $100, I could get an Ontario license. TB work is the thing I am supposed to do well, and have every qualification

for it, and plan to keep up my reading. Please do not think of us having to leave our mission, but pray with us that we all get back to our posts as soon as the way is open. My article on early diagnosis of TB has been accepted by the Canadian Medical Journal for publication, with a nice letter from the editor. The article was the study of two hundred and sixty cases of early TB. There are many Presbyterians and other missionary families from Korea and other countries in this town.

Phyllis has not been well since last March following scarlet fever and may have to have a sinus operation. Glad to hear Miss Lawence is out of prison. A Mr. Benson, British, at Kalgan, North China is in for seven years. A Manchurian jail with no heat.

When I get better some—I shall write for the church papers.

It is good we are living in Wilmore, as Asbury will cut tuition in half while children are living with their parents in the town. Asbury College has the greatest number of missionary children next to Wheaton College. The grass is green here and I have been sitting on the porch of a Canadian friend's house. He is Dr. Wiseman a professor at Asbury.

Please excuse this jumbled letter from a "tired hand" but it's still British and will later on grasp your own in Toronto, if the doctors let me go back and finish up my job in Korea.

Best regards to Dr. Arnup and Miss Cranston from us both.
Cordially yours,
S. H. Martin

The Martins found a place to rent and Stan and the children settled in. Mother Margaret then left them and went to do private nursing in Boston for a few months, while Stan was having his prescribed rest period. She planned to stay with her daughter Ruth.

When son Jerry transferred from Wooster College in Ohio, and daughter Margie came from Nyack Missionary Training Institute, Nyack, New York, they joined Edna, Phyllis, and Betty to make a raucous, bubbling, happy household for Stan. Each sibling had a share in the cooking and other house work. There was never a dull moment, with violin and piano music, with the radio which was always fascinating to them, and swarms of college and grade school friends coming and going.

The Kilbournes lived across the way, and that made Ed Kilbourne and Edna very happy. Margie and Edna started their last quarter of college together, while at the same time Jerry began his pre-med courses in earnest.

Stan prepared for possible medical practice in America by applying for a non-quota visa which would be required as he was not an American. He was receiving the recommendations from fellow doctors that were necessary for this.

Of the many doctor recommendations that came to him, he cherished one from Dr. W. T. Reid. Stan had installed the x-ray machine years ago at Reid's Methodist Hospital in Songdo, Korea. Songdo is now called Kaesung. Their families had had good times together at Wonsan.

1/27/41

I have known Dr. Stanley Haviland Martin for many years as a close personal friend, and I am proud to count him as a friend of mine. He is a true Christian, a man whose quality of unselfish kindness is rare indeed, a true physician to whom the well being of his patient is his paramount consideration. He has worn himself out in the service of the poor and needy who could never repay his invaluable medical service except with thanks from grateful hearts.

Margaret, who was now in Boston, wrote to Dr. Armstrong.

My plan was to bring Phyllis here with me, to put her through Lahey Clinic because of her sinus trouble, but two days before I left, Phyllis begged to stay with Edna for these last few months before Edna's marriage. So that matter was settled.

I have found my daughter Ruth well, and constantly busy. The prospect for nursing employment is good. We realize we have been hit by the war, but we can take it on the chin as well as the rest. Until Stan has had his ordered rest, and we find out whether he will be able to return to the field it seems best for me to work here with Ruth.

Jerry's college has to be paid and we need every cent we can save. He wants to study medicine. Stan will have access to the college library, and any college functions he desires when he is not resting. He asked me to handle the accounts from here.

Her letter closed with the recent financial accounts. It had become more complicated because of the Canadian to American exchange.

E. J. O. Fraser the Korea Mission Treasurer wrote to the Martins from Wonsan January 11th, 1941.

Hope that after Stan gets a good rest, he will be able to carry on somewhere for a good long time yet. We here go along very quietly, and since the rush of folks getting away has passed, we are wondering what it is all about. Too bad so many left from other Missions, but things did look worse then than now.

In March Stan was invited to go to Florida for another fund-raising trip for Chinese orphans. It was with Rev. Percy Culver, "Uncle Putts" the one with whom he had traveled on his recent furlough. He wrote to Margaret.

"We have done well here. We are here in the center of the most sympathetic wealthy group in North America. There are hundreds of Canadians down here."

"I have just walked out on a "Bayou" looking towards the Gulf of Mexico – cranes, gulls, pelicans, palm trees, bamboo etc. Flaming bushes – sweet singing birds and all the other things you would enjoy. I have been praying for a car, 1ˢᵗ to take you out into the fresh air and sunshine – 2ⁿᵈ to take the kids on picnics in the country and by the water, 3ʳᵈ to save my pump."

"I ate tangerines, oranges etc. from the trees on Sunday. Am enclosing orange blossoms, a palm frond and apron leaf such as they used in the Garden of Eden. We are all well, and I get some rest in the daytime – busy at night but all in good cause. Thinking and praying for you all. Cheerio. Love, Stan"

Dr Murray who was still in Hamheung, Korea frequently conferred with Dr. Armstrong in Canada about Stan's health.

She wrote to Dr. Armstrong, March 13, 1941:

> I am glad to hear that Dr. Martin is improving but fear that complete recovery is too much to expect in his case. I hope that he may become well enough to do some light work where he is. If he could get a place in a sanatorium it might suit him very well.
>
> We have had several leave-takings on this station and they were not easy ones. This is a much more tragic affair, I almost said debacle, than a return home on furlough where there is a good deal of anticipation in connection with the home going and the prospect of a speedy return to work after a well earned rest. Meeting and parting is the way of the world, and one expects it, but lately it has been all parting and that is not so good. Our hearts have been warmed, however, by the kindness of our Korean neighbors. Some whom we had not even known before, have stopped us on the street with cries of joy, exclaiming, "We heard you had all gone, and here you are! I am so glad you have not gone. It is good to have you here."
>
> Our hospital staff came to us with the proposition that if we would remain with them and funds were no longer forth coming for our salaries that they would reduce theirs enough to make up the amount that we should receive. Naturally we could not agree to such a proposition but we appreciate the fact that they are willing to make the offer.

Dr. Murray's suggestion that Stan should find work in America came true almost right away. In March, on his return from Florida he received word from his missionary doctor friend, R. M. Wilson, that a position was available at the Pine Camp Sanatorium in Richmond, Virginia. Dr.

Wilson was now with the Richmond Health Department. He requested that Stan come to be interviewed by Dr. Welchon of the sanatorium.

Stan gladly made the trip in April, and wrote a full report afterwards to his wife Margaret who was in Boston.

The radio is playing "Beautiful Dreamer." Betty is listening to a mystery story. Jerry is reading in a big armchair, Margie and Edna are curled up in bed surrounded by Margie's bridal shower presents, including a big silver teapot from Mr. T. Delos Crary. Margie is writing to her Jim.

I have been in bed all day up to now, resting from my <u>most</u> <u>strenuous</u> bus trip. 48 hours with one hour's sleep, and only orange juice and coffee and toast at bus stops – through winding roads of W. Virginia whose roadsides flamed with blast furnace's glow, and the valleys were filled with the smoke of defense production. Inside the bus, women and men smoke and chew, and men joke with silly college girls who throw up beer and coca cola from car sickness. There were sailors and soldiers among the Duke University students at bus stops, showing war has already entered America.

But to business – Dr. Welchon is a perfect Southern gentleman about thirty-eight years old—very kind. After he met me he drove me around the Pine Camp grounds. He told me there is a great shortage of nurses in Richmond, the greatest shortage in years. The nurses at the sanatorium consist of five graduates and twenty probationers or undergraduate nurses. The nurses and the secretaries also repeated the problem of the nursing shortage as we visited there. The patient population is about 300.

We drove around for half an hour looking at apartments. Rent was high $50 per month but not furnished and $65 furnished. Dr. Welchon says he will be glad to hold the job until June 1st for me and has instructed secretaries to look for a suitable house.

One of the nicest grammar schools in the residential part of Richmond is a five minute walk from the hospital. The high school is at some distance, but he says he could send the hospital car, and there are buses.

The question is have I got enough strength to go over to Richmond in May to earn money to help pay your travel? The way I feel now, I need two more months of rest as the summer will be very hard on me.

XXVII

The Shining Glory Shore

It was a beautiful spring day. The gardens of Wilmore had never been more beautiful, with forsythia, red bud and pear trees blooming everywhere. The birds were singing.

Stan and daughter Margaret were taking a stroll in the sunshine. Suddenly he stopped and looking down at her with a troubled look in his blue eyes, he said, "There ought to be a law! – ought to be a law that when body strength goes down, the will to work and make plans, ambition of any kind should go down too!"

Plans had been made, however, with the Martin household bustling with activity. Young Margaret's wedding dress was hanging in her closet. The Hughes Auditorium at Asbury College had been reserved for the wedding, and all plans for bridesmaids and ushers were complete. Three of Jim's Crusader Quartet members and Ed Kilbourne would be ushers. Frex Culver was to be his best man. Frex was the son of Rev. Percy Culver who was Stan's companion on mission trips. The music and musicians were chosen. On top of this, there were the last weeks of intensive studies for all of the family. Margaret and Edna would graduate from college the morning of Margaret's wedding day, June 4th.

That morning, in addition to the wedding, Stan was thinking of his family's future and the move to Richmond. Would he have enough strength for this new challenge?

Mother Margaret and daughter Ruth, had come from Boston, to attend and help with the wedding, and to pack up the family for the move to Richmond. June 4th came and all went well – the graduations, the wedding and the reception. Young Margaret left for a new home and church in New Jersey with her newlywed husband, James H. Moore, a minister of the Christian Missionary Alliance Church.

The rest of the family, except for Jerry and Edna, did last minute preparations and were off to Richmond, VA, and the next chapter of their lives. Friends helped them in many ways and were sorry to see them go. Jerry stayed for summer school pre-med studies, and Edna went to Cincinnati to be with Ed's grandparents for a visit. Ed's parents were in a prisoner of war camp in Shanghai.

In Richmond, Stan's family was given a royal welcome by the R. M. Wilsons the missionary friends from Korea. A house had been rented, and Stan began his medical work at Pine Camp Sanatorium.

News came in a letter from Stan, to the Crarys in Wilmore, written June 28, 1941.

1410 Claremont Ave.
Richmond, VA

My dear Mr. and Mrs. Crary,

We had such a lovely visit from your daughters Nancy and Sunny, and Mrs. Crary's sister. They are such a nice party. People are more important than buildings. I introduced them to one of my best Christian patients. She said, "I know you are Christians as I can tell by your faces."

I am speaking tomorrow at the Sunday school hour over the microphone to the 300 patients in the hospital. I tell stories to the kids at night, and hope to have an African American church group sing hymns after 7 PM. Many said they were helped. Three of the patients have been led to Christ before they died.

It has been hot in the day time, but the nights are quite cool with a breeze from the sea. We visited Jamestown and Yorktown last Saturday. The history is most fascinating. The Crary party looked well. I felt so homesick to see them go.

I get off every second weekend and one half day a week. Hours are 8:30 AM to 4:30 PM. We have good food provided from the Sanatorium supply center. We have met new friends at the Baptist and Presbyterian churches.

Betty won second prize in a church poster contest showing the evils of alcohol. [He sketched the pictures as she had drawn them.] Phyllis and Betty are enjoying summer vacation

We are keeping our house here for three months – hoping to pay all our debts and get back to Kentucky to practice.

With kindest thoughts,

SHM

Margaret wrote to the family in July that their father seemed to be standing his work fairly well and that Edna would be coming to them the next week. The Virginia State Agency said that Edna could probably get an assistant dietician job easily, as there is a demand for it. Mother Margaret and Ruth were busy in private case nursing duty.

The Wilson family was in constant touch with them and they spent much of their free time together. Edna arrived and the summer was going along very well for all of them.

July 23rd was Stan's fifty-first birthday and the Martin family was invited to the Wilsons for a birthday dinner for him. Margaret wrote to Dr. Armstrong the next evening at 10 PM, July 24th, 1941.

> Your two telegrams received, also the one from the Korea missionaries in Toronto. Thank you all for your sympathy.
>
> Stan went home to Heaven quickly and peacefully this morning at eight o'clock. He had listened to the radio news at seven, and we had our coffee together. He was planning to take his exam for a Virginia driver's license today. I had his breakfast all ready when Betty called me and said "Daddy wants you." I ran upstairs and caught him in my arms and eased him to the floor so he didn't fall. There was a little flicker of a smile as I kept saying "Jesus loves you" and he was gone.
>
> Please mimeograph this letter and send it to the friends from Korea and relatives. We have selected a lot at Riverside Cemetery on a hillside above the beautiful James River, and just across is a bronze caribou like the Newfoundland Memorial in France. The Presbyterian minister has invited us to have the service in his beautiful church, Saturday morning at eleven.
>
> Dr. Wilson has been a tower of strength to us all. He came at once at eight, but Stan was really gone before he arrived. Last night we had had such a happy birthday for my husband at Dr. Wilson's house in Mission Court. The young people sang and Stan told stories. Dr. Wiseman [a Canadian friend from Asbury College and Toronto] is motoring from Kentucky with Jerry and will arrive tomorrow. He will take the service.
>
> Jerry sent his Dad a birthday telegram which was under his [Stan's] pillow last night. Dr. Wilson advises me not to do anything hastily but to remain where we are until we can decide what is best.
>
> Stan's brother Bill and his wife Laura, Margaret and Jim Moore, and Edna and Ed Kilbourne are arriving tomorrow. All my neighbors and the Methodist, Presbyterian and Baptist ministers have been so kind. I am deeply grateful to have the service in a lovely church instead of the funeral home. Dr. Wiseman will be in charge assisted by the Presbyterian minister.
>
> I was expecting this, but not so soon. He was <u>so brave</u>.

The Lord has greatly sustained us all.

Sincerely and gratefully,
Margaret Martin

Tributes came in from all parts of Korea, Canada and the United States. One, from Edna Hylton, Margaret's dear friend in Yong Jung, Manchuria, seems to have said it the best. "He was about fifty years old, but he lived at least three times as much as the average person."

KOREAN PAGODA GARDEN

This stone monument was constructed in the Republic of Korea by the alumni of Yonsei University Medical College and shipped to Canada in 1985. It was moved to this site in 1998.

It expresses the great honour and respect in which three early Canadian Christian Medical Missionaries are held for their dedication and service to the people of the Korean peninsula.

Dr. Oliver R. Avison (1860-1956) Born in Yorkshire, England, he was both a graduate of and a teacher at the Toronto School of Medicine, affiliated at the time with Victoria University. He served Korea from 1893-1934 in Seoul, founding Severance Union Medical College and Hospital, and Chosun Christian College, now Yonsei University. His work in Korea was continued by his son, Dr. Douglas Avison, who was born in Pusan in 1893, was trained at the University of Toronto in pediatrics, and served at Severance Hospital until 1940.

Dr. Stanley H. Martin (1890-1941) Born in St. John's, Newfoundland and a graduate of Queen's Medical College, he was designated as a missionary from the Orillia Presbyterian Church. He served Korea from 1916-1940 in Manchuria and in Seoul. He was a pioneer in the field of tuberculosis and was a doctor at Severance Hospital, now Yonsei Medical Center.

Dr. Florence J. Murray (1894-1975) Born in Pictou Landing, Nova Scotia, she served Korea from 1921-1969 in many districts from north-eastern China to Hamheung, Wonju, Seoul and Taegu. She was a doctor at Severance Hospital and started its Medical Records Department.

The garden surrounding the monument honours the Very Rev. Dr. Sang Chul Lee Born in Siberia in 1924 and educated in Korea and Canada, he served as Moderator for the United Church of Canada from 1988-1990 and as Chancellor of Victoria University from 1992-1998.

Further information is available in the United Church of Canada/Victoria University Archives.

Korean Pagoda Garden plaque which stands near the Pagoda Memorial
at Victoria College at the University of Toronto, Canada.

Epilogue

Awards

The first recognition of the Martins' part in the Korean Independence Movement were the gold medals that Stan and his wife Margaret received from the Shanghai Provisional Government, a temporary Korean government led by Kim Koo and Syng Man Rhee. Maud MacKinnon, a nurse of their mission also received a similar medal.

In 1968 his daughters Margaret and Edna were missionaries in Seoul. Margaret was with the United Methodist Mission Board (BGM), and Edna and her husband Edwyl were with the Oriental Missionary Society.

One day Margaret received a phone call from Rev. Moon Ik Whan, a friend of her father's during his time in Manchuria. "Go to the Government General Building, to the second floor, to the Independence Movement Memorial Office. They are looking for information from all who aided Korea in her struggle for independence from Japan. They want to know about your father."

The sisters went immediately to the designated place and were met by a large group of Korean newspaper reporters. They were so excited to see them, to hear the story and see the pictures of their father's work in Manchuria.

After receiving their information, the official in charge said "Please come to the 49th Anniversary Independence Day Celebration tomorrow morning, at ten o'clock. It is to be held at the large stage, on the grounds of the Government General Building." He then gave them special entrance passes for their car.

Margaret and Edna arrived the next morning and were amazed to see hundreds of people gathered on the capitol grounds. A man came up to them saying, "President Pak Chung Hi read your father's story in the newspaper and one of you is to represent your family on the platform." Margaret being the eldest was escorted up to the stage to sit with a long line of dignitaries, while Edna watched from below.

Margaret continues the story.

"Soon the ceremonies began. Those of us on the platform were asked to stand. The President and his beautiful wife Yuk Young Soo were coming down the row greeting each one of us, one by one. A Chinese man was standing at my right. I would have loved to hear his story. When the President and his wife came before me I bowed to them and spoke in Korean.

"My family and I thank you for this great honor to my father."

Immediately the first lady said, "To the contrary, our country thanks you and your family for what your father did for us."

President Pak shook my hand, then hung a large gold medal, on a blue and white ribbon around my neck, he then pinned another large gold medal to my coat. Then he handed me a scroll. The scroll and the medals were for the "Order of Merit for National Foundation."

Prime Minister Chung Il Kwon was at the President's side. We both recognized each other. We both were born in Yong Jung, Manchuria and had met on an earlier occasion in Seoul. It was a nice surprise.

The pride and joy of our Korean friends at this recognition, made me realize the love they had for their country and their gratitude to those who had helped them in any way.

A Korean writer Ahn Su-gil wrote a book "*Puk Kando*" (North *Kando* Province) telling of the suffering of the Koreans in Manchuria, including the account of our father's medical help for them. A drama was made of the story and performed by the National Theater Group. Edna and I attended one of the performances. Afterwards we went back stage to thank the actors, telling them that we were the daughters of the missionary doctor. They were surprised.

Daughter Margaret receiving her father's medals from President Pak Chung Hi.
First lady Yuk Yung Soo and Prime Minister Chung Il Kwon on the left.

The Martin Children

It was suggested that further information be provided about the six Martin children.

The eldest, Ruth Martin, was born in Yong Jung, Manchuria where her parents were serving as medical missionaries. Her early schools were Seoul Foreign School and Pyeng Yang Foreign School. After a year at Ricker College, Houlton, Maine she took nurses training at the New England Baptist Hospital in Boston. In 1949 she was appointed as a missionary of the Methodist Church Board of Global Ministries to Severance Hospital, Seoul, Korea.

In Korea, it was a post-war period, and the wards were in shambles. One of her early problems was separating the tuberculosis patients from the new mother's ward. The Koreans said, "She speaks Korean better than we do!" The Communist Invasion, June 25, 1950 interrupted her missionary service and she spent her later years in private nursing in the United States.

The second daughter, Margaret, was born in Yong Jung. The family moved to Seoul in 1927. There she attended the Seoul Foreign School through high school and took violin lessons from Mr. Joseph Huss a German violinist. She had one year at the New England Conservatory in Boston, and then attended Asbury College in Kentucky where she graduated. She married Rev. James H. Moore and they were sent to Korea also with the Methodist Church. After the Communist Invasion they served in the Philippines for three years and then returned to Korea. Margaret's work was with the Methodist Women's Missionary Society in the Philippines and Korea. In Korea she did juvenile delinquent rehabilitation work with girls who had been released from prison. She directed drama, both religious and secular, including Shakespeare in Korea. She travelled with her drama troupe to Hong Kong, Taiwan and the Philippines. Her husband, James, was Chairman of the Audio-Visual Department of the Korean National Christian Council. He taught Audio-Visual Methods in the Methodist Seminary and had a fleet of six mobile units showing Christian films throughout South Korea.

Edna, the third daughter is remembered as "Nanoo", a nickname given to her by her sister Margaret. She too was born in Yong Jung. She had most of her schooling in Seoul, but had two years at Pyeng Yang Foreign School, when Ruth Bell (who later became Billy Graham's wife) was attending there. Edna married Ed Kilbourne, a missionary's son. Further description of Ed's work is included in the chapter *Jerry's Story*. They were appointed as Oriental Missionary Society missionaries to Beijing, China, later to Seoul, Korea. They too escaped at the time of the Communist Invasion of South Korea. When they returned, Ed taught and gave leadership to their Seminary. Nanoo worked with the blind, and two leper colonies (Hansen Disease). She checked to see that they had blankets and food supplies. She was especially known for what she did at Severance Hospital in Seoul where she was in charge of Housekeeping and Sanitation. Nanoo had the workers wear special uniforms and she wore one too. They took pride in their work and Severance was soon known as "the cleanest hospital in Seoul!"

Jerry's life is described in *Jerry's Story*.

Phyllis, the fifth in the family was born in Yong Jung. When they moved to Seoul she attended Seoul Foreign School through high school. She later graduated from Asbury College and married Dr. Walter Harrison from Moultrie, Georgia an obstetrician. She had a beautiful contralto voice, and was well known and loved in the community.

Betty, the youngest of the Martin children, was born in Seoul, Korea and attended Seoul Foreign School and Asbury College. She married Rev. Woodrow Smith a Methodist Minister. They served in many different churches in several different States. Woody was District Superintendent part of the time. Betty taught junior high school for a period of time. She was an ardent supporter of the work in the churches where they served.

The Pagoda Memorial

Years passed, and in 1984 when Margaret was still on the mission field in Seoul she wrote this story.

"One evening I was standing on the street on Yoido Island in Seoul. I had just been interviewed on KBS television about my father. They had asked me to bring pictures of him and his work and to tell of his part in the Independence Movement of 1919. There was a distinguished looking Korean gentleman standing nearby and I asked him, "Is this a good place to get a taxi?"

His eyes widened as he looked at me, and he said, "Miss Martin!" He was thinking of my sister Ruth who had been a nurse at Severance Hospital.

I said "No, I'm Dr. Martin's second daughter Margaret Martin Moore. Ruth is my sister."

I showed him the large picture of my father that I was carrying.

"Why, he was my medical professor at Severance Union Medical College! My name is Yu In Soon."

He was so excited. He asked me to come right then to his apartment which was nearby because his son, a neurosurgeon from Rochester, NY was due in from the United States in just a little while. We walked to his apartment and waited for his son's arrival. There we met his wife Mrs. Yu who served us refreshments. Dr. Yu told me that he was a heart and lung specialist, working with tuberculosis patients just as my father had. He also said that Dr. Florence Murray had helped him to get to Canada for further studies. Then he said solemnly, "You know, the people of Canada should know what some of their citizens have done for Korea. I'd like to place a monument somewhere for Dr. O. R. Avison, for your father, Dr. Martin, and for Dr. Florence Murray. Perhaps it could be at the University of Toronto."

Later that evening, Dr. Yu's son and family arrived from the airport, and the doctor enthusiastically told his son about his plan. The son was pleased with the idea, and said he was in a position to contact a network of Korean doctors who were Severance Medical School graduates, and could help fund the project.

Not long afterwards, I contacted Rev. Don Irwin a United Church of Canada missionary in Seoul and told him of the plan. Don and I met with the president of Yonsei Medical College and with Don's help, a letter was written to the University of Toronto proposing that a monument be placed there, memorializing the three doctors. Later, an acceptance letter was received.

In June 1984 I retired from my missionary work and moved to Wilmore, Kentucky the town where my alma mater Asbury University is located. The next year an invitation came to me for the dedication of a pagoda to be placed at Victoria College at the University of Toronto on October 19, 1985.

It was an exciting time when I arrived in Canada. Family members of Dr. Florence Murray were there, also a granddaughter and great grandchildren of Dr. O. R. Avison. I represented the Martin family. A large group of Koreans from the churches of Toronto, former Canadian missionaries to Korea and their relatives, and other interested friends had gathered for the dedication. A representative from the Korean Embassy and the chancellor of the University made speeches. We learned that the funds for the ten ton pagoda, and for its transportation to Canada, were raised by former Severance Union Medical college graduates as well as current Yonsei Medical College students. It had to be shipped across the ocean in a special container.

Years passed and I made a trip to Toronto with my son Ron, and my brother-in-law Dr. Walter Harrison and his grandson Colby. We were searching our family history in the United Church of Canada Archives at Victoria College, which is a federated college of the University of Toronto. I was preparing to write my father's biography. The archivists were interested to learn that I was related to one of the doctors honored by the pagoda, which by then had become something of a campus landmark.

"They are going to be moving the pagoda to a new place sometime soon," they said.

"Oh that's interesting" we said, and went on with our work.

The next day as I was standing in the archives library, thirteen-year-old Colby came dashing in the front door.

"The pagoda is here!" he exclaimed.

"What?"

I went out to see what was going on, and there was the enormous, ten ton pagoda lying in sections on a truck. The University bursar and architect were supervising the work of placing it in its new location in front of the Archives at Victoria College.

When they heard I was the daughter of one of the doctors whose name was on the monument they came over to me. It was then that I told them of the chance meeting of the Korean, Dr. Yu In Sun, by the KBS-TV station, and how the pagoda came to be there at the University. They knew little of its origins and were thrilled with the story.

"We have an appointment with the president of Victoria College at 2:30 today and if you will come to her office then, we will introduce you!"

Thus we met the gracious President Roseanne Runta, who was amazed at the story and especially that we should be there just at the moment of the arrival of the pagoda at its new location. She called it, providential. Now it is where people pass constantly, either driving or walking on the busy street. Already we have heard exclamations of delight from passers-by. It does look magnificent with its Oriental charm against the quiet grey stone university buildings. They'll be planting trees and flowers around it. We suggested planting Korea's national flower the *Moogungwha* (Rose of Sharon). As we surveyed the memorial in its new location, we were thankful for all that had transpired, and especially thankful to God for the three doctors who represented the saving of thousands of Korean lives.

Since then, a fine big plaque with information describing the three doctors' work has been placed on a stand near the pagoda. The place is now called "The Pagoda Memorial, University of Toronto," and photos of the pagoda may be seen on the internet.

On September 23rd, 1998 there was a ceremony honoring the life, work and memory of Dr. Stanley Haviland Martin at Yonsei University in Seoul. Part of the ceremony was the turning over of Dr. Martin's medals and citations from the Korean government to the Yonsei University Museum, in light of the fact that he was a professor at the University's Severance Union Medical College.

Edna Martin Kilbourne, her husband Ed, and Margaret Martin Moore with her son David went to Korea to transfer the memorabilia.

The Pagoda Memorial at Victoria College at the University of Toronto, Canada.
A gift of the alumni of Yonsei Medical School in honor of the missionary doctors:
Dr. O.R. Avison, Dr. Florence Murray and Dr. Stanley H. Martin.

OCTOBER 20, 2005 DEDICATION OF NEW PLAQUE AT KOREAN PAGODA PARK, VICTORIA UNIVERSITY /U OF TORONTO, CHARLES STREET, TORONTO. RELATIVES OF ALL 3 DOCTORS ON PLAQUE PRESENT.

The Pagoda Memorial with members of the Murray, Avison, and Martin family.

(Dr. Martin's only son Gerald, followed in his footsteps as a doctor to the Korean people, therefore, we include *Jerry's Story*.)

Jerry's Story

Gerald Arthur Martin, Lieutenant in the U.S. Navy Medical Corps, was born in Boston, November 29, 1922, when his missionary family was on furlough from Manchuria. In spite of the dignity that naturally surrounded both his profession as a doctor and his rank as an officer in the Navy he was still known as "Jerry" to all his friends. Jerry's parents, Dr. Stanley Haviland Martin and Margaret Rogers Martin, were medical missionaries with the Canadian Presbyterian Church, later the United Church of Canada. They were sent first to Yong Jung, Manchuria, then to Seoul, Korea. Jerry lived in Manchuria until he was four-years-old when his parents moved to Seoul. His father was to serve at Severance Hospital. So it was really in Korea that Jerry spent most of his childhood and youth. He graduated from high school at the age of sixteen. It was during these years he learned the Korean language which was to be such an added contribution to his work for the Navy.

After graduation from high school he attended Wooster College in Wooster, Ohio, a Presbyterian school. At the end of his freshman year, he transferred to Asbury College, Wilmore, Kentucky, where two of his sisters, Margaret and Edna, were attending. During this time he began pre-med courses and after a year transferred to the University of Kentucky to work toward his Bachelor of Science degree. It was also while Jerry was at Asbury College that he met Virginia Stevens from Maryland who later became his wife. They met in chemistry class and were lab partners.

Meanwhile his mother and father had returned from Korea, and his father was serving as a doctor at the Pine Camp Tuberculosis Sanatorium in Richmond, Virginia. From Richmond came the tragic news of his father's death, July 23, 1941. It came as a tremendous blow to all the family. Jerry attended the funeral and after staying awhile with his mother and sisters he decided to continue his medical studies.

He entered the Medical College of Richmond, Virginia, under the Navy Medical Training Program V-12 from May, 4 1943, until December 2, 1945. After graduation he received his MD degree and enlisted as an officer in the United States Navy Lt. j. g. USN Reserve May 5th, 1943. The V-12 was an accelerated program. Jerry laughed as he told us later, that the students lived on coffee and aspirin. His fellow students made a ceremony of lining up to sniff at his drink, to see what he had put in it because he was among the top ten of his class. They nicknamed him "Parson," but not in a derogatory way. He married Virginia Stevens at her home church in Street, Maryland, in September 1944. They lived in Richmond for over a year while he was at the Medical College. Virginia worked as a supervisor of three child care centers to help financially. They then moved to Windsor Hills in Baltimore while Jerry did his internship at the University of Maryland Hospital. Virginia then worked for the Baltimore City Department of Public Recreation.

Sometimes during his grueling studies he and Virginia would look at various germs through the microscope together. Virginia made excellent sketches of them, but when she tried to pronounce the names, she couldn't say them very well. Jerry laughed at her pronunciation but those were the germs that he remembered the best. He did well in his exams.

After his internship he accepted a commission as Lt. j. g. USNR on January 15, 1946, at Annapolis. There he was doctor to a brigade of midshipmen and was back in uniform. Virginia said she traveled with him, along with members of the football team. He was the team doctor 1947-1948.

Virginia also told of another activity. "We enjoyed sailing in Annapolis on a yawl. It is two-masted, and had three sails, foremost, mainsail and mizzen sail. The mizzenmast is located aft the rudder post. Yawls could not be taken from the mooring unless there was someone aboard with a "Yawl Command." Jerry passed a seamanship test and earned his Yawl Command. His experience with his *Sweetie Pie* sailboat as a teenager had helped to prepare him for this.

In 1947 they were blessed with their first son, Robert, who was born at the University of Maryland Hospital and taken home to Annapolis.

After Annapolis they returned to the University of Maryland Hospital for Jerry to begin his medical residency in internal medicine. They bought their first home, a town house in Loch Raven Village in Towson, Maryland. Their second son, Gerald Arthur Jr., was born in December 1949. His father, Jerry, was ordered from the Naval Reserve to the U. S. Navy the same year.

The outbreak of the Korean War naturally placed in great demand all doctors in the Armed Services, and Lieutenant Martin was especially qualified to work in the Orient. He had mixed feelings, however, when he was called to leave his young family and serve with the Fleet Epidemiological Unit No. 1 at Yokosuka, Japan. On the way, prior to going overseas in1950 he received special training in epidemiological diseases, at the George Hooper Foundation at the University of California.

When Jerry arrived at Yokosuka, Japan, his assignment was on the Laboratory ship LSIL 1091, which was outfitted to deal with the epidemic diseases that were ravaging the Far East. When disease broke out in an area, his lab ship would dock, and he and his staff would diagnose and treat the afflicted people. His specialty was infectious diseases of all kinds. The lab ship's territory was also Korea and its environs.

On Koje Do Island off the coast of Korea near Pusan there were about 140,000 North Korean and Chinese prisoners of war. They were in camps managed by the U. S. Army Logistical Command. There were also thousands of Korean civilians who worked at the camp, plus many refugees from the main land. The Army authorities there requested that Navy Lieutenant Gerald Martin be loaned to them because of his special training. The Navy Medical Research Laboratory ship 1091 was then docked at the Koje Do port. Special research was to be done on plague, cholera, and dysentery. There Jerry became "Co-director of the Joint Dysentery Study." Jerry's work on the island became very close to his heart, not only from the point of making a contribution to the Navy and to the medical profession, but because he was able to work with and minister to the needs of the Korean people, whom he loved so dearly and who loved him with deep devotion. Reports of some of his research were published in *The American Medical Journal*.

When Jerry first arrived on the island, he found that the North Korean prisoners, who were of high rank, tightly controlled every movement of the prisoners of lesser rank.

They said, "Don't take the Americans' medicine. They are trying to kill us!"

But Jerry went to those who were sick, and made friends with them. Sitting on an army cot he would laugh, tell jokes, and sing songs with them in the Korean language. There was a saying among his fellow American servicemen, if there was happy shouting, singing, and clapping of hands somewhere, "Oh! Is that where Martin is working today?"

Besides typhus and dysentery there were many other diseases. Jerry was able to slip the needed medicines to those who needed it. Fortunately the new chloromycetin became available. [His wife Virginia said, "Jerry helped develop the drug chloromycetin, and gave me a big bottle of capsules, which I still have. The label says, 'Caution, new drug limited by federal law to investigational uses. Parke-Davis and Co.' He was an intern at that time at University of Maryland Hospital."] He was also asked to report to senior doctors about his amazing experience of saving the life of a tetanus patient.

So many prisoners began to be healed, that those who would prevent Jerry's medical help were silenced. Several months passed.

During his time at Koje Do, the North Koreans accused the Americans of using germ warfare. There was an epidemic of some kind in their territory. In order to investigate the diseases, Jerry and some Severance medical students were landed in a rubber boat near Wonsan, North Korea, behind enemy lines. Because he spoke fluent Korean he gained the trust of those he met. He also told them his father had been a missionary doctor at Severance Hospital. He asked to see some of the sick people, and was able to examine them and bring out medical specimens. They found cases of typhus, but also found "hemorrhagic fever," a disease that was also prevalent in South Korea. This disease is carried by nits in the fur of field mice or other small animals. As the soldiers moved through grass some of them became infected by the nits. His findings were announced and it helped to disprove the germ warfare theory.

Unfortunately, after his trip behind enemy lines in the spring of 1951 Jerry contracted typhus fever. It was during those critical days, so near death's door that he gave the most clear-cut testimony concerning his Christian experience. In Navy terminology he said to his brother-in-law Ed Kilbourne, who visited him on the Hospital ship Repose near Pusan, "Well, Ed, I've gotten everything 'squared away' with God. He's been very near to me during these hours."

Rev. Ed Kilbourne an Oriental Missionary Society missionary was also working on Koje Do Island. As a missionary's son he was fluent in Mandarin and was able to speak to the Chinese prisoners there. He was part of an education program sponsored by the United Nations Civil Assistance and Far East Command's Civil Intelligence and Education Service. Ed was considered one of the most effective representatives.

It was amazing that the two men could be together as Jerry lay there so sick. After recovering, the medical staff and the prisoners welcomed him back to his ministry of healing on Koje Do.

These times were ended when on September 27, 1951, Jerry took the blood bank courier plane to Tokyo and lost his life in an air crash near Mount Fuji, Japan. The tragic news of his death reached his wife, Virginia, and their two little sons, Robbie and Gerald, in Maryland. Jerry was twenty-seven years old. He would have turned twenty-eight years old in November of that year.

His fellow American servicemen and the prisoners who knew him were devastated! They had lost a friend. At that time, a Health Care Center was being built by the United Nations Civil Assistance Command for the Korean civilian workers who worked at the POW camp. Jerry had treated many civilians as well as the POWs. It consisted of a fifty-bed hospital flanked by a dispensary on one side, and a lab and x-ray building on the other. His friends and co-workers were anxious to do something to honor his memory, so it was decided to name this center for him. Colin M. MacLeod, M.D., Chairman of Armed Forces Epidemiological Board proclaimed it this way:

"We by common consent rise to place in our official record this memorial to one of our medical officers most deserving of our honors. Dr. Gerald A. Martin. His name be forever honored as a great physician and a noble man." He was awarded the Legion of Merit with combat "V" posthumously by the United States Navy.

Some of the grieving North Korean prisoners were anxious to have a part in the project, and carved the words on the memorial stone. The so called "enemy" carved the stone.

Several years went by and word came that the buildings of the Health Center were destroyed by typhoon winds, but the memorial stone was still there.

When Jerry's wife Virginia, now a school teacher, heard this, she was determined to go to Korea to find the stone. She knew that Margaret Moore, Jerry's sister, was a United Methodist missionary in Seoul, Korea, and could probably help her. Margaret's husband, the Rev. James H. Moore, had also been a missionary there but had died in 1967 after twenty years of service.

Margaret continues the story.

When Virginia arrived, we showed her many of the places of Jerry's childhood, including our Canadian Mission house where we had lived, the old Seoul Foreign School grounds at Chung Dong, where we all attended school, the beautiful Korean palaces and the markets. We even took her north by train to Whachinpo where Jerry and the family had spent some summers. It was there he had sailed his boat the *Sweetie Pie*. Virginia enjoyed seeing all of these places but whenever I asked her, "What are your priorities? What else do you want to do?"

She always said, "I want to go to Koje Do."

Each time she said this I was concerned because I had never been to Koje Do and I wasn't sure how to get there. I knew it was an island off of the Korean peninsula somewhere near Pusan. In the past, I had heard some Canadian missionary nurses speak of their trip to Koje Do. They said that you take a little Korean boat from Pusan which smells of fish and bobs around on the water like a cork, for a <u>long</u> trip to the island. These wonderful nurses, Beulah Burns and Ada Sandell, had been working at "Severance in Exile" on Koje Do when Jerry was there.

I envisioned going to Pusan and staying in a hotel, because our Methodist friends, Jeff and Shirley Jeffery, whose work was in Pusan were on furlough. We would have to find the dock of departure for Koje Do, and take the long trip. At Koje Do we would have to find a Korean inn and sleep on the floor. <u>Above</u> <u>all</u> there would be no one to help us find the POW camp area and the stone!

One day we were invited for dinner to my dear friend Mrs. Kim Chong Hi Pahng's home. She was General Secretary for the National Christian Council Home and Family Life work. She and her husband spoke fluent English. As we ate a delicious dinner they asked Virginia, "What have you seen of our country?"

She told them of all the places she had visited, but ended with "But I want to go to Koje Do to find my husband's memorial stone!" Hearing this, Mrs. Pahng got up from the table immediately and went to her telephone. In a few minutes she came back with a piece of paper. She had a time-table for trains to Pusan, and departure times for two kinds of ferry boats to Koje Do Island.

She also said, "Call my friend Mrs. Choi at this number when you know what day and what time you are going." We were surprised. We went home and made plans to go right away.

The wind was blowing hard in Seoul when I made plane reservations to Pusan. Then I called Mrs. Choi in Koje Do to tell her our plans.

"Don't come today," she said. "The weather is bad and the boats won't go today." So I cancelled the air reservations.

A few days later I was surprised when a phone call came from our Methodist office saying that the Jefferys were returning from furlough the next day and might they spend the night with me before going on to Pusan? Of course I met them and welcomed them to my home. They were thrilled with our plans for Koje Do and promised to help us. How fortunate this was for us. I called Mrs. Choi again to give the new plans. Virginia and I and the Jefferys all flew together to Pusan the next day. We stayed overnight with them, and the next day a Korean friend of the Jefferys took us to find the ferry for Koje Do. We had dreaded this part of the trip but when we reached the dock we were dumbfounded! There was a beautiful hydrofoil, outfitted with air conditioning and color TV! We made the trip in comfort on calm seas over to the island in less than two hours. The people on board told us that the hydrofoil crossings had just started two months before.

A tall Korean man met us at the Koje Do pier.

"Are you Mrs. Martin and Mrs. Moore?" he asked in English. When we said, "Yes," he said, "Follow me. We have had two calls from Seoul today to say you were coming."

Soon we were in a jeep traveling along an island road with beautiful scenery on every side. We drove up a hill to a group of fine-looking buildings. We learned that this was the *Ae Kwang Won Center* for care of handicapped children. It was sponsored by friends I knew in Seoul. Our driver friend, Mr. Choi, took us to the guest house, where we were met by a smiling Kim In Soon, the hostess. We were shown upstairs to a guest room with twin beds, overlooking the harbor. Later we found she was a graduate of the Home Economics Department of Ewha Woman's University. I had been teaching there in the Christian Studies Department.

That evening during dinner, we shared our story about Jerry and the POWs, and also my father's work in Manchuria and Seoul. We found that Mr. Choi had studied English with Dr. William Scott, a Canadian missionary, who had been in Yong Jung on the United Church of Canada Mission station where I was born. He was a member of my parent's mission denomination. Using excellent English, he told Virginia and me, that he had been on Koje Do, since refugee days from Hamheung, North Korea, when the POW prisoners were there. He remembered hearing about a memorial stone for an American doctor, but he didn't know if he could find it. We were discouraged, but he said we would go the next day to look for it.

The next morning there was a gentle rain as we started out in the jeep. After winding along on a road by the grey sea we went down a long valley.

"To our right is where the POW cemetery was," he said.

There was nothing but a rough surfaced bare field. Later we heard that the bodies had been dug up and sent to North Korea. Then we came to a small stone bridge.

"This is the check point for the beginning of the POW camp."

Here we looked across a great flat area of rice paddy fields, like a bowl surrounded by low hills.

"There were about 140,000 prisoners in this place during the war years."

I tried to imagine the tents and quonset huts jammed into that place. In my mind I heard clapping and singing as Jerry did his work. We passed on from there by the sea, and suddenly Mr. Choi stopped the jeep. He sat and thought for a minute. Then he started to drive forward a few feet, and then stopped again. Without saying a word, he jumped out of the jeep and scrambled up a bank by the side of the road. He slipped in the mud and slid down about six feet but caught himself. Then he disappeared into the trees on the hill. Virginia jumped from the jeep and followed him. She was wearing a raincoat and hat, and could move quickly, but I was carrying an umbrella and followed more slowly. It was hard to climb the muddy bank. Then I heard Virginia's voice calling.

"I think he's found it!"

I hurried, but I still had to cross a steep rocky ravine.

Suddenly a young Korean came to me out of the woods. He came right to me to help me. He was wearing a yellow shirt and I noticed he was dry although it was raining.

"Good old polyester," I thought. I was also surprised that he was not shy of a foreigner.

I can still remember his brown thumbs pressing down some barbed wire to help me over a fence. Virginia said later that the man had helped her too.

Suddenly we came to a clearing and I saw Virginia in front of a large grey stone. She was leaning forward to read the inscription on the stone, and I knew this was it. Behind it where the small hospital had stood, there was only a rice paddy field with young green blades blowing in the wind. Tears mingled with the rain on our cheeks, as we read the inscription. We could read the words although lichen covered part of it.

Gerald A. Martin Memorial
Health Center
Dedicated in Remembrance of
Lieutenant Gerald A. Martin
Medical Corps US Navy
Gave His Life For KOREA
September 27, 1951
United Nations
Civil Assistance Comm. Korea

Mr. Choi was taking pictures of us and a few minutes passed. Then the young man in the yellow shirt spoke to me in Korean.

"This land will be leveled and they will be building something here."

"Oh, is that so?" I responded.

We continued to examine the stone. After a little while, I turned to the young man to thank him for helping me. He wasn't there. He had disappeared without saying a word. Korean etiquette requires that if you have to leave early from a group that you have been with, you say, "I am being very rude, but I must leave now," and then you leave.

Mr. Choi then took us to see the governor of the island in a little town a few miles from there. We were escorted into a large building to an inner office. Virginia and I entered, and Mr. Choi stood in the doorway.

He said, "I have brought you some important guests. May I introduce them to you, and tell you their story?"

The Governor was seated behind a large desk with photographs of former leaders above his head. He looked up and listened as Mr. Choi spoke.

"This is Mrs. Moore, the daughter of a doctor who worked for our Korean people. Her brother was also a doctor who worked here on Koje Do with the POW, and died for our country. This is Mrs. Martin, the wife of the doctor who died for our country."

Upon hearing this, the Governor got up and came around to shake our hands. His whole attitude changed. He invited us to sit with him at a table and ordered coffee for us. Mr. Choi told him more of our story, especially of Virginia wanting to find the memorial stone, and that we had found it that morning. When Mr. Choi told of the young man who met us near the stone and said that the land there was to be leveled, and something built there, the Governor was surprised.

"I haven't heard about these plans," he said. This was unusual for him not to know news of this importance.

"But if this happens we will move the memorial stone to a new and beautiful place."

He gave us beautiful little flags, post cards, and other souvenirs, and it was time to go.

As we left, the Governor accompanied us to the front door of the building. We passed through a large area with many workers at their desks. As we went by, all of the workers stood to their feet. Standing in the rain, the governor waved to us as we drove away.

We went back to the *Ae Kwang Won*, where a surprise awaited us. While we were gone, our hostess had placed gardenias in little bowls on every step of the stairs going up to our room. We were wafted up on gardenia fragrance. Our hostess didn't know that on special dates Jerry would always bring Virginia a gardenia. The fragrance was a blessing.

"And what about the man in the yellow shirt?" our Korean friends asked us as they heard the story.

"I don't know," I answered, "but he, too, was a blessing."

What was to be a sad journey was full of blessings. With God's amazing help we had made the pilgrimage to Koje Do. We found Jerry's memorial stone.

Jerry with son Rob

Lt. Gerald Martin, j. g. USNR (Epilogue**Jerry's Story)

Jerry with the Admiral on laboratory ship LSIL 1091 in Yokosuka, Japan, 1950.

Printed in the United States
By Bookmasters